VENEZUELA

REVOLUTION AS
SPECTACLE

RAFAEL UZCÁTEGUI

TRANSLATED BY
CHAZ BUFE

SEE SHARP PRESS ♦ TUCSON, ARIZONA

For information contact:

See Sharp Press
P.O. Box 1731
Tucson, AZ 85702

www.seesharppress.com

Uzcategui, Rafael.
        Venezuela : revolution as spectecale / by Rafael Uzcategui ; Intro-
duction, by Octavio Alberola ; translated by Charles Bufe.– Tucson, Ariz.: See
Sharp Press, 2010.
Includes bibliographical references and index.
ISBN 1-884365-77-9   9781884365775
Contents: Map of Venezuela -- Introduction -- Preface -- Translator's Note --
Chapter 1. Leftist Reaction to the Bolivarian Government (Noam Chomsky and
Gabriel Muzio) -- Chapter 2. Daily Life in Revolutionary Venezuela -- Chapter
3. The Devil's Excrement -- Chapter 4. Populism -- Chapter 5. The Social
Movements -- Chapter 6. The Bolivarian Political Process -- Chapter 7. The
Challenge of the Future -- List of Acronyms that Appear in the Text .
1. Chavez Frias, Hugo. 2. Venezuela -- Politics and government -- 1999-
3. Venezuela -- Economic conditions -- 21st century. 4. Petroleum industry
and trade -- Political aspects. 5. Petroleum industry and trade -- Venezuela.
                                    987.0642

CONTENTS

For those no longer here, but whose shining example and spirit live on:

Emilio, Antonio, Yolanda, Simón, and Daniel

Thank you for being an inspiration.

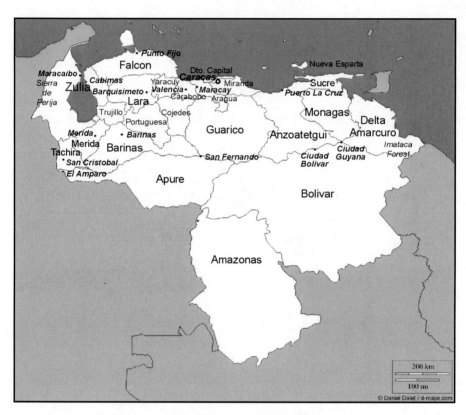

Outline map of Venezuelan states courtesy of d-maps.com

INTRODUCTION

After the fall of the Berlin Wall and the implosion of the Soviet Union and totalitarian socialism—which up to that time had presented itself as the driving force of modern history—political bipolarity ended. The world was now unipolar, and some called it "the end of history." Upon the ruins of the "real socialism," capitalism stood triumphant, and only bourgeois democracy remained as the paradigm of the "social contract." [Who drafted and who signed this "contract" remains a mystery.—tr.]

Class struggle continued, but now it did not have the goal of revolution but rather of electoral triumph. Both the left and the right assumed the victory of the capitalist system (the "free market"), and both made a tacit "historic promise" to compete for political power exclusively through universal suffrage as an expression of the "will of the people."

As one consequence, during the two decades since the end of the Cold War, almost all of the dictatorial regimes have disappeared in Latin America. So, with the sole exception of Cuba, electoral democracy has become the means of political management of society, and the "free market" the means of economic management of society. From this grows the symbiosis between capitalist business and state funding, a symbiosis that grows ever stronger. And this does include Castro's Cuba, that Cold War anachronism that demagogically tries to maintain the old political bipolarity.

So then it's not strange that, from the arrival in power of Hugo Chávez and other populist Latin American leaders, we've seen the pretended renewal of the bipolar political struggle. Both the left and the right do everything possible to convince us of its existence, and to convince us that there is no alternative to it. But this time it's presented as the irreconcilable political bipolarity of the "new" socialism ("socialism of the 21st century") and imperialism.

This is a comprehensible coincidence of interests between those on both sides who aspire to govern. They reduce past and present history to this duality, because both left and right need to legitimize and justify their struggle for institutional control. But this is not comprehensible from the standpoint of those who continue to be the victims of exploitation and domination, given that the "socialism of the 21st century," like "real socialism," is simply a type of state capitalism.

There's no doubt that the desire for guiding lights and certainty impels many leftists to seek refuge in any discourse that promises change, no matter how rhetorical and demagogic that discourse might be. This is particularly so when leftists have a follower mentality and understand neither what's happening around them (in China, for instance) nor recent history (that of the Soviet Union and other "existing socialist" countries, for instance). Given all this, it's not surprising that new dreams of collective paradise have appeared, and that they assume the form of a "revolutionary" delirium with millenarian overtones. At present, these dreams center on Venezuela and, to a lesser extent, Bolivia. And these dreams uniformly have one truly revolting feature: fervid support for the regimes in power.

Neither is it surprising that the recipe of leftist populism has once more been found wanting, has once more demonstrated its incapacity to deliver on its emancipating promises. Instead, when one looks beyond the rhetoric and spectacle, one finds that the leftist regimes show their true face: authoritarianism and the cult of personality, with authority exercised at the convenience and desire of those holding the reins of government.

Springing from the failure of the neoliberal policies that the social democratic parties made their own, and with the advent of the anti-globalization movement of the 1990s, the new Latin American populism promised to reconstitute the social-welfare state and in the longer term to construct "socialism" compatible with representative democracy. This would all be done to cure the ills of unemployment and the precariousness of life and the misery that neoliberal economic policies had created or worsened.

This new populism reawakened the appetite for political struggle among the young, and also the old, who in many cases had begun to lose confidence in electoral games and institutional promises, and who rejected this dog-eat-dog world without understanding that there truly is "another world possible." Those supporting the new populism believe that they can reach paradise through the new electoral "radicalism."

But in the hour of truth, and as many of us have pointed out, this electoral "alternative" that pretends to be anti-capitalist, far from breaking with capitalism, instead adapts itself to the established order and submits to the imperatives of the market. In the process, it fails to fulfill its promises, or is incapable of doing so because of bureaucratic corruption. And it continues and amplifies the development policies that it had formerly called "devastating," and which it had denounced for being in the hands of the transnational capitalists.

So, the "alternatives" have failed, not only because of not having known how to, or not wanting to, create a new form of political empowerment for the exploited—while exercising power in a near-authoritarian manner, and without opposition worthy of the name—but also because they are responsible for the continued devastation of the planet. As well, they're also complicit in the destruction of the natural, social, and cultural environments of the indigenous communities to which they had promised the preservation of their lands and traditional ways of life.

This then is what the new populism has delivered. A populism that at times is xenophobic. A populism that pretends to be leftist, but that has contributed decisively to the disarming of the people and to the reintegration of the popular movements with the capitalist system of domination and exploitation. A populism that has almost annihilated the visions of authentic anti-capitalist alternatives.

All of this is put in concrete terms, with objective evidence, in this book. Even though the subtitle makes it clear that this is an anarchist critique of the Bolivarian government, this book is not an ideological analysis, but rather it's the result of long and rigorous empirical investigation—it's filled with first-hand accounts and is also extremely well documented. And the references (documentation in the form of hundreds of endnotes) allows the reader to not only verify the information presented here, but to learn much more if he or she wishes.

Here, the Chávez movement is considered from its origins and analyzed in all its complexity. But, above all, this book analyzes at length what gives Venezuela its political and economic identity: the extraction and export of petroleum and other energy resources.

This book traces the history of Venezuela and the consequences of historical events for the Venezuelan people—and the other peoples of Latin America. This book is, in the words of the author, a mixture of "history, political analysis and journalism, based in the testimony of participants." It's not possible, in this introduction, to provide a summation of its informational and contextual richness. Nonetheless, I'm convinced that the reader will appreciate it, and that the reader will come away from it with a healthy increase in understanding of the "Bolivarian process," whose sad consequences, for both the people of Venezuela and social emancipation, are becoming ever more apparent.

—Octavio Alberola

"They say that 'peaceful' protest is their right.
And [what about] my right to private property?"

Poster produced in 2002 by the Venezuelan Ministry of Communication and Information

PREFACE

Much has been written—and there's been even more discussion—about the political development in Venezuela that began in 1999 and is commonly called "The Bolivarian Revolution." Two gross oversimplifications about this process vie for hegemony on the world stage: A) that the government in Caracas has initiated a series of radical transformations that will lead to "21st-century socialism," a development inimical to the politics and values of imperialist capitalism; B) that President Chávez is a dictator who is imposing Communism by force in Venezuela.

As we'll demonstrate, both of these ideas are false.

In the midst of this polarization, some are attempting to reconstitute horizontal social movements among the oppressed, attempting to resurrect the solidarity exemplified by the old slogans Social Justice, Liberty, and Equality. In the years since 1999—the years of the manufactured dichotomy produced by the struggle over Venezuela's oil riches between the Chávez regime and its right-wing opposition—these voices of dissent have been silenced, ridiculed, and criminalized. This book will make audible the voices of those who dissent as much from the policies of the Chávez government as from those of the rightist opposition parties. This book will attempt to present the true situation in Venezuela in all its complexity.

The principal error of those who are attempting to interpret the "Bolivarian" phenomenon is that they focus on what is being said about it, forgetting—unconscionably at times—the political and social history of Venezuela. We believe that it is impossible to understand the significance of the Chávez presidency without understanding the profound cultural influences generated by the petroleum economy as well as the overwhelming role of the military and the concomitant cult of the strong man, to name but two examples. Any review, no matter how careless, of the history of Venezuela in the 20th century will show that Hugo Chávez is much more a logical outgrowth of the development of the nation over the last 100 years than a radical break with its past.

This book doesn't pretend to be objective. Rather, it's based in anarchist argument. Its starting point is that old utopian socialist vision, that attempt to construct a society based on human equality and solidarity, a society with neither coercion nor authoritarianism—that is to say, a society with neither the state nor capitalism. But, of course, an exposition of anarchist theory is beyond the scope of this book. For that, please see the bibliography.

Having said that, we again must emphasize that the arguments in this book are based on well documented facts, primarily on governmental sources and sources affiliated with the Chávez regime. A large majority of the data cited from periodicals came from the pages of *Ultimas Noticias* ("The Latest News"), a nationally circulated Venezuelan daily paper that, even though owned by a Venezuelan family with roots in the oligarchy, functions as the mouthpiece of the regime. There are two reasons for this: 1) *Ultimas Noticias* is edited by a veteran leftist journalist who has reiterated in print his unconditional support of President Chávez; and 2) *Ultimas Noticias* has a virtual monopoly on the government's press publicity budget—it's virtually the only recipient of those funds. Beyond this, we directly present the voices of those activists who passionately participated in the Bolivarian Movement during its first years, but who are now critical of it.

As we break down the continual paradoxes, phantasms, and epic pyrotechnics of Venezuelan history and society, we'll attempt to place them in context. But reality can never be forced into the Procrustean bed of a particular theoretical category, as many attempt to do. In contrast, all these things can be seen through the lens of what Guy Debord more than 30 years ago called "the spectacle"; we also maintain that the Chávez regime's development has validated Debord's postulates. To that end, we suggest that the so-called Bolviarian Revolution is a spectacle for the global audience, a spectacle that has unfolded without material benefit to the daily lives of the people.

We need to dispel a possible objection to the approach we take in this book: Is it contradictory for an anarchist analysis to favor things such as the construction of schools and housing for the poor, or the founding of public hospitals by the government? The answer is No.

In the classic text, *Anarchy*, the Italian anarchist Errico Malatesta (1853–1932) describes the function of a liberal government as part of the state apparatus:

> We even admit that never, or hardly ever, has a government been able to exist in a country that was civilized without adding to its oppressing and exploiting functions others useful and indispensable to social life. But this fact makes it nonetheless true that government is in its nature a means of exploitation, and

that its position dooms it to be the defense of a dominant class, thus confirming and increasing the evils of domination.

The government assumes the business of protecting, more or less vigilantly, the life of citizens against direct or brutal attacks; acknowledges and legalizes a certain number of rights and primitive usages and customs, without which it is impossible to live in society. It organizes and directs certain public services, such as the postal service, preservation of the public health, benevolent institutions, workhouses, etc., and poses as the protector and benefactor of the poor and weak. But to prove our point it is sufficient to notice how and why it fulfills these functions. The fact is that everything the government undertakes is always inspired with the spirit of domination and intended to defend, enlarge, and perpetuate the privileges of property and of those classes of which the government is representative and defender.

A government cannot rule for any length of time without hiding its true nature behind the pretense of general utility. It cannot respect the lives of the privileged without assuming the air of wishing to respect the lives of all. It cannot cause the privileges of some to be tolerated without appearing as the custodian of the rights of everyone.

Anarchism is not an ideal opposed to common sense, nor does it deny certain aspects of reality, nor is it reductionistic—it doesn't simplify reality in order to validate its premises.

This book owes much to the experiences and debates over the last decade of different actors on the Venezuelan stage, some of whom are specifically cited in the text. In this sense, a good part of the arguments presented here is not the work of the author. At the same time, I should acknowledge all those who have helped to make this work possible. I'd particularly like to thank those who went to the time and trouble of reading the manuscript as it was being written. I'd also like to thank the compañeras and compañeros of *El Libertario* [Venezuela's longest-running anarchist periodical], who have taken part in many social campaigns and initiatives over the last ten years. As well, I'd like to thank the Venezuelan human rights groups, a movement whose dedication and perseverance have been exemplary and instructive in many senses. Finally, I'd like to thank my compañera and confidant Lexys Rendón, who did the tedious but necessary job of checking all of the sources cited and of putting the citations into the proper format.

To all, Love & Anarchy.

—Rafael Uzcátegui, Caracas, September 2009

Photo by Rafael Uzcátegui

Hugo Chavez announcing a deal with the Spanish
multinational oil company Repsol-YPF

TRANSLATOR'S NOTE

Those familiar with the Spanish-language version of *Venezuela: Revolution as Spectacle* (*Venezuela: Revolución como Espectáculo*) will notice differences between it and this English-language version. There are a number of reasons for the differences. The first is that the author wrote this book for a Venezuelan audience and assumes that the reader is already very familiar with Venezuela. One cannot assume this for North American readers. So, the author was good enough to furnish additional background material which appears in this version of the book.

The second reason that this book differs significantly from the Spanish-language version is that I edited the book as well as translated it, and in the process made many changes. The most obvious is that I rearranged the structure of the book. It was originally organized into three long sections divided internally by subheads. I reorganized the entire text and broke it down into chapters.

As well, given that he's flying in the face of leftist political orthodoxy, the author did the right thing, providing extensive documentation and a large number of lengthy quotations from a large number of sources. Many of these (especially the quotations from government and corporate sources) share a common characteristic: they're written in bureaucratese. To spare the reader, I've shortened some of these quotations by deleting irrelevant portions. Where I've done this, I've inserted ellipses.

The alert reader will also notice that there are fewer endnotes in this version than the approximately 600 in the Spanish-language version of the book. There are several reasons for this: 1) I worked almost all of the lengthy endnotes into the body of the book; 2) Where there were multiple consecutive citations of a source, sans page numbers, I collapsed the repeated citations into single endnotes; 3) In other places I worked citations into the body of the book; 4) In a very few places I deleted small amounts of material and the accompanying endnotes for editorial reasons; and 5) I deleted a few endnotes that referenced web pages on sites that are no longer available.

Some readers will wonder why the only Spanish words italicized are book, magazine, newspaper, and film titles. The reason is that a large number of such titles appear in the text, as do a great many organizational names, and if all of the Spanish terms in the text were italicized it could easily have led to confusion. As well, the United States is to a great extent a bilingual country, and therefore there's little need to italicize Spanish-language terms.

As for the book and film titles, when there are English-language versions, the English titles have been italicized; when there are no English versions, the English translations of the titles appear, for informational purposes, in plain text within quotation marks.

On a more political note, this book gores a leftist sacred cow, so it's certain to provoke protest in both the U.S. and Europe. There's a long, unfortunate history of American and European leftists—including some anarchists—serving as loyal followers of leftist strong men, from Lenin and Stalin, with their Potemkin villages, to Castro and the Venceremos Brigades, to Hugo Chávez and the Chavistas of today. Decades ago, a maoist friend who had participated in a Venceremos Brigade in Cuba in the 1960s told me that the response of the brigadistas when Castro appeared before them reminded him of nothing so much as the reaction of 14-year-olds to an appearance by the Beatles. Unfortunately, that type of hero worship continues to this day.

And many leftist hero worshipers will attack the author, translator, and publisher of this book as "counter-revolutionary." This is to be expected. It's a standard charge. It's a standard, reductionist attempt to establish a false dichotomy: "If you're not with us, you're against us," to use the words of Mussolini, or, to use the words of George W. Bush, "Either you are with us, or you're with the terrorists." That leftists—who in theory support free speech—would (and will) take up this authoritarian shibboleth as a means of stifling dissent is saddening.

On a related note, the author takes to task American intellectuals who support the Chávez regime, specifically Noam Chomsky and Michael Albert. These two are significant in that they have done exceedingly useful political work for decades, and hence are among the most difficult American intellectuals to criticize. But at the same time both self-identify as anarchists, yet support a government.

It seems condescending and contradictory for anarchists to support any regime (which by definition rules from the top down, in the process creating a new privileged class). Essentially, the support for Chávez by American and European intellectuals is telling Venezuela's anarchists (who want genuine, up-from-below, revolutionary social change, and who oppose the Chávez regime—as they would any regime) that "the government knows what's good for you." One expects this sort of thing from authoritarian leftists, not from anarchists.

One point of political clarification is that there are numerous references in the text to *El Libertario* ("The Libertarian"), Venezuela's longest-running anarchist periodical. Readers should understand that "libertarian" has a very different meaning in the U.S. than in the rest of the world. There, the term is used as a synonym for "anarchist," one who believes in equal freedom and therefore rejects all forms of coercion and domination—most notably what Ricardo Flores Magón called the "three-headed hydra" of government, religion, and capitalism.

In contrast, here the term was hijacked by right-wing, *laissez-faire* capitalists in the 1960s and 1970s. "Libertarian" now refers, in the U.S., to a supporter of capitalism who is liberal on social issues, such as legalization of drugs and prostitution, but who wants to do away with all social welfare functions of the state (social security, medicare, unemployment benefits, etc.) while retaining its repressive functions (the police, military, prisons, etc.). Unfortunately, this grotesque redefinition of this formerly useful term appears to be a permanent part of the American political landscape.

Finally, I would like to thank five individuals who helped to make this English-language edition possible: Sonya Diehn, for putting me in touch with the author; Jean Michel Kay of *Cahiers Spartacus* (the French publisher of this book) who was of great help in a number of ways—providing the English translations of quotations from French authors (notably Guy Debord), pointing out a number of errors in my translation, and making a great many useful suggestions regarding the book's structure and contents; Ken Knabb, who helpfully and promptly provided the original English versions of two quotations from his works; Lynea Search, who did a wonderful copy editing job; and the author, Rafael Uzcátegui, who promptly provided additional information and clarification during the translation process.

—Chaz Bufe, Tucson, Arizona, November 2010

Photo by Rodolfo Montes de Oca

March of the Committee of Victims Against [police and military]
Impunity in Caracas on June 12, 2008

CHAPTER 1

Leftist Reaction to the Bolivarian Revolution

Noam Chomsky's vision of Venezuela is shared in large part by leftist intellectuals and political and social organizations throughout the world. This is no accident. The American writer and academic, whose discoveries in the field of linguistics are an important contribution to contemporary science, is one of the keenest critics of U.S. foreign policy. His critiques of the imperialist maneuvers originating in Washington, DC, and played out in the rest of the world, are a guidepost for dozens of revolutionary publications, hundreds of web sites, and innumerable individuals.

The political process that has played out in Venezuela since 1999 has been among those analyzed by this MIT professor. However, some of the data cited by the author of Manufacturing Consent are incorrect, and have affected his conclusions. At the same time, many of his assertions about the anti-capitalist nature of the present Venezuelan government are contradicted by a broad spectrum of Venezuelan revolutionary and anti-capitalist organizations, ranging from traditional marxist-leninist, to (Che) guevarist, to trotskyist, to anarchist. Why has an intellectual of the stature of Noam Chomsky misread the situation in Venezuela?

In many writings and interviews, Chomsky has constructed an image of Venezuela for American and European leftists. In describing this image, we're synthesizing six of Chomsky's declarations on the topic that are available in Spanish.[1] These are its features:

1) Venezuela remains in the United States' backyard;

2) From approximately 1920, with the discovery of major petroleum deposits, Venezuela has been part of the area controlled by the U. S.;

3) The strategy for this control unfolded in different parts of Latin America rich in natural resources;

4) Those resources have provided a good part of the United States' wealth;

5) Venezuela is the only Latin American member of OPEC and has by far the largest petroleum reserves outside of the Middle East;

6) for this reason it has been an important source of oil for the U.S. since the middle of the twentieth century;

7) Venezuelan petroleum has both enriched the local elites and flowed via the transnational corporations to the West, where it has contributed to industrial development;

8) In Venezuela the petroleum economy has produced a handful of the super-rich, but at the same time fully a quarter of Venezuelan children under 15 go hungry.

There is little to object to in this general characterization of Venezuela. The problems commence when Chomsky gets more specific about the present situation. To sum up his position: Owing to the democratic election of leftist governments in several countries in South America, the continent's countries have begun to move toward varying degrees of independence—which Washington can't tolerate—and for the first time in its history South America has begun political integration.

Historically, Latin America has had enormous resources, extreme inequality, oppression, violence, and very little interaction among its peoples, but that is starting to change. And of all the Latin American governments, Hugo Chávez's has delivered the greatest blow against U.S. domination—for the first time, Venezuela is using its energy resources for its own development. Only now have public health services begun to become a reality for a majority of the poor in the rich but profoundly divided country; since Chávez became president there has been slow but perceptible progress in the public health and social assistance services, which have so poorly served the people. Venezuela is smashing the model imposed by the U.S., breaking with the so-called Washington Consensus (neoliberal economic "reforms") and utilizing its resources for the benefit of its people. As a demonstration of the transformation and democratization the country is undergoing, a certain measure of workers' control of the oil industry—the principal source of revenue for the Caracas government—has been introduced.

Remember that this description of Chomsky's position is taken from six interviews translated into Spanish, in which the MIT professor places Venezuela in the vanguard of what can be termed the outcry against the system of U.S. domination. And if this outline of Chomsky's thought seems a bit hazy, a bit general, it's simply because there is no more precise elaboration.

If the Venezuelan government is neither a dictatorship nor a replica of Cuban-style Communism—as the conservative opponents of President Chávez say—neither is there substantive evidence that the country is undergoing a revolutionary transformation, whatever that term might mean. Despite Chomsky's having recognized, barely, that the so-called Bolivarian Process has authoritarian tendencies, there is no doubt that he's become a promoter of the "great goals of the Bolivarian Revolution" and has become a tactical ally of the Venezuelan government, as can be seen in the costly ads in Venezuelan periodicals featuring the prominent linguist's image, his appearances in the U.S. at presentations on Venezuela, and the continual diffusion of his speeches and interviews by the various ministries and governmental institutions in Venezuela. Nonetheless, Chomsky's opinions are based almost exclusively on secondary sources, such as the mass communications media in the U.S., and on information supplied by the governmental bureaucracy in Venezuela. Chomsky has spent only two days in Venezuela, in August 2009.

In contrast with Chomsky, there are activists interested in the "Bolivarian Process" who have directly investigated the construction of "twenty-first century socialism." Some of them have taken the officially sanctioned tours and have gone to various social enclaves supported by the government. The circuit of such tours includes campesino start-ups, "domestic developments," and urban and rural (indigenous) sites where the tourist can sample "the flavor of the Venezuelan Revolution." Other travelers come in search of a more authentic vision of the situation, one based in the daily life of the people.

Gabriel Muzio, an Italian documentary filmmaker, was one of these travelers. He's a member of the militant film production company, Gattacicova Films, whose focus is on documentaries about popular movements in Latin America. Muzio won a degree in economics in England, worked for years as a banker in London and Paris, where from the belly of the beast he witnessed "the [ongoing] great wave of financial innovation that took place in the capitalist world beginning in the 16th century," that is to say, the present-day reality of speculative capital operating without borders in a globalized economy.[2]

But Muzio retired from that comfortable life and returned to the passion of his youth: supporting popular movements in Latin America. In Columbia he began to tie together the issues of biological and cultural diversity, issues that would help humanity survive the depredations of capitalism. After eight years of crisscrossing the continent, attending conferences, and realizing the connections between the fate of the Amazon jungle, indigenous peoples, biodiversity, and the political/social-resistance community, he participated in the Social Forum in Porto Alegre, Brazil in January 2005.

I interviewed Gabriel one hot afternoon in March 2005, shortly after the premiere of his second documentary on Venezuela, *Nuestro petróleo y otros cuentos* (*Our Oil and Other Tales*, Gattacicova Films, 2004). In the heart of the Sarria barrio in Caracas, Gabriel related his initial fascination with and subsequent disillusionment with the potential revolutionary qualities of the so-called Bolivarian Process. From Columbia, he had closely followed the Caracazo popular uprising that took place in February 1989,[3] as well as the two attempted coups d'etat that took place in 1992, the first of which was led by Hugo Chávez. Years later, back in Italy, he watched the coup attempt in April 2002. In June 2002 he visited Venezuela for five days: "I met many people then, and became convinced that something new was going on here." Upon returning to his native country, the filmmaker attempted, without much success, to convince the Italian left to turn its attention to Venezuela.

Then, following an encounter with video-activist Max Pugh, who showed how quickly video documentaries can be made with the aid of digital technology, he turned to that medium, because "there was no other way to convince people that what was happening in Venezuela was different from what was being described in the corporate media." This was the origin of his first film on Venezuela, *Venezuela: otro modo es posible* (*Another Way is Possible . . . in Venezuela*, Gattacicova Films, 2002), which was produced in only five weeks of shooting and editing.

This film was made in a moment of intense social-movement support for President Chávez. At the same time, many popular organizations were attempting to bring about new social forms that, in the view of Muzio, deserved support: "Our film became, to a certain extent, a type of rallying flag. It circulated in many countries and was translated into five languages. It helped to organize groups in Europe and, especially, in the United States that supported the Bolivarian Revolution."

Despite the dizzying schedule of presentations of the Venezuela documentary, Muzio and his team recorded two more documentaries on conflicts in Latin America: *Bolivia no se vende* (*Bolivia Is Not for Sale*, Gattacicova Films, 2003); and *Como Bush ganó las elecciones en Ecuador* (How Bush Won the Ecuadoran Elections Gattacicova Films, 2003). However, Muzio's heart remained in Venezuela. During the filming of these other documentaries, he returned to Venezuela in order to follow the evolution of events and to meet with the various social groups and movements with which he was in contact. Also, as the producer of *Another Way is Possible . . . in Venezuela*, he was welcomed with open arms by several Venezuelan governmental institutions. His film, along with *Chávez: The Film* (Bartley & O'Brien, Ireland, 2003) and *Puente Llaguno: Claves de un Masacre* (*Puente Llaguno: Keys to a Massacre*, Angel Palacios, Venezuela, 2002), was part of the invariable trilogy shown at the time at forums and video showings organized by the state, and also by support groups, both inside and outside of Venezuela.

But Muzio was becoming uneasy about some of the things going on in the country. He commented, in 2005, on his personal journey of encountering the contradictions inherent in the Chávez movement:

> In those times, especially in 2004, I saw things that I didn't like at all. Things were moving away from autonomous movements, away from the idea of popular power, and toward a situation in which the bureaucracy and, especially the political parties, were delivering favors, dispensing with what little there was of power sharing [with the people]. It was totally the reverse of what was happening in 2002, when things seemed like they were flowing from the bottom up. . . . We've returned to a top-down situation, in which the political parties and president choose the candidates, and then the political parties decide where local power lies, who controls it, where economic resources go, etc. Where PDVSA (Petroleos de Venezuela, Sociedad Anónima)—the Venezuelan state petroleum company—is the entity that delivers the money for social investment, they deliver it as if it were a form of charity. Everything is from the top down.

For Muzio, it wasn't sufficient to visit Venezuela for five or thirty-five days in order to get an idea of what was going on in the country. Neither did he take a photo or make another film at a specific moment and then insist that it was the immutable reality in the country, while receiving the applause of the international leftist audience. The economist and video activist compared what appeared in his 2002 film with developments he observed directly--not from an office in American academia. And when things had taken a turn in a different direction than that portrayed in his first film on Venezuela, Muzio decided that the hour had come to make a second film to bring his audience up to date on what he had seen:

People in far off lands had begun to look at Venezuela through the lens of our [2002] film, believing in what was really a snapshot of a dynamic, of a movement. And then, with the passage of time, I simply had to better things. . . . People weren't bothering to investigate what was going on. They were looking at the situation in Venezuela uncritically, without raising doubts or questions. It was simply support! support! support! It was as if people always need to have some kind of faith.

The second film focused on the matter which concerns Chapter 3 of this book: Petroleum. Muzio puts it like this:

It's said, "PDVSA is of the people." But at the same time it makes agreements with international petroleum companies without consulting the people. Bolivia, at the end of 2003, had a popular revolt against the delivery of natural gas to the United States via a pipeline that ran through Chile. The Bolivian president was removed, but here in Venezuela, at the same time, [PDVSA] signed over the Deltana Platform, which has more natural gas than in all of Bolivia, to Chevron-Texaco, and nobody said anything.

Political reasons weren't Muzio's only motivation for making *Nuestro petróleo y otros cuentos*:

When I took my first journey through the petroleum-producing zone in the state of Zulia, on the eastern side of Lake Maracaibo, I was absolutely astonished by what I saw, by the misery, the resignation of the public, the public health problems, the environmental degradation. It was incredible. Then I thought, "The great majority of Venezuelans don't know about this." I wanted to shine a light on the costs of petroleum, because all people ever hear about are its benefits. If people continue to think that the Venezuelan model, the extractive model, should be that which reigns, I don't see any [chance of] change.

The Gattacicova film group changed its perspective: if the purpose first film was intended to inform the world about what was occurring in Venezuela, the purpose of the second was to introduce a heterodox viewpoint about the Bolivarian Revolution. *Nuestro petróleo y otros cuentos* is a 90-minute documentary that provides a quick history of the Venezuelan energy industry, and then builds upon that to cover the energy-company policies of President Chávez, including a subject that has become taboo among state functionaries: the environmental costs of energy extraction, with, as Muzio puts it, a focus on "the daily life of the communities that live and die by petroleum." The images are eloquent, contrasting clips of speeches by President Chávez and his ministers with clips taken at the conclusion of negotiations between the Venezuelan government and multinational corporations such as Chevron,

Repsol YPF, and British Petroleum—negotiations at which the parties acknowledged that their commercial relationships are profound and historic. As Noam Chomsky explained in another context, in order to maintain the propaganda line that Venezuela resists U.S. domination "it's necessary to suppress a great number of facts." [4]

The response of high government officials to the new documentary was furious. Francisco Sesto, then-Minister of Culture, called the documentary "intellectual yellow journalism and a manipulation of reality." In addition, given that a number of official institutions had partially financed the film, he asked that the institutions withdraw their logos [from the credits], and that state television refrain from showing the film. He added, "[Muzio] was not sufficiently professional, in the sense of abiding by the rules of the game, to be honest about his intentions." [5] Other statements by government officials suggested that the producers of the film had been bribed, that it was advancing the dark agenda of the opposition political parties, or that, simply and plainly, the producers were "counter-revolutionaries." One official asserted that Venezuelan problems were no business of foreigners. Néstor Francia, former leftist intellectual and later the spokesman for PDVSA, called the film "an act of piracy," assuring listeners that revolutionary marxists, such as himself, were "struggling against the deviations of the ultra-left." [6]

But we should clarify the nature of then-Minister of Culture Sesto's accusations, since they're good examples of the manner of debate typical of the politics of the so-called Bolivarian Process. Let's remember that Gabriel Muzio's film crew had the institutional approbation of the Bolivarian government, owing to its having produced *Another Way Is Possible . . . Venezuela* and its other previous documentaries. The National Council of Culture (CONAC—Consejo Nacional de la Cultura), an office of the Ministry of Culture, had a program that supported audio-visual productions, and through it had offered economic support for any project that the Italian film company wanted to shoot. Muzio delivered a project that was pre-approved by that government sub-agency, which provided half the funds for its production. So, is there, as Sesto's denunciation alleges, a lack of honesty?

We posed this question to Muzio, who responded as follows:

> I don't know exactly what they expected, because the proposal that I delivered to CONAC described practically everything that ended up in the film. The only difference, if one could even call it that, is that my viewpoint stemmed from the desire to introduce alternatives for the people beyond that of [being dependent upon] petroleum. Then, I thought those alternatives fell under two rubrics: small-scale fishing and sustainable agriculture. During the course of

the filming, we realized that [outlining alternatives] should be the object of another film, because otherwise it would be too complex, too ambitious. Only then did we concentrate on the petroleum situation.

One of the articles of faith in the Bolivarian Process is that there are two and only two positions regarding the government. The one on the left sympathizes with the construction of so-called 21st-century socialism, with its epicenter in Caracas. The other, which is critical and questioning, unfailingly is on the right and stems from the opposition political parties. This is a false dichotomy, for reasons that will be explained in the course of this book. But on this point it's important to emphasize the hostility and ostracism that meet any criticism whatsoever, be it from the left wing of the Chávez movement itself or from further-left groups attempting to build a revolutionary, anticapitalist movement in Venezuela. All criticism is treated as if it comes from the right-wing opposition.

This was the case with *Nuestro petróleo y otros cuentos*. The arguments in it were hardly debated by the Chávez partisans. Instead, Gattacivoca Films and Gabriel Muzio were the objects of a defamation campaign, based mostly on personal attacks. The film, contrary to the original agreements, was not shown on any of the state television channels. It had become a prohibited, politically incorrect film, rejected by Chavez supporters worldwide.[6] (Fortunately, Indymedia Arizona's Sonya Diehn produced a version subtitled in English, which is distributed through anarchist and autonomist channels by the German group Rebel Cinema.)

The experience of Muzio is not unique. But it is significant because he provides a critical view of the Bolivarian Revolution, seen through the perspective of the daily life of the people of Venezuela, not through the lens of government ministries and "revolutionary" tourism.

1. All of these positions were outlined in the following sources:
A. Democracy Now: "From Bolivia to Baghdad" http://www.democracynow.org/2006/12/19/from_bolivia_to_baghdad_noam_chomsky
B. Agencia Bolivariana de Noticias: "Noam Chomsky: Venezuela Deasfió con éxito a EEUU" (Link no longer available; web site has been renamed Agencia Venezolana de Noticias, http://www.avn.info.ve)
C. Pensa Consulado de Venezuela en Boston. "Noam Chomsky en el MIT: Venezuela es ejemplo de verdadera solidaridad y el mundo entero lo esta viendo" http://www.aporrea.org/tiburon/n73200.html
D. Miguel Vera, "Noam Chomsky analiza políticas de Venezuela y EEUU" http://www.radiomundial.com.ve/yvke/noticia.php?24062
E. La Jornada, "El petróleo de Venezuela y las chimeneas de Massachusetts" http://www.rebelion.org/noticias/2005/12/24003.pdf
F. Simone Bruno, "In América Latina se agrieta el sistema de dominación de Estados Unidos." Diagonal, Massachussetts: 2006, pp. 4–5.
G. Samaeer Dossani, "Guerra, imperio y neoliberalismo. Noam Chomsky establece las conexiones." *Contacto con la Nueva Pdvsa*, Numero 16, Caracas, 2007.
2 Rafael Uzcátegui, "Interview with Grabriel Muzio: el silencio favorece al enemigo no a la crítica," held in the Centro de Estudios Sociales Libertarios in Sarria, Caracas in March 2005.
3. The Caracazo consisted of rioting protesting the neoliberal austerity policies of then-President Carlos Andres Pérez; the rioting was followed by a massacre by security forces on February 27/28 that killed at least several hundred people.
4. Sameer Dossani, op. cit.
5. Claudia Furiati, "El cuento de 'Nuestro petroleo . . ..". Aporrea, December 2005. Available on the web at http://aporrea.org/actualidad/a13403.html
6. Nestor Francia, "En torno a nuestro petroleo y otros cuentos." Aporrea, December 2005. Available on the web at http://aporrea.org/actualidad/a12844.html

CHAPTER 2
Daily Life in Revolutionary Venezuela

"Those who speak of revolution and class struggle without alluding explicitly to daily life, without understanding what's subversive in love and what's positive in the refusal of duties, have a cadaver in the mouth."
—Raoul Vaneigem, *The Revolution of Everyday Life*

According to the traditions of the entire left, from social democrats to anarchists, the antisocial instincts that bring humans to commit violent acts against their fellows are as much the natural consequence of the alienation of labor as of the injustice inherent to capitalism. Inside the anarchist movement, Peter Kropotkin (1842–1921) laid the building blocks, in a conference held in 1877, of anti-authoritarian thought about crime and punishment. In *Prisons and Their Moral Influence on Prisoners*, Kropotkin said:

[I]f physical causes have so strong an influence on our actions, if our physiology so often becomes the cause of the anti-social deeds we commit, how much more potent are the social causes . . .

Year in and year out thousands of children grow up in the midst of the moral and material filth of our great cities, in the midst of a population demoralized by hand-to-mouth living. . . . These children do not know a real home. Their home is a wretched lodging today, the streets tomorrow. They grow up without any decent outlets for their young energies. When we see the child population of large cities grow up in this fashion, we can only be astonished that so few of them become thieves and murderers.

And at the other end of the ladder, what does the child growing up on the streets see? Luxury, stupid and insensate, fashionable shops, reading matter devoted to flaunting wealth, a money-worshiping cult with a thirst for riches, a passion for living at the expense of others. The watchword is: "Get rich. Destroy everything that stands in your way, and do it by any means save those that will land you in jail." Manual labor is despised to the point where our ruling classes prefer to indulge in gymnastics than handle a spade or a saw.

Society itself daily creates these people incapable of leading a life of honest labor, and filled with anti-social desires. It glorifies them when their crimes are crowned with financial success. It sends them to prison when they have not "succeeded." . . .

We will no longer have any use for prisons, executioners, or judges when the social revolution will have wholly changed the relations between capital and labor, when there are no more idlers, when each can work according to his inclination for the common good, when every child will be taught to work with his hands at the same time that his mind and soul get normal development.

Man is the result of the environment in which he grows up and spends his life. If he is accustomed to work from childhood, to being considered as a part of society as a whole, to understanding that he cannot injure anyone without finally feeling the effects himself, then there will be found few cases of violation of moral laws.

If it was completely certain that since 1999 Hugo Chávez has undertaken a wide-ranging transformation of Venezuela, and that his principal object was to better the living conditions of the poor and the working class, then why do there continue to be so many robberies and murders in the country? The coherent leftist response is, "If conditions had improved, there would be fewer of them." A more cautious though less direct answer would be, "At least they haven't gone up since 1999." But, taking our information from the Venezuelan government itself, we see that the latter answer is absolutely incorrect. Things have gotten worse.

The Homicide Epidemic

In 1999, coinciding with the government's bureaucratic renovation, Venezuela had the same homicide rate as countries such as Mexico and Brazil. The homicide rates in those countries have remained virtually flat since 1999, while in Venezuela the homicide rate has tripled.[7] According to Venezuelan government data, Venezuela is the most violent country in South America and Caracas has the highest homicide rate on the continent. The murder rate in Venezuela in 2007 was 48 homicides per 100,000 inhabitants. [Translator's Note: The rate in 2008 was considerably higher than in 2007, and dipped back down to just barely above the 2007 level in 2009.] By way of comparison, the murder rate in Brazil in 2007 was 25 homicides per 100,000 inhabitants; in Colombia 38 per 100,000; and in Peru 10 per 100,000.

The rates in 2007 for the major cities in the region are consistent with these figures: Caracas had 130 homicides per 100,000 inhabitants; Rio de Janeiro 62.9 per 100,000; Bogotá 23 per 100,000; Buenos Aires 9.9 per 100,000; Lima 2.4 per 100,000; and Santiago de Chile 2.2 per 100,000.[8]

All of the opinion polls conducted in the country show that Venezuelans consider personal safety the primary national problem. And it would be surprising if the result were different. The number of homicides has increased, virtually without interruption, since 1989, when the number of homicides was 2,513 in the entire country. In 1999, the date that President Chávez assumed power, that number had risen to 5,968 homicides, and it continued to rise through the next decade: 8,022 in 2000; 7,961 in 2001; 9,617 in 2002; 11,342 in 2003; 9,719 in 2004; 9,964 in 2005; 12,257 in 2006; and 13,156 in 2007.[9]

In the face of this social catastrophe, the Bolivarian authorities have denied the situation or have even insisted that the homicide rate is falling because of their efforts. Ramón Rodríguez Chacín, then-Minister of Popular Power for Interior Relations and Justice, provided an example of this disingenuousness when, on April 16, 2008, he proudly stated that there had been an 8% reduction in the homicide rate in Caracas.[10] He didn't point out that the number of homicides in the country as a whole had not diminished, and that in fact the homicide rate was increasing. By the end of 2008, it was 10.9% above the 2007 rate, and the total number of homicides had increased to 14,600.[11]

The principal victims of violence in Venezuela are the poorest people, especially those who live in slums. According to the figures from the Body of Scientific, Penal and Criminality Investigations (CICPC—Cuerpo de Investigaciones Científicas, Penales y Criminalistas), as diffused by the Center for Peace of the Central University of Venezuela, in Caracas murders are concentrated in the poorest parts of the city. In Chacao, a middle to upper class district, there were 21 homicides per 100,000 inhabitants in 2007. The rate was several times higher in Caracas's slums: Coche, 101 per 100,000; 23 de Enero, 113 per 100,000; San Juan, 90 per 100,000; Petare, 84 per 100,000; and El Valle, 75 per 100,000.[12] Homicide far exceeds heart attacks, cancer, and accidents as the leading cause of death of Venezuelan men ages 15 to 35.[13]

The homicide rate increase is not an anomaly; the rates for other types of crime have also risen. To cite an example, in 2008 robberies increased by 8% from the previous year, while kidnaping went up an alarming 101%. In 1998, a large majority of crimes were property crimes—69.3% versus 18.3% crimes against persons. By 2007, the rate of crimes against persons had increased alarmingly to 29.8% of the total (versus 54.3% crimes against property).[14]

The fracturing of the social system and the deepening of anomie in Venezuelan society, which is an obvious problem after more than a decade of the so-called Bolivarian Revolution, offers much material to analyze. Either all of the intellectuals of the left, including anarchists, who have theorized for well over a century about the causes of crimes are wrong, or those who insist that the Chávez government has revolutionized daily life for the vast majority of Venezuelans are wrong.

The Causes of Violence

Despite the graveness of the situation, neither the government nor its followers, nor the intellectual defenders of the Bolivarian Process, have attempted to understand or seriously debate the causes of the continuing increase in criminality. In the face of the number of crimes, and also the pain of families suffering the loss of a loved one, the reasons offered by the regime and its defenders are unbelievable:

A good part of the crimes that occur in Venezuela, especially those in the last three years, are in response to a political strategy designed by the U.S., the bourgeoisie, the Colombian oligarchy, and are executed in Venezuelan streets by Colombian paramilitaries and by mercenaries hired with the objectives of creating terror, systematically weakening Chávez and the people's Revolutionary Process, and of projecting through the national and international communications media a negative image of Chávez and Revolutionary Venezuela.[15]

This denial of reality is also expressed via the neglect of the matter in the different state and para-state media outlets.("Para-state media" include all of the propaganda communications media outlets financed by the government, masquerading under the labels "alternative" and "community.") On the web site of the state radio chain YKVE, if you type in "insecurity" ["inseguridad"–what this corresponds to is fear for personal safety], one gets 362 results, a bit less than the 387 results for "Ché" Guevara, and far less than the 5,467 results for "Hugo Chávez."[16]

The most rigorous attempt to understand the spiral of violence in Venezuela has been undertaken by the Laboratory of Social Sciences, an academic group linked to the principal public university in the country, the Central University of Venezuela. The model the Laboratory uses to explain the phenomenon of violence in Latin America, which holds for Venezuela, has three levels.

The first level is structural in nature, and consists of major and long-term social processes; these are considered the basis of the origin of violence. There are six factors:

1) the increase in urban inequality;

2) [poor] education;

3) unemployment;

4) rising aspirations;

5) changes in the nuclear family;

6) the weakening of Catholicism as a means of social control.

The second level is also based in the structure of society, but is less deep rooted than the first. These factors consist of specific situations or conditions that contribute to the growth in crime by encouraging antisocial behavior. Specifically:

1) segregation in urban areas;

2) overcrowding in urban areas;

3) drug trafficking;

4) a patriarchal and macho culture.

The third level is composed of micro-social factors, individual factors, that facilitate violent behavior, making it more damaging and more lethal. These are basically personal enabling factors:

1) the increase in firearms possession among the population; it's estimated that in Latin America somewhere between 45 million and 89 million guns are in the hands of civilians;

2) excessive consumption of alcohol, which acts as a disinhibitor, reducing cultural social-norm behavior; and

3) the inability to express sentiments and emotions; those who can't express their anger in words–a widespread problem in macho Latin America—express it through acts, and in this way create a mechanism that bypasses [dealing with] their emotions and desires.[17]

Fear and violence have noticeably changed Venezuelans' way of life. One of the visible effects is the abandonment of public spaces and migration toward private ones, reinforcing the global trend toward large business/commercial centers [in which there are few if any places for public socializing] as the new "public plazas" in the Bolivarian Revolution. There's a mall for every fifty thousand Venezuelans, and according to Arnold Moreno, president of the Venezuelan Chamber of Malls, the goal is to have one for every six thousand.[18] Approximately 85% of the urban population patronize malls–526 million visits per year–and they spend $4 billion to $6 billion annually.[19]

According to the report, "Interpersonal Violence and Citizens' Perception of Personal Safety in Venezuela," produced by the Venezuelan Observatory of Violence, during 2008, 62.4% of those they interviewed said that they had limited their leisure time away from home for fear of being the victim of violence. Also, 63.3% said that they had limited the hours in which they went shopping.[20] Another study, conducted in 2006 by Community Voice, revealed that 42% of children in Caracas never played in the street. And 63% of adults thought that the city was not a good place for children, citing as the principal reason the possibility of violence.[21]

The Tentacles of Violence

Fear and violence have combined to become one of the principal violators of human rights in the country. Stories about robberies from the schools appear every day in the communications media—robberies that reduce the amount of equipment and furniture that took years to arrive in the schools. Also, a study conducted by the Centro Pumilla reported that 73% of the students they questioned had witnessed violent incidents on school premises. [22] This has caused the public schools to take measures intended to reduce the amount of fear and violence. One example of this is prohibiting students from using cloth or canvas backpacks, or backpacks made from any other nontransparent or nontranslucent material.[23]

There are similar problems in the public hospitals. Fear of violence in medical centers is one of the reasons that health professionals are refusing to work in them. Assaults or gunfire exchanges among gang members have limited work hours in emergency rooms and made it necessary for hospitals to hire guards. During 2009, doctors and hospital workers used pressure tactics and work stoppages to demand safety in their workplaces.[24] Doctors in

Caracas witnessed, from the end of 2008 through mid 2009, three murders in which gang members finished off other criminals in hospitals; and in the same period nine other potential victims were saved in hospitals by armed commandos. In the interior cities, during the same period, there were seven homicides in medical centers.[25]

If there's one sector in which the violence underlying Venezuelan society is especially evident, it's in the jails and prisons. At the close of 2008, there were 23,457 inmates in Venezuelan prisons; and, over the entire country, there were 30 penitentiaries, all of them suffering from overcrowding. For example, the Internado Judicial de Falcón held 332% of its planned capacity; El Centro Penitenciario de Occidente held 144%; the Internado Judicial de Valencia held 121%; and the Cárcel Nacional de Maracaibo held 119%.[26] In 2008 there were 422 murders in Venezuelan jails [roughly one in 60 prisoners], and 854 assaults resulting in injuries. This corresponds to a murder rate of 1799 homicides per 100,000 population, a rate 33 times higher than the overall homicide rate in Venezuela in that same year (54 per 100,000). The Venezuelan Observatory of Prisons (OVP), a nongovernmental organization, calculated that, for the same year the rate was 44 times higher. This means that every two years the equivalent of the entire population of one of Venezuela's 30 prisons is murdered, which is why the OVP says that Venezuela's prisons are the most violent of any in South America.

In contrast, between the years 2000 and 2007, there were 494 murders within the walls of Colombian prisons, which housed 70,000 inmates. During the same period, the Bolivarian government's prisons, which held on average four times fewer prisoners, recorded 2,852 murders. More recent figures from the OVP indicate that the number of prisoners increased sharply in 2009, with the number being 35,600 in early 2010. Despite the drastic increase in overcrowding, the number of homicides in Venezuela's prisons decreased slightly to 366 in 2009, which still yields a very high homicide rate slightly in excess of 1% annually.[27]

Simón, a Life Senselessly Taken

If death is absurd, how much more senseless is it to bid goodbye to life as the victim of a robbery? In such senseless crimes, here in Venezuela we're losing many of our fellow citizens, one of whom was Simón Sáez Mérida (1928–2005). Simón was a professor in the School of Sociology at the Central University of Venezuela, and was well known as a rigorous historiographer, for his dedication to polemics, and, despite his years, for being a great agitator. I saw him in an assembly of professors in the mid-1990s, where they were discussing calling a strike to demand a larger budget for the university, along with the paying of past-due salaries to academic personnel. The theme that predominated at that meeting of more than a thousand was the calling of a standard strike—simply folding one's arms and staying home. In contrast, Simón proposed a strike with propaganda picketing throughout the city. Then there was silence. When it broke, Simón's proposal was labeled "adventurous" and went down to defeat. Three months later the strike ended, the professors went back to work, and the university continued to be plagued by the same problems.

Simón was born in 1928 in Maturín in eastern Venezuela. In 1949, under a military dictatorship, he joined Democratic Action (AD—Acción Democrática), which was an illegal organization at the time. While the most well known AD leaders directed the party from exile, Simón organized armed resistance inside the country, for which he was detained in 1954 and exiled in 1956. A year later, he entered Venezuela clandestinely to participate in the resistance, and in 1958 he was one of the protagonists of the insurrection that took down the dictator Marcos Pérez Jiménez

Simón left the AD in 1960 to found the Movement of the Revolutionary Left (MIR—Movimiento de Izquierda Revolucionaria). He was subsequently elected to the National Assembly, while he simultaneously organized an armed insurrection against the AD government of Rómulo Betancourt. In May 1962, he participated in the civilian-military insurrection called El Carupanazo, after which 400 militants were arrested and the MIR and the Venezuelan Communist Party (PCV—Partido Comunista Venezolano) were both outlawed. Even after that defeat, both organizations continued armed resistance. In 1964, Simón was jailed, and he spent five years in prison before being exiled to Europe in 1969. In that same year, the government adopted its Democratic Pacification Program, which allowed Simón to return to Venezuela.

In the following decades he dedicated himself to teaching, to union activities, and to editing leftist magazines such as *Reventón* ("The Burst"), *Al Margen* ("To the Margin"), and *F27* [a reference to the Caracazo uprising on February 27, 1989]. In 1998, he sympathetically observed the candidacy of Hugo Chávez, and he voted for the candidate from Sabaneta [Chávez]. However, the gap between the words of President Chávez and his actual governing policies made Simón begin to question Chávez, to the point where, in the year 2000, he denounced Chávez as a continuation of the past, as carrying out the neoliberal "Agenda Venezuela" of former president Rafael Caldera, deepening the subordination of the country to economic globalization.[28] His leftist friends who formed part of the Bolivarian government condemned him. Five years later, well into his eighth decade, the release of his final book, *Domingo Alberto Rangel Parliamentario* took place in the Center of Libertarian Social Studies in Caracas. It was Simón's final public appearance.

Simon was killed in 2005 during an apparent attempted robbery. It had become common for thugs to throw objects at cars in order to force them to stop and discharge their passengers, so that the thugs could rob the passengers. On April 23, a hunk of steel smashed through the windshield of Simón's pickup truck on the Valle-Coche highway in Caracas. It destroyed his jaw and disfigured his face, sending him to the hospital and the intensive care unit. Even so, he clung to life for 37 days.

Simón's killer was never arrested. And the number of those killed and wounded during robbery attempts against car drivers and passengers continues to mount in these times of the Bolivarian Revolution.

Police and Military Impunity

The tendency toward growing social decomposition is amplified by the active participation of police and military officials in human rights violations. This is nothing new, of course; there were plenty of abuses of authority in the 40 years prior to Hugo Chávez's rise to power. Nonetheless, one would suppose that the revamping of the bureaucracy and the implanting of a different model of government, self-proclaimed as humanitarian and respectful of human rights, would have minimized abusive practices.

On December 15, 1999, after a dizzying "constituent process" that lasted four months, 71% of the Venezuelan electorate approved a new national Constitution that went into effect five days later. Local activists hailed it for its important advances in the area of human rights. Despite the government's promotion of what it called "the best constitution in the world,"[29] one of the sacred rights enshrined in that document soon became a dead letter.

A guarantee of personal safety is one of the rights proclaimed in the Constitution of the Bolivarian Republic of Venezuela. The definitive version of the document stated in Article 46 that "No person can be subjected to inhumane or degrading punishments, tortures or cruel treatment." Nevertheless, in September of 2000, according to human rights groups, there were 527 such violations: 21 cases of torture; 333 instances of cruel treatment; 72 cases of personal injury; 71 cases of threats or harassment; and 30 cases of illegal detainment [by Venezuelan authorities]. Poor young people were, as always, the principal victims. Almost half of the cases—241 of the 527 (45.7%)—were the responsibility of regional police forces; municipal police forces accounted for 58 cases (11%); the Directorate of Intelligence and Security Police (DISIP—Dirección de Inteligencia y Seguridad Policial) accounted for 22 cases (4.1%); the army nine cases (1.7%); and the Technical Body of the Judicial Police (CTPJ—Cuerpo Técnico de Policía Judicial) accounted for six cases (1.1%).[30]

In a report presented in 2007, the nongovernmental human rights organization Red de Apoyo por la Justicia y la Paz (Aid Network for Justice and Peace) stated that between 2003 and 2007 they had examined a total of 143 cases of torture. Of the 143 victims, 113 (79%) were men and 30 (21%) were women. Students formed the largest single bloc of those tortured (18%), while workers accounted for 15%, persons in miscellaneous occupations accounted for 10%, and salespeople and housewives accounted for 7%. [It's reasonable to assume that common criminals accounted for the other 50%.—tr.] One of the findings of the report was that the great majority of torture was conducted for the purpose of obtaining information, and that the principal organizations involved were those responsible for the initial investigation of crimes: CICPC (Cuerpo de Investigaciones Científicas, Penales y Criminalistas—Body of Scientific, Penal and Criminality Investigations) accounted for the largest number of torture cases (23%). It was followed by the Caracas Metropolitan Police and the National Guard (15%), which in turn were followed by the army (10%).

Among the methods of torture employed by Venezuelan authorities were blows, kicks, verbal abuse, death threats against those being tortured or those they held dear, the use of handcuffs, plastic bags over the head to produce asphyxiation, guns held against the head or against other parts of the body, and the constraining of the victim in uncomfortable positions [as at Guantánamo].[31] By June 2009, the number of cases of torture that had come to the awareness of the Red de Apoyo had risen to 237 during the first six months of that year.[32]

Article 43 of the 1999 Constitution established the inviolability of the right to life: "No law can establish the death penalty, nor the authority to apply it." A report from the Venezuelan Program of Education on Human Rights (PROVEA—Programa Venezolano de Educación de Derechos Humanos), a nongovernmental organization similar to the Red de Apoyo, stated in September 2000 that in the previous 12 months there had been 104 instances in which state authorities had violated this fundamental right. Nearly half the victims (47) had been executed; 22 died while in custody; 15 from abuse of power; five died from torture or other mistreatment; six died in military custody; six died from excessive use of force; and three from indiscriminate use of force. In order of importance, the principal organizations responsible were the state police, the municipal police, the Caracas Metropolitan Police, the Technical Body of the Judicial Police, the National Guard, the armed forces, and the Directorate of Intelligence and Prevention Services.[33]

The numbers cited above continued to grow over the following years. In September 2008, PROVEA's annual report cited 247 instances in which the right to life had been violated by the authorities. As in previous years, extrajudicial executions accounted for the largest number of victims, comprising 85% of the whole. Next came death through negligence at 6%, death through excessive use of force by state security forces at 4%, and death through indiscriminate use of force at 3%. Various state police forces were responsible for 46% of the deaths; following them came the national police, the CICPC, the army, and the National Guard.[34]

These figures correspond with those cited by government authorities. In May 2009, Attorney General Luisa Ortega Díaz revealed that between January 2008 and March 2009 there were 755 incidents of homicides presumably committed by police. The Attorney General said that in the period cited 10,103 investigations were opened regarding injuries, abuse of authority, unlawful home intrusions, illegal detentions, torture, and "disappearances." Ms. Ortega Díaz added that these investigations resulted in the arrest of 22 policemen, while 2,655 cases had been filed away.[35]

In June 2009, the Minister of Popular Power of the Interior and Justice, Tareck El Aissami, estimated that 20% of police were involved in crimes and murders.[36] And on July 13, 2009, the Vice-Minister of Citizen Security of the Ministry of Justice and the Interior, Juan Francisco Romero Figueroa, revealed that of the 9,000 members of the Caracas Metropolitan Police, 1,800 were under investigation.[37]

Growing police corruption and impunity form part of the picture of fear and violence in Venezuela. The police and military participate in kidnaping, extortion of businessmen and workers, drug trafficking, smuggling gasoline across the border between Colombia and Venezuela, and they also collect protection money from gangs for allowing them to control territory. When a police functionary is investigated for engaging in criminal activities, there's a show of expelling him, and then he's rehired by another police agency in another state. Pablo Fernández, coordinator of the Red de Apoyo, has called this practice "police recycling." One example: "A group of officers were expelled from the Polianzoátegui [police force], were absorbed by the police of Puerto La Cruz, and later were apparently involved in grave human rights violations."[38]

Corruption is not confined to low-level officials; rather, it's especially serious with high-level bureaucrats who coordinate police bodies, who, despite repeated accusations, not only enjoy impunity, but also continue to climb the state's hierarchical pyramid. The governor of Lara State provides a notorious example. Lara State is the fifth most economically important region in Venezuela, and its capital Barquisimeto has more than a million inhabitants. In the period 2000–2008, Air Force Lieutenant Colonel Luís Reyes Reyes, who had the political capital of having participated along with Hugo Chávez in the attempted coup d'etat in April 1992, was the governor of the state.[39] After four years of Reyes' government, people with few resources organized themselves to denounce violations of human rights in the state. In 2004 they formed the Committee of Victims Against Impunity (CVCI—Comité de Víctimas contra la Impunidad), which has stated that Reyes Reyes is directly responsible for the human rights situation in Lara. In 2009, they declared: "Eight years were sufficient for the State of Lara to come to occupy first place on the index of drug-trafficking crimes, and the police in command were vying with Anzoátegui, the Capital District, and Zulia in extra-judicial executions."[40] The Committee also stated in a different declaration: "We want to expose the total impunity that exists in the State of Lara regarding the evident and multiple crimes committed by the police. Through [2007], the state attorney registered 273 cases of presumed extra-judicial executions; this year there were 30 more."[41]

The statistics cited by the CVCI indicate that the Armed Police Forces of Lara (FAP—Fuerzas Armadas Policiales), under the control of the state's governor, are responsible for a staggering 49% of the total crimes in the state. Of the crimes committed by the police, 69% were homicides. Another 7% involved drug trafficking; 7% involved "disappearances"; 5% involved incitement to crime; and 3% each involved aggravated assault, rape, and sexual molestation.*

---

* Translator's Note: One suspects that the statistics cited in the previous paragraph are in part the result of sampling error, that is, CVCI probably hears disproportionately about the most serious crimes and about crimes committed by the police. Among other things, this would in part explain the very high police homicide rate cited above. Regardless, the human rights situation in Lara State is undoubtedly grave, as witnessed by the hundreds of individual cases of extra-judicial homicides that CVCI cites.

In June 2008, the CVCI along with other popular groups in Barquisime-to, delivered a document to the Venezuelan Attorney General in Caracas, in which it detailed 237 extra-judicial murders committed by a group of state police.[42] In July 2008, a journalist who worked for a daily paper sympa-thetic to the regime tried unsuccessfully to interview Reyes Reyes in order to get his version of events. Reyes' secretary for citizen security, General Car-los Enrique Colmenares Camacaro, responded to the accusations: "Publish what you want. The governor has nothing to say because it's not his duty to do so. Besides, all of the dead were criminals who died in confrontations. I don't understand your interest in interviewing the governor when this matter doesn't have the least importance to him nor to us, given that all the acts were done within the law."[43]

Despite this sorry record, on December 10, 2008 Luís Reyes Reyes was designated by Hugo Chávez to be the Minister of Popular Power for the Of-fice of the Presidency, a post in which Reyes Reyes sits as I write this.

Luís Reyes Reyes is not the only high functionary of the Bolivarian gov-ernment accused of serious human rights violations. A formerly obscure mili-tary officer, who has twice filled the role of Minister of Interior Relations and Justice, is directly tied to massacres in 1988 which killed, at a minimum, 34 innocent persons who were made to appear as if they were Colombian guer-rillas. This mass murder is known as the El Amparo Massacre, and the man who led it is Hugo Chávez's Minister of Interior Relations and Justice, then-navy captain, Ramón Rodríguez Chacín.

The El Amparo Massacre

Venezuela and Colombia share 2,216 kilometers of border. On the Ven-ezuelan side, there are three border states: in the north, Zulia, which is rich in gas, oil, and coal deposits; in the middle, Táchira, which was the epicen-ter of Venezuelan coffee production a century ago; and in the south, Apure, which marks the beginning of the Venezuelan savannah, with cattle ranching, wide open spaces, and rich biodiversity. This infinite green plain was the set-ting for the most well known Venezuelan novel, *Doña Bárbara* (1929), by Rómula Gallegos, who in that book's prologue describes the area as well as it possibly can be described:

Searing sun and copious rain, with all the thunderous ostentation of a savannah downpour, where among the storm clouds and the plains a single thunderclap rings on, accompanied me on my journey on one of the thousand paths across the savannah . . . half dry plains, with mirages of torrents of water brought on by the thirst of the traveler, and wide expanses of water, from mountain to mountain in the rivers, and from one end of the sky to the other in the estuaries.

The capital of Apure State is San Fernando, which is divided into seven municipalities, of which one, Municipio Páez, is bounded by the Arauca River, which marks the frontier between Colombia and Venezuela. The most important towns in the Municipio Páez are Guasdualito, Palmarito, El Nula, La Victoria, and El Amparo. Municipio Páez accounts for 15% of the border between Venezuela and Colombia. Despite having 8.35% of Venezuela's territory, fewer than half a million people live in Apure, according to the 2000 census, which counted 466, 931 residents; this makes the state population the sixth lowest in the country with less than 2% of the total. [44]

In 1987, when this story begins, a report from the Ministry of the Office of the Presidency diagnosed the problems that afflict the area: lack of electricity and infrastructure that would stimulate economic productivity, lack of adequate schools, lack of studies and planning to address cultural and social problems, lack of adequate housing, lack of medical equipment and medical services, high incidence of diseases such as malaria and yellow fever, and chronic malnutrition. The data revealed an area with a dramatic lack of basic services, lack of development of the regional educational system, and a health situation that reflects the abandonment of the region by the state health programs. As might be expected, 59.5% of the area's land was in the hands of 6.3% of the producers.[45]

In October 1987, then-President Jaime Lusinchi signed Decree 1810 that created the José Antonio Páez Commando Unit (CEJAP—Comando Específico José Antonio Páez) with the purpose of "guaranteeing the integrity of the land border in its jurisdiction and to plan, organize, and conduct operations to combat and eradicate drug trafficking, subversion, smuggling, and common crime in the southwest border strip."[46] This commando unit was attached to the President of the Republic and, in operating terms, to the Ministry of Defense. It was comprised of units belonging to the four branches of the Venezuelan armed forces (army, navy, air force, and coast guard) along with security arms of the state: General Sectorial Directorate of Military Intelligence (DIM—Dirección General Sectorial de Inteligencia Militar), DISIP, General Sectorial Directorate of Identification and Foreigners, and the CTPJ.

Between January 16 and October 6, 1988, CEJAP reported six "confronta-tions" with "Colombian guerrillas" in which at least 20 "guerrillas" died. The operatives of the commando unit operated with unusual efficiency, given that they suffered not a single casualty and completely dismantled the enemy's subversive plans. CEJAP planned its greatest success, dubbed "Anguila III" ("Eel III"), for October 29. In an ambush conducted in the Caño La Colo-rada, near El Amparo, CEJAP killed 14 people. Barely two hours later they described to the media those they had killed as "Colombian guerrillas," who intended to dynamite the Gaufitas de Apure oil field.

But, in contrast with CEJAP's previous operations, there were two survi-vors of Anguila III. Protected by the people of El Amparo, they provided a very different version of events. Subsequent investigations confirmed what these survivors said: autopsies revealed that all of the victims had been shot in the back, and the majority killed by subsequent shots to the head. The scene of the crime had been staged, with the cadavers hurriedly costumed with guerrilla-style clothes, and with arms that had never been fired strewn about the scene. The vision of a military confrontation vanished, with its place being taken by that of a massacre.

Despite the fact that the victims were civilians, the investigations of the crime were conducted by the military. The human rights group PROVEA, which was founded and incorporated to defend the survivors and families of the victims, stated: "In the case of the El Amparo massacre, the actions of those comprising the tribunals, the councils of war, and the courts martial which sat in judgment were oriented toward the clear purpose of producing impunity. With only a few exceptions, the military attorneys and judges com-mitted an innumerable number of irregularities intended to favor those who conducted the massacre."[47]

The case went to the international level, and on January 18, 1995 the Inter-American Court of Human Rights (CIDH) rendered its first judgment against the Venezuelan state, holding it responsible for murdering 14 innocent per-sons. The government acknowledged the verdict, in doing so recognizing its culpability, and completed in part what the CIDH ordered: it compensated the families of the victims, but it didn't punish the intellectual and physical authors of the crime.

The El Amparo Massacre become, along with the military repression un-leashed on February 27, 1989 ("El Caracazo"), an emblematic case of human rights violations in the 1980s. In addition, it revealed a sinister modus ope-randi carried out by CEJAP, repeated decades later by the Colombian army of Álvaro Uribe, in cases dubbed "false positives": murder innocent persons, and then present them before the public as guerrillas. One of the hypotheses about the motivations of CEJAP is that it wanted to create the appearance of growing guerrilla control in the zone where the massacre took place. In this manner it would stimulate fear, which in turn would stimulate the private security-protection business, controlled by the top brass at CEJAP, which wanted business from cattlemen and large landowners. Another theory (reported by PROVEA) points to the creation of conditions conducive to the elevation of one of the spokesmen for the commando unit to the position of Minister of Defense.

What can this crime, which occurred ten years before Hugo Chávez came to power, reveal about the Bolivarian Process? One of the intellectual authors of the crime has become, twice, Hugo Chávez's Minster of the Interior and Justice.

On October 25, 1988, three days before the El Amparo Massacre, a CEJAP helicopter crashed while on an intelligence mission. Among those injured was the National Chief of Operations of DISIP, commissioner Henry López Sisco. The other injured crew included a minor navy functionary, Captain Ramón Rodríguez Chacín. The crash made it impossible for López and Chacín to be present at the massacre, undertaken as operation "Anguila III," and which was conducted by 19 army, DISIP, and CTPJ personnel. The intellectual participation of Rodríguez Chacín in the massacre can, however, be seen in court documents on the case (number 1644, folios 42–45), which was handled at the time by the Military Court of First Instance of Táchira. Henry Salinas, an inspector in the Division of Military Intelligence (DIM), declared before the military tribunal that "I was a witness that the R2 and R3 [presumably 2nd and 3rd in command; "R" probably stands for "Responsible"] of CEJAP, Lieutenant Colonel Clavijo Forero and Navy Captain Ramón Rodríguez Chacín, called us together days after 'Hipolito'—the alias of DISIP inspector Celso Rincón Fuentes—and I spoke about preparing this confrontation [Anguila III]."

Barring the helicopter crash, it seems probable that, as had occurred in previous operations, Chacín would have been directly involved in the ambush. Those prior murderous actions can be generically grouped under the name "Los Amparitos" ("the little Amparo" [massacres]). The "Los Amparitos" crimes include the Isla de Charo massacre on January 16, 1988, in which 10 persons died; Caño Las Gaviotas on April 22, 1988, in which two died; Los Totumitos, on July 8, 1988, in which five died; and El Vallado on October 6, 1988 in which three died. It was for those crimes that on June 20, 1994 a military court investigating the "Los Amparitos" crimes, presided over by General Ubaldo López Barrios, issued arrest warrants against 11 former members of the commando unit. These included Commissioner Henry López Sisco (who, years later, would become security advisor to the governor of Zulia State, Manuel Rosales, an opponent of President Chávez) and Captain Ramón Rodríguez Chacín.[48]

In 2002, the Chávez regime appointed Rodríguez Chacín Minister of the Interior and Justice, a post which he held for several months. In December 2007, it appointed him Special Coordinator of Operation Emmanuel.[49] And on January 4, 2008, Rodríguez Chacín was named Minister of the Interior and Justice for the second time. At the time of this writing, he also performs functions within the Coordinating Commission of the PSUV (Partido Socialista Unido de Venezuela—United Socialist Party of Venezuela), the principal government party.

In July 2008, the author of this book made two trips to El Amparo—in order to produce a video that would document 20 years of impunity following the El Amparo Massacre—traveling 14 hours on the only bus line that connects Caracas and Guasdualito, and from there it was another 30 minutes by taxi to El Amparo, a community of 9,000 frozen in time. At that moment Rodríguez Chacín was still in office. I talked with or interviewed the victims' family members, and the two survivors of the massacre, and they all remembered Rodríguez Chacín. The majority of them didn't hide their sympathy for the Chávez government, but they also asked me why the Bolivarian Revolution would name a murderer to the position of Minister of Justice. In the 34-degree centigrade (93-degree Fahrenheit) heat, that question hung in the air.

Labor Conditions

A second indicator of the material conditions of existence in Bolivarian Venezuela, beyond fear, crime, and related factors, is the situation of the country's workers. Let's first compare the figures for the years 2000 and 2008 in order to assess the quantitative advances and defeats in the labor sector.

According to the Central Office of Statistics and Information Sciences (OCEI, now the INE—Instituto Nacional de Estadística/National Institute of Statistics), at the close of the first quarter of 2000 the rate of unemployment was 15.3%, which corresponded to 1,554,606 persons without employment, based upon the Economically Active Population. Eight years later, according to data supplied by officials from the INE, the unemployment rate was 7.2%, corresponding to 922,503 out of a workforce of 12,812,548. A report distributed by the INE in May 2009 said that the state employed 2,244,000 workers—an increase of 220% in ten years, from the 700,000 it employed in 1999.[50]

Since the 1980s, a high proportion of Venezuelans have been involved in the "informal sector" of the economy. This informal sector is a result of the high level of unemployment in Venezuela, and is comprised of small scale and individual enterprises with low levels of organization and technological expertise. Most workers in the sector have few job skills and do not receive the benefits due them under Venezuelan law, notably participation in the social security system and vacations. In 2000, according to the OCEI, the percentage of workers involved in that sector—in other words, workers who work for themselves or others and who do not enjoy the labor rights established by law—accounted for fully 52.6% of the total number of workers in Venezuela. Eight years later, the situation had improved slightly, with the informal sector accounting for 43.2% of workers.[51] Nonetheless, after ten years of the Bolivarian Process, and after the highest national income in the last 30 years, there still existed 5,535,020 persons who worked in precarious conditions in the informal sector.

In 2000, Venezuelan human rights organizations recognized that the increase in the minimum wage ordered by the national executive, an increase which amounted to 20% in the public sector, would compensate for the inflation that occurred during 1999: "[It's a] fact that this is the first time this [an increase in the minimum wage that kept up with inflation] has happened in a decade characterized by the progressive deterioration of real wages."[52] Things changed for the worse in subsequent years.

In 2000, the minimum wage bought 71% of the Venezuelan "food basket," a "basket" (rice, black beans, potatoes, bananas, powdered milk, eggs, chicken, sugar, corn flour, and cooking oil) sufficient to feed a family of five with a breadwinner working eight hours per day. By 2009, the minimum wage bought only 52.7% of the "food basket." In other words, the 29% gap between the minimum wage and the cost of the "food basket" had risen to a 47.3% gap.

On May 1, 2009, the Chávez government raised the minimum wage to the equivalent of $409 (US) per month, which it said was the highest minimum wage in the region.[53] The aggressive publicity campaign that accompanied this wage raise was refuted by the leftist Venezuelan web site laclase.info, a site tied to the Socialist Union of the Left. (All of the statistics laclase.info cites come from official sources.) We've included their full analysis here because of its clarity and eloquence:

One can't consider wages in simple absolute terms. Neither can one compare [wages in Venezuela] to wages in countries that have less inflation than ours. In the case of the Venezuelan minimum wage, it's necessary to compare it with the level of inflation in order to know its real value. If it's true that Venezuela has the highest minimum wage in Latin America, it's also true that Venezuela has had the highest inflation of any country in the region over the last three years, and in the last decade [Venezuela] has on more than one occasion closed the year with the highest level of inflation on the continent. [Cumulative compounded year by year] inflation rose 556.41% between 1999 and 2008. In comparison, cumulative inflation in the price of food products during the same period was 922.38%. [In this period] wages didn't keep up with inflation.

Between 1999 and 2008 there was double-digit inflation every year. The lowest rate was in 2001 at 12.%, and the highest rate came [in 2008] at 30.9%. It's necessary to underline that while inflation in Venezuela was 30.9% last year, inflation in food prices . . . was 43.7%. . . . [H]owever, real wages hardly rose at all—1% annually over the last 12 years. And in accord with this it's evident that the increases in the minimum wage have been "swallowed" by the elevated inflation we've suffered.[54]

It's worth noting that the poorest wage earners spend, relatively, the most on food (the price of which rose far above the overall rate of inflation). So, the 1% annual increase in real wages—an *average* increase—was, for the poorest wage earners, almost certainly a net *decrease*.

In Venezuela there are always arguments about the manner in which the government collects information about and calculates the rate of unemployment. Many of these arguments coincide with the traditional anarchist practice of doubting what the government says. In this respect, economist Domingo Maza Zavala has written:

Jobs or employment—categories that should technically be differentiated–according to the official indicators have risen to the point at which unemployment can be placed this year [2008] at 6% or 7%. However, it's necessary to take three things into account: "informal" occupations, which account for about 45% of the active work force; public-sector work, which in good part is disguised unemployment; and independent investigations which cite unemployment as an obvious cause of social deviations . . . One can make proclamations utilizing conventional indicators, but that won't improve the [actual] situation; neither will it fool the unemployed.[55]

A polling company whose results have been hailed at various times by the Bolivarian government, the Venezuelan Institute of Data Analysis, in March 2009 placed unemployment—behind only fear for personal safety—as the second most important problem to Venezuelans.[56]

If the Chávez government has significantly decreased unemployment, why does the public continue to cite it as one of Venezuela's principal problems? Either the figures from the government or public opinion must be wrong.

Professor and economist Miguel Angel Santos has alerted [the public] to the definitions used by INE in the collection of information on employment. The procedural manual used by the organization classifies working-age (15 or over) persons as "inactive" (that is, not seeking work) who, during the week of the survey, attended as students any of the social programs implemented by the national government. Santos says: "The most important thing is the fact that those questioned were not permitted to distinguish if, despite participating in these programs, they had (or had not) continued to actively seek employment." This would have the effect of lowering the number of those classified as actively seeking employment, and would thus artificially lower the calculated unemployment rate.

As well, the INE uses the criteria of the UN's International Labor Organization to determine whether someone is employed or unemployed. Those criteria classify a person as being employed if he or she, during a reference period (usually a week), works one hour for (monetary) pay.[57]

Even if we assume that the government has not manipulated the figures, even if we take its statistics as valid, it's evident that, despite the economic bonanza [from petroleum], the high rate of inflation and the continued presence of a huge "informal" sector are evidence that the Chávez government's concrete results do not match the huge income it's had to work with.

Unionism Impelled from Above

If one listens to the declarations from high officials in the Chávez government regarding unions, one finds common threads: "The working class should adhere to the Bolivarian union organizations, not only to better procure what belongs to it, but also to impel the political struggle for the construction of socialism."[58] These words were spoken on April 30, 2009 by the Minister of Labor, María Cristina Iglesias. Later, she stated: "In 1998 there were barely 1,300 unions, and today almost 6,000 organizations have registered with the Ministry of Labor, a surprising increase, in a decade, of 460%."

Unfortunately, there are no public reports on the names and nature of these organizations, on the companies in which they operate, or on their membership figures. And it appears as if the government itself cannot confirm the Minister of Labor's statistics. The newspaper *Ultimas Noticias* attempted to ascertain the true figures, and, starting with the Ministry of Labor, received the run around, from one government agency to the next. In the end, the newspaper obtained no firm figures from the government.[59]

Nonetheless, the promotion of union organizations on the part of the Chávez government has continued the patrón politics of Venezuela's past—the creation of labor federations from above and by decree. In 1947, after participating in the coup that brought it to power, the Democratic Action party (AD) instigated the calling of a national union congress that, with the participation of 15 regional federations and seven professional federations, founded the Venezuelan Workers Confederation (CTV—Confederación de Trabajadores de Venezuela), with an executive committee consisting of AD militants. In 1948, after a new coup that overthrew the AD's Rómulo Gallegos, the CTV was banned. But in 1958, with a return to democracy and a new government presided over by AD member Rómulo Betancourt, the CTV began to function again, with its executive committee controlled by the two parties that had made a pact to alternately rule the country, the AD and Social Christian Party (COPEI). Over the following four decades, the CTV was the principal union organization in the country, monopolizing labor representation, and being clearly subordinate to the government of the day.

When Hugo Chávez assumed office, his intent to control the labor movement was evident from day one. In 1999, he quickly confronted the CTV [leadership]. Despite questions about irregularities and problems in the organization, despite the lack of a self-directed labor movement, the government participated in the union's elections scheduled for October 1999, but which were delayed for two years on orders of the National Electoral Council (CNE—Consejo Nacional Electoral). In the CTV elections, Aristóbulo Isturiz was the candidate of the government's Bolivarian Workers Front, running a campaign that typified the political strategy that began in 1999 [with Chávez's election]: "The government backed Isturiz' campaign in all its aspects: the campaign's propaganda tied it to the popularity of the president; the use of state resources in the campaign was evident in the mass meeting held in the Caracas Polyhedron–a venue for major events—with participants transported from all over Venezuela in thousands of buses, with famous musicians and musical groups which transformed the event into a celebration of the anticipated victory."[60] Nonetheless, the Bolivarian candidate was defeated by Carlos Ortega, the candidate of the Unitary Front of Workers controlled by Democratic Action.

After the defeat, the government decreed the organization of a new union organization, the National Union of Workers (UNT—Unión Nacional de Trabajadores), which held its founding congress on April 5, 2004. However, the UNT was more focused upon defending the government than upon advancing the interests of the workers. In 2006, the opinion of Venezuela's anarchists was as follows:

> What is known of the UNT is, principally, its vassalage to government officials–a vassalage that exceeds that of the CTV to previous governments. Its street events are mere demonstrations of adhesion to Chávez and his measures . . . [I]ts concrete actions in regard to collective bargaining or other confrontations are ruled by a conciliatory zeal . . . Except for giving uncritical, after-the-fact approval to decrees, the UNT has had nothing to do with setting the minimum wage . . . [S]ave for some generalities, no one knows what the UNTistas say about immediate labor problems such as the . . . super-exploitation of women and minors . . . or inflation and the loss of purchasing power of wages."[61]

It could be objected that the opinion of the anarchists couldn't be anything but this, given that they distrust all state organizations. Even so, they're not alone in this attitude. A leftist current, Labor Option (Opción Obrera), that took part in the creation of the UNT, said this four years after the organization's founding:

> The UNT was born beneath accords from above, and it put on a show for the base; in its executive there were very few authentic directors from a labor background. Fourteen national coordinators, from diverse founding currents, expressed the accord. At its foundation, it was decided to wait a year to convoke a congress and to hold grassroots-level elections. After three years a plenary was called in May and a congress was held in September in a treacherous, antagonistic atmosphere that didn't permit the approval of the statutes under discussion. This was in keeping with the fact that the original directors did not yet have the legitimacy that they would have derived from being representatives chosen by the base; instead, their strength was measured by their prostration before the government. The internal crisis in the UNT persists and worsens to this day with, at the national level, diverse currents disputing the positions of power. . . . The UNT was born under the government's shelter. The pro-government CTV practices that were criticized are now being repeated by the leaders of the UNT, who deliver themselves unconditionally to the government.[62]

Paradoxically, given the limited acceptance of the new labor organization (UNT) by the mass of workers and the resistance of some sectors to this cooptative entity, the Chávez government in 2007 promoted new labor organizations to displace the UNT, such as the Bolivarian Socialist Workers Front (FSBT—Frente Socialista Bolivariano de los Trabajadores).

A second mechanism intended to control the labor movement—justified by the argument that it weakened the CTV—was the promotion by the government of so-called "union parallelism," which created artificial "unions" outside of the organized unions in the principal companies in the country. In this manner, the Chávez government could brag about the high number of registered unions, and that the Bolivarian Process [i.e., the Chávez government] had promoted like no one before the organizing of the workers. However, this increase in unions did not signify greater labor power. One indication of this is the paralysis of collective bargaining contract negotiations with public enterprises: at the end of 2007 there were 243 expired contracts.[63]

The decisions regarding wages, work conditions, and the laws regulating the work world are made unilaterally by state institutions, after which they're ratified by the spokesmen of the UNT. "Union parallelism" has augmented the fragmentation and division of workers' initiatives. Here I'll cite the opinion of Labor Option:

> Parallel unionism is a wild card, at first used against the old CTV bureaucracy and now for more fragmentation; it continues in the ambient of the officialist unions, that now must deal with diverse internal currents–some with the blessing of the authorities of labor administration, and others that are marginalized. Unionism, following this course [parallel unionism], has fractured even more, owing in part to the proliferation of unions in single enterprises to the detriment of labor federations.[64]

A third element in the government's control of the labor movement was the creation of the PSUV, a body which, in the words of its first chief executive, had to absorb all of the organic initiatives that supported the Bolivarian Process—and that included union organizations. Few defended the independence of the labor movement, and dissent was not tolerated. In March 2007 Chávez said in a speech: "The unions should not be autonomous . . . [I]t's necessary to do away with this."[65] He reaffirmed this in successive statements along the same line, arriving at the zenith of these proclamations in March 2009, when after mocking the labor demands in the Guayana region in Venezuela's south, he threatened to use the police to repress strikes or other mobilizations in the region: "Some unionists go around inciting the workers; I'm going to start calling them by first and last name; I'm going to wade into this battle heart and soul."[66] For the revolutionary Venezuelan unionist Orlando Chirino, this was insupportable. He said that Chávez's statement "constituted a declaration of war against the working class."[67]

If the previous facts and arguments aren't enough to suggest that the Bolivarian Process [i.e., the Chávez government's policies] has worsened the perversion of Venezuela's labor movement—"atomized, dispersed, disarticulated, weakened—that is to say, in its worst crisis"[68]—the antagonism among the unions (which involves a high number of deaths) over the control of workplaces speaks for itself.

Corrupt Labor Practices

Before he became president, Hugo Chávez denounced the trafficking in workers in the petroleum and construction industries by the principal union organizations. That was a demonstration of the degradation of union activity in Venezuela and the abandonment of the struggle for workers' rights by the unions. In 1999, when Chávez assumed power, there was a makeover of the government bureaucracy, a makeover accompanied by talk of transformation and renovation; this generated expectations about the rebirth of the Venezuelan union movement.

But since 2003 the well-intentioned talk has melted away in the heat of reality. Worsening violence introduced a new element into the labor arena: the murder of unionists and workers for the purpose of controlling the labor market. In the construction sector—one of the two areas where the situation is the worst—since 2003 clause 53 in the collective bargaining agreement specifies that the unions provide 75% of workers.

Human rights organizations such as PROVEA have denounced this clause, in that it destroys the essence of unionism [to combatively assert workers' rights *against* employers] and instead makes the unions into organizations that *cooperate* with employers—and that the unions' control of who gets jobs can easily lead to corruption. For example, in some cases employers have used "irregular" channels in reaching understandings with the unions, without open conflict such as strikes; and many times these "irregular" arrangements have not been to the workers' financial advantage.[69] This situation repeats itself, on a smaller scale, in the petroleum sector.

Between the years 1997 and 2007, Venezuelan human rights organizations recorded 52 murders of unionists and 87 murders of workers over control of workplaces (that is, workplace hiring), for a total of 139 victims. Hit man-type murders were in the majority, and there were heavy indications of the participation or complicity of the police in those murders. The states with the highest number of workplace-control-related murders were Bolivar (42.3% of the murders), Aragua (14.6%), Caracas (11.4%), Anzoátegui (8.9%), and Zulia (8.1%).[70] According to the figures compiled by the Human Rights Vicarage of Caracas, the problem continues. Between June 2008 and May 2009 there were 52 murders of unionists and workers in cases clearly related to the control of workplaces.[71]

In the construction sector, prior to the beginning of the work day, there are hundreds of workers knocking on the door seeking employment. Officials in the various unions, in accord with the number of workers they have or their ties to the construction companies, provide the workers. In exchange, they get substantial commissions from the companies and kickbacks from the workers to whom they give work.. (In Bolivar State—in which 42% of murders are over control of workplace hiring—the largest union organizations, such as the Union of Construction Workers of the State of Bolivar, are self-proclaimed as "Bolivarian" and "revolutionary.")

There are two things that we should highlight about this terrible situation. The first is the high level of impunity. Of murder cases involving corrupt union officials between 1997 and 2007, only three of the material authors [union officials] were sentenced to prison, which equates to a conviction rate of only 5.8% in cases involving union officers.[72] The second is that, despite the gravity of the situation, none of union federations—CTV, UNT and FSBT—have as one of their goals the stopping of violence over workplace control, or even to investigate and punish those materially and intellectually responsible for these crimes.

Breaking the Fake Union Consensus

I first became aware of unionist Orlando Chirino at a birthday party in 2001 at the home of Gonzalo Gómez, a militant trotskyist I'd come to know a year earlier in the Venezuelan Network Against External Debt. The network was a coalition of diverse individuals who united around a critique of the economic globalization process and the subordination of the countries of the so-called Third World via indebtedness to the international financial organizations.

Despite their long and fractious history, the Venezuelan trotskyists, after the change in government in 1999, regrouped in order to insert themselves into the Chávez movement. Gonzalo was a part of this, as a member of the group that produced the magazine *La Voz de los Trabajadores* ("The Voice of the Workers") and also as a popular singer. In the small room of Gómez's apartment that served as a library, with a portrait of Trotsky beaming down, several students and professors announced what, to an outsider such as myself, sounded like the imminent assault on the Winter Palace. And, they concurred that the man leading the charge was a combative textile worker from the state of Aragua named Orlando Chirino.

Chirino was born in Falcón, a coastal petroleum area neighboring the State of Zulia. He became involved in the leftist political struggle when he was 17, and participated in the MIR, a part of the Democratic Action party, which conducted armed resistance in the country, primarily from 1960 through 1969. When the MIR began to run out of steam, amidst the contradictions and internal fighting that followed the cessation of armed struggle, Orlando became involved with the trotskyist tendency that came to call itself *MIR Proletario*, which combined with the Socialist Workers Party (PST—Partido Socialista de los Trabajadores) to form PST-The Spark (PST-La Chispa), which in turn put out a militant union magazine called *La Chispa*. In 1974, he began working at Cenalese, a textile-chemical company in the city of Valencia in Carabobo state, where he labored for 27 years and founded the union local. In the 1980s, he struggled actively against the CTV bureaucracy in the states of Aragua and Carabobo, in the central part of the country, where there's a significant industrial belt. In 1984, he was nominated as a candidate for president of the National Federation of Textile Workers and ended up being elected as its Secretary General.

Chirino was enthused by the progressive rhetoric of the [Chávez] government elected in 1998, and became part of the wide pro-Chávez movement promoting the renewal of unionism in Venezuela. In 2002, when the failed coup attempt against President Chávez occurred, Chirino denounced the attempt to tear apart the country's constitutional fabric, and months later fought the PDVSA "petroleum strike" [which temporarily paralyzed petroleum/gasoline supplies; see pp. 112–114] in dozens of workers' assemblies and mobilizations.

His experiences in 2002 motivated him to become a key player in the formation of a new union federation intended to displace the CTV. On August 11, 2003, he became the National Coordinator of the Provisional Directing Committee of the UNT at its founding congress, the union federation promoted by the Bolivarian government. The UNT had five tendencies at its core; one of them was the Class-Conscious, Unitary, Revolutionary, and Autonomous Current (CCURA—Corriente Clasista, Unitaria, Revolucionaria y Autónoma), headed by Chirino himself.[73]

Two years later the CCURA promoted the holding of a UNT congress to end its provisional directorship via elections and at the same time to elaborate a specifically labor-oriented program. That's when confrontations began with the union functionaries appointed from above, and for whom the campaign to re-elect Hugo Chávez took precedence over everything else. This meant postponing the agendas of all of the social movements, including the unions.

Despite the fact that there were already criticisms of the Bolivarian Process, the UNT largely went along with this, lending "critical" support to Chávez at the polls. Despite this, Chirino's breach with the Chávez bureaucracy grew because of his independence and defense of the unions' autonomy. In December 2007, he was dismissed from his position at the time of Secretary of Safety and Health for the Sinutrapetrol union; this provoked protests from many organizations worldwide, which considered his firing as political retribution.[74]

Simultaneously, Chirino was demanding that President Chávez fulfill all of the promises he had made to Venezuela's working class. He later denounced the government's inaction as well as the sudden enrichment of a new bourgeoisie under the shelter of the Bolivarian government. And at that time, he recommended abstention in the referendum on the constitutional reforms proposed by President Chávez [which, among other things, would have removed Venezuela's term limits on the presidency]. Venezuela's anarchists also recommended abstention in the referendum, and it was at that time their paths began to cross with Chirino's.

In a March 2009 interview with the Caracas anarchist paper, *El Libertario*, Chirino didn't mince words: "This is a government, [including] the president, that has had an anti-labor policy for a long time. Beyond that, it's necessary to say that it's also anti-union. The government has a policy of dismantling the unions."[75] Chirino, who had been the spokesman of the Bolivarian labor federation (UNT), which had at its beginning more than a million members,[76] enumerated the contradictions of the government that said it defended the country's workers:

> I want to indicate the most important collective accords that have been violated. We'll start with the public workers, approximately two-and-a-half million workers. It's been five years, from December 2004, since their contract standards have been discussed, and this is very grave. This has resulted in 70% of public workers being minimum-wage workers, which is to say that we're a country of minimum-wage workers. It's been three years since the educators'

collective bargaining agreement expired; the electrical workers, approximately 36,000 of them, had their contract expire last year; and the petroleum workers over the last ten years have lost important gains.[77]

This last point, about work conditions in the country's principal industry, is paradigmatic. In a denunciation published on the leftist web site laclase. info, an oil worker enumerated eight violations of working conditions by PDVSA:

1) Failure to supply safety equipment, such as work coveralls, helmet, gloves, uniforms, insulating boots, and the tools necessary for daily labor;

2) The deterioration of infrastructure, such as storage tanks and measuring devices in bad condition. Lack of response to these problems has been a roadblock to production;

3) Wages have not risen for two years, while between 2007 and 2009 inflation ran to 66.5%. Because of this, many workers hold second jobs such as taxi driver or cleaning-product salesman;

4) Elimination of overtime pay, without compensation in daily wages;

5) Inequities and discrimination in the payment of wages;

6) Criminalization of labor demands by the workers;

7) Postponement of union elections by the bosses, as well as the imposition of company men in the unions;

8) Absence of social safety policies, such as transparent mechanisms to help workers attain housing or health services.[78]

In other sectors of the economy the situation is equally complicated. In his interview with *El Libertario*, Chirino describes government actions that weaken the power of the unions, citing concrete examples:

The workers of the Caracas Metro have held talks about their collective bargaining agreement, which had lapsed for a year and a half. They arrived at accords with the representative of the Procurate, which is supposed to be the entity that safeguards and cares for the interests of the state. Later, the president of the republic and his new director of the Metro, refused to recognize these accords and resorted to a terrible method, one used only by dictators or authoritarian governments: it threatened the workers. If they demanded their legitimate rights by striking, it would militarize them and then fire them.

. . . It had [the police agencies] DISIP and DIM, as well as the government-controlled Community Councils threaten the workers with being booted out. A government press release stated that in case of a strike Chávez would "militarize the Metro," because he would not accept a work stoppage. He said that some unionists had managed to have the board of directors of the Metro, under pressure, sign an unsustainable contract, and that he would not accept it.(79) And so, without consulting with the workers, in an anti-democratic manner, the directors of the union who were members of the PSUV [Chavez's party], behind the backs of the workers, acceded to a new agreement that rolled back most of the gains won [with the previous, non-implemented agreement], and that left them with only 30% to 40% of the gains previously agreed upon.(80)

On November 23, 2007, President Chávez ordered, from the largest theater in Caracas, the Teatro Teresa Carreño, the creation of a new method of organizing the working class: Workers Councils. "It's necessary that work sites be related to the community, and the popular-power Workers Councils can exist, as much in the factories, as an internal organ of the factories, as much as they ought to exist out there in the community; they're the arms of the working class in the social battle, in the ideological battle."(81)

Anyone who was listening to President Chávez for the first time would have concluded that his proposal was revolutionary. However, after dozens of similar proposals, [which when put into practice] were all controlled and manipulated by the state, many people doubted Chávez's good intentions. Orlando Chirino is one of them:

If for the workers, in order that the debate be more fluid, in order to be more efficient, in order to deepen democracy and [popular] participation, they [the Chávez government] decided to form workers councils, socialist councils or whatever, we'd be heading this up with them. But this proposal has nothing to do with that. The proposal for workers councils is an instrument, in my opinion a para-political one, of the government whose purpose is to subjugate the workers and to guarantee to the new bourgeoisie stability and well-being. The purpose of these workers councils is supposedly to advance the construction of socialism, but as you see, [its true purpose] is to combat, discharge, persecute from within all those union officers who have distinct opinions from them, who truly believe in socializing [the workplace], who truly believe in a redistribution of wealth.(82)

Chirino goes on to make comparisons between the Bolivarian shackling of the working class and the repressive mechanisms of the past:

I've been a union representative. In the 34 years I've been involved, I've never seen the extreme to which we've arrived today with the criminalization of protests. On the extreme, there's an element that has never been used before. For example, when you're doing proselytizing work, as in handing out flyers at a factory gate, speaking through a megaphone, participating in an assembly, they use the repressive bodies of the state to detain the leaders, take them to jail, and while in jail they accuse them [of crimes]. This ends up with [union militants] being prohibited from going near to the businesses where they do their political work under the legitimate rights of free expression and organization. These are very serious, concrete things. . . . We denounce today, as we denounced when we've had anti-worker and anti-union governments, the concrete things that are happening.

On November 27, 2008, three comrades of Chirino, who had been participating in acts of solidarity with the workers of the Alpina Dairy, in the midst of a labor conflict, were murdered by thugs in the city of Cagua in Aragua state. Their names were Richard Gallardo, Luis Hernández and Carlos Requena. The indications, which have not been officially investigated, point to the complicity of the owners and the state security agencies in the murders.

The Flexibility of Globalized, Bolivarian Labor

One of the elements of the present process of globalization of the economy and the unstoppable flow of capital is the flexibility of relations of capital and labor. Spanish anti-globalization activist Ramón Fernández Duran says that "social and labor conquests, obtained after more than a hundred years of struggle by the labor movement and the various social movements, are being dismantled by the deregulation of the labor market and the parallel dismantling of the social safety net provided by the state."[83]

During most of the 20th century, the organization of work unfolded along the lines established by Frederick Taylor and Henry Ford. Taylor was an economist and mechanical engineer who proposed that the production process be managed scientifically, achieving efficiency through having a very high degree of managerial control over the work process, using such tools as time-motion studies. The industrialist Ford is considered the father of the assembly line, which breaks down the production process into repetitive small tasks performed in sequence by individual workers. The approaches of Ford and Taylor combined in the factory model that became dominant during the First World War: a huge infrastructure where primary materials entered on one end and came out the other as finished products after passing along an assembly line.

This method was dominant through most of the twentieth century, but began to go into decline toward its end. The huge traditional factory, with its rigid organization and hierarchy, with the specialization of its parts, including the workers, lost competitive capacity. Business terrain was conquered by new companies which had incorporated into the production process advanced technologies provided by telecommunications, microelectronics, biology, and genetic engineering, among others.

The convergence of these practices left the Ford/Taylor model behind, and enterprises that wanted to survive in a highly competitive market were obligated to modernize via policies that implemented industrial reconversion. That is, they had to develop the capacity to vary the production process and the volume and design of their products very quickly and at minimum cost, via flexible structure and technology, and a workforce with flexible capabilities, a workforce which could be changed (or abandoned) as needed. This recasting of the productive model—given the disposability of the labor force—began to negatively affect working conditions and at the same time diminish the gains labor had made over the previous century. In sum, the new industrial model was flexible enough to transplant itself quickly and relatively easily, especially to those countries with the lowest wages and fewest regulations.

Venezuela was not immune from this trend in the 1990s. It reached its zenith with the elimination of the Social Security System and the Social Services System in 1997. The government also diminished substantially the amount of compensation for those dismissed from their jobs. Human rights organizations such as PROVEA called this measure "the greatest retreat in history in this country as regards human labor rights. This is a result of the continued application of policies oriented toward obtaining greater flexibility in labor relations."[84]

In 1998, with the election of a new government that denounced the policies of its predecessors as subordinate to international capital, many believed that the harmful labor practices would reverse, or at least come to a stop. Ten years later, the situation of the laboring masses, Bolivarian rhetoric aside, demonstrates the contrary. In the concrete case of the relation between workers and their bosses, there is more "flexibility" than a decade earlier, especially in the public sector. The government itself has promoted labor deregulation in order to prioritize individual contract labor for fixed terms, with no social safety net. At the same time, it employs cooperative firms to execute public policies, which may then subcontract to individuals without having to supply the benefits established by law [for wage workers]. Finally, the state has postponed indefinitely the renewal of collective bargaining agreements with its employees, so that the conditions under which they work remain at the discretion of their bosses.

The prior analysis is not exclusive to Venezuela's anarchists. In November 2008, Topo Obrero (The Laboring Mole), a union current that defends the Chávez government, released an analysis in which it describes the different types of labor flexibility in the country:

> It's important to take into account that this phenomenon–deregulation–if we relate it end to end in the present Bolivarian socialist system, the EPS (socialist production businesses), the cooperatives, the social missions, create false systems of safety and labor protection, falling quickly into a system of [government] assistance. . . . The situation presents itself today in Venezuela of "clandestine" jobs that worsen the general condition of Venezuelans . . . the small jobs and illegal scavenging, the maquiladoras, contraband trafficking in basic products, the subcontracts that are grasped at even though [they're not worth much], day labor agencies, the tricks and traps, etc., are part of the progressive degeneration of a progressively neocolonial epoch . . . [There are] taboos observed by labor inspectors in the entire country, ministries, mayoralties, governorships, universities both experimental and autonomous, autonomous institutions, factories and state enterprises, as in the entire private and commercial sector, the state enterprises and all their derivatives, producing "diverse" workers in various social conditions, subdivided in an illusory, alphabetical manner (divide and conquer), creating different types of workers in generally precarious situations.[85]

Another article published on the pro-government web site APORREA, affirms: "The truth is that the bourgeoisie of the day in Venezuela advanced their tropical New Deal, with considerable labor flexibility, hazardous jobs, company unionism, always beneath a nationalist discourse and false confrontations with bankers, land holders, transnationals and imperialism–for whom they guaranteed their piece of the pie of surplus value extracted through the exploitation of the labor of wage workers."[86]

Johan Rivas is a worker and unionist in the Dr. José Ignacio Baldó Hospital Complex, located in the western part of Caracas. He's also a leftist militant, a member of the Socialist Revolutionary Collective (CSR—Colectivo Socialista Revolucionario, which considers itself a part of the Bolivarian Process, but is critical of the government), and was an unquestioning follower of President Chávez until 2007. Rivas tells us in an interview for this book about the conditions of healthcare workers:

The divisions [among workers] have deepened, sadly. In the case of health workers, they have increased. That is to say that now, even though I don't have the exact figures at hand, a high percentage of workers, more than 20% or 30% in [this] hospital are not regular workers. . . . They're not called "substitutes" as in the past, but now, rather "special contractors," and they're nothing but substitutes under another name. Pay and work conditions have improved, but they're the result of the struggle of the workers. According to the figures that we have, which are not denied by the government, there are presently more than 25,000 workers in the health sector in Caracas and more than half of them are contract workers. . . .

[T]his is part of a [government] labor agenda, an incredible social drama. I can cite cases of women who were discriminated against because they became pregnant, and so had to abandon their contracts. Infirmary workers who've worked three or four months receive their wages a month or two late. Or they work for a weekend, and they're paid their wages as the law prescribes, but only after delays of one or two months. . . . People wait up to two years for a contract and receive permanent pressure in the sense [of pressure] not to participate in such-and-such a political organization or not to do such-and-such a thing. They don't say so directly, but they've been imprisoned by this blackmail that's so disastrous and lamentable: "If you don't do this, you won't get work." [This is] a tough burden that contradicts revolutionary practice, because the practice [today] continues being that of the past.

The situation described by Johan Rivas can be found in all of the institutions of the Bolivarian state, where the hiring of new workers is done via temporary contracts, which in turn has enabled an old practice in Venezuelan politics: obligating public employees to participate in political demonstrations. These practices have "normalized" to such an extent that they no longer scandalize anyone in the country. The different electoral events or mobilizations supporting the government have attendance lists, which must be signed by the employees of the different ministries, institutions, and by those who benefit from social policies. As well, it's common in employment interviews for state jobs for those applying to be quizzed about their political opinions. Another form of control in the workplace is the perusal [by government authorities] of data lists provided by the National Electoral Council (CNE).

The most well known data list is the "Lista Tascón." In 2004, a group of Venezuelans, in accord with Constitutional Article 72, formally requested that the CNE call a referendum to recall President Chávez. To do this, they had to deliver the signatures of 20% of those registered to vote. One National Assembly deputy, Luis Tascón, put up on a web site the complete list of those who had signed the recall petition. To make things worse, anyone [i.e., employers, including the state] could search the list for a national i.d. number to discover if the i.d. number [of a job applicant] corresponded to anyone who had signed the petition. So, the Lista Tascón, and other similar lists, have become instruments of political blacklisting.

Despite the preceding, no labor-flexibility situation created in the years of the Bolivarian Revolution could surpass that in the mixed-enterprise Venezolana de Telecomunicaciones (Vetelca), which assembles the cell phone popularized by President Chávez called, incredibly, the Vergatario. ["Verga" has several meanings, among them the mainmast of a ship. However, it's normally used as a crude sexual term. —tr.]

Vetelca, the History of a Bolivarian Maquiladora

On May 10, 2009, President Hugo Chávez, speaking from the El Tigre sector of the State of Barinas, presented on television the cell phone made in Venezuela under the tutelage of his government, the Vergatario, produced "with the highest technology." It had such features as a "simple video camera, games, watch, text messaging, radio," and was offered for a low, low price equivalent to $15 US. Given the Venezuelan appetite for cell phones, which are status symbols in an underdeveloped country, and given the wide publicity for the product featuring the Bolivarian leader, it was foreseeable that the Vergatario would be a rousing success.

On that May 10, President Chávez stated: "This telephone not only will be the best seller in Venezuela, but in the world."[87] He announced that it would soon be exported, after satisfying the domestic market and that of the Andean countries, Caribbean, and the Southern market (Brazil, Argentina, and Uruguay). Given such ambitious objectives, the question arises: "How will this become the best seller in such a competitive branch of the telecommunications industry?" The answer is obvious: "Reduce, as much as possible, the cost of labor." And the expert in doing that—as companies such as The Gap, Nike, and Adidas well know—is China; and China is precisely the associate that the Bolivarian state chose as its partner in the Vetelca mixed enterprise, which was established in January 2009 in the Franja de Paraguaná zone in the State of Falcón. The first challenge was to deliver 10,000 units to Movilnet (the state cell phone provider) so that the Vergatario could be offered on Mothers' Day, as President Chávez had promised. Even so, the workers in the factory were unhappy with the short deadline, and said so through the government's media channels.

Levy Revilla Toyo, one of 56 workers who were fired by Vetelca, has written a detailed account of the beginnings of the company.[88] According to Revilla Toyo, the company began hiring in October 2008 through the Ministry of Light Industry and Commerce; and the government selected the board of directors, with Carlos Audiles Flores as the chair. Conditions of employment and classification/status of workers were nebulous, which would shortly lead to trouble.

On May Day, Vetelca began producing Vergatarios: "[I]t was necessary to labor until far into the night; this labor was done without logistical preparation, which caused dismay among some comrades because of lack of nourishment and trouble with transport." However, the workers were compensated with a productivity bonus and the satisfaction of having made good the word of the President, and had the devices ready in ten days.

In compliance with the Organic Law of Prevention, Conditions and Work Environment, put in effect by the Bolivarian government in 2005, the Vetelca workers elected "prevention" (safety) delegates, despite the negativity of and the obstacles imposed by the enterprise's board of directors. On July 7, 2009, Vetelca fired eight workers, among them the three safety delegates who had been elected at a workers assembly.

The fired workers went to the authorities, who visited Vetelca in order to investigate. Revilla Toyo recalls what management said: "[T]he workers are apprentices, [and] the pay is not pay but support, and they had no organizing structure." Later, the Vetelca management asked the National Guard to protect the factory from the workers, while the bureaucrats accused those fired of being counter-revolutionaries. In the end, the company fired 56 workers, who were forced to sign resignation letters as a condition of receiving their final paychecks.

On July 29, 2009, the Minister of Science and Technology, Jesse Chacón, visited the Vetelca factory in order the dispel the uncertainty of the remaining workers. The official press release states: "The minister looked through the factory and met with the workers in order to tell them that no more than 15 days later they would be able to sign their collective bargaining agreement."[89] The press release also contained this gem: "Until these moments the employees went to their workplaces in the capacity of volunteer operators, receiving a monthly production bonus of 1,300 Bolivars."

The minister added, "One is dealing with a model of socialist production with 'integral' workers who perform different jobs on a daily basis, in order that each will know the steps of the production process and the complete function of the plant. In addition, they participate in the planning of the production process, which clearly shows the difference between this and the capitalist model."[90]

The reports in the state media stuck tightly to this story. Carlos Audiles, the president of Vetelca, declared: "It was a dismissal of persons who were in the process of organizing, because of nonncompliance with norms. . . . I would note that one can't speak of the firing of persons who weren't on the payroll . . ."[91]

In another declaration, this time in the daily paper *Ultimas Noticias*, Audiles surpassed himself: "These fifty-six [fired] persons had the intention of creating a union [for the purposes] of agitating or of procuring jobs, [and] with an aggressive, instigating attitude."[92] The article in which this quote appeared added, "Audiles explained that Vetelca is not registered as a company, and because of this there is no contract."

Audiles also stated that after a test [period], and once the enterprise was constituted, it would form a security department, "because in a socialist enterprise there's no room for the word 'union,' because this would break with the concept that everyone is equal, and in a socialist system there's no need for a union." Responding to the accusation that the fired employees performed maintenance functions, Audiles replied that "because they couldn't count on resources, the participants worked in a voluntary manner performing cleaning [functions]." But with the launching of the Vergatorio things changed, and "the mothers of the local community [were hired] to carry out these activities."

Analyzing all this, we see that Minister Chacón's "integral model of socialist production" is a euphemism for "polyvalent labor," a term which describes labor flexibility in the age of information-capitalism. In the "polyvalent" model, workers must be capable of working at different tasks, going from one to the other according to the needs of the productive process. (This is in sharp contrast to the Ford/Taylor system of production, in which workers perform a single repetitive task.)

As well, it's by no means certain that the Vetelca workers are familiar with the "complete function[ing] of the plant" nor that they "participate in the planning of production." The workers of Vetelca are simple assemblers and packagers of a product whose parts are fabricated in China.

Vetelca, despite the epic descriptions delivered by high officials in the Chávez government, is a simple *maquiladora* that serves the needs of the state cell-phone company. In an interview, Audiles himself confirmed this: "Vetelca, in its total capacity, satisfies Movilnet's demand for products."[93] Movilnet decides the quantity of phones that will be assembled, the date on which they'll be delivered, and the distribution network, three things in which the Vetelca workers have no say. If the Venezuelan President suddenly decides to launch a promotion of Vergatarios to celebrate the birth of Simón Bolivar, and so increase production rapidly, the Vetelca workers will have no choice but to repeat the days of overwork described by fired Vetelca worker Levy Revilla. This, of course, corresponds to the flexibility of work hours typical of the present stage of capitalism.

The statements of economist/company head Audiles also reinforce the view that the "Bolivarian Process" is more one of economic globalization than socialism. It's revealing that he fired the "aggressive, instigating" organizers of a union intended to ensure continuing, stable employment–a goal of virtually every worker in the world. And his confession that Vetelca will not permit union organizing, "because it's contrary to socialism," needs no further comment.

President Chávez, Jesse Chacón, and Carlos Audiles can assert, a hundred times over, that the Vergatario is a socialist telephone fabricated in a "socialist enterprise" by "salaried volunteers." Even if they repeat that lie a thousand times, the facts speak for themselves: Vetelca is the first *maquiladora* in Venezuela, one that copies the Chinese model, a model in which interchangeable workers serve the interests of today's savage capitalism.

The Social Policies of the Elitist Post-1958 Democracies

When an intellectual of the stature of Noam Chomsky, referring to the government headed by Hugo Chávez, makes statements such as "For the first time, the country is using its energy resources for its own development–we can debate with how much or how little success–in reconstruction, health . . ."[94] he's putting at risk his reputation for rigorous analysis. Why? Because the preceding statement isn't true. It's one thing to recognize the social development policies of President Chávez, which have had varying degrees of success, and it's another to maintain that never before, under any of the governments that preceded Chávez, were there education, health, or housing policies aimed at helping the poorest classes.

Is the Chávez government really something new under the sun? No. Populism has been one of the principal features of many Latin American governments. And a form of populism all its own has characterized Venezuela since 1958, given Venezuela's unique status as a country almost entirely dependent on hydrocarbon extraction. This condition has molded the relations of society, the state and its institutions, and political movements. Venezuelan democracy has based its modernization projects, as we've explained earlier, on hydrocarbon exploitation. In this manner, it's obtained sufficient resources to extend wide client networks emanating from the state, and to develop social policies intended to benefit the poorest classes.

These policies, which neither formerly nor now provide structural solutions to poverty and lack of opportunity in Venezuelan society, were interrupted in 1983. The abrupt devaluation of the Bolivar (the basic unit of Venezuelan currency) vis a vis the U.S. dollar in that year—an event known as "Black Summer"—inaugurated 15 years of economic crisis in Venezuela. As with every economic crisis, it fell hardest on the poor, with dismantlement of the public policies and programs implemented by previous governments. Because of this economic crisis, there's a substantial difference between the social policies implemented between 1989 and 1999 and those of the Chávez government; but there are more similarities than dissimilarities between the policies implemented between 1958 and 1988 and those of the Chávez regime.

It goes beyond the scope of this book to make a detailed analysis of the social policies implemented by Venezuelan governments between 1958 and 1988. Nonetheless, we'll offer some examples from different areas. In their book *Política Social en Venezuela* ("Social Policy in Venezuela")[95] Lissette González and Tito Lacruz sum up Venezuelan state social policies implemented since the 1960s:

1) free public education on all levels;

2) free health services;

3) subsidies for the principal services necessary to daily life (provision of gasoline, water, electricity, natural gas, telephone, etc.);

4) price controls and control of the labor market;

5) subsidies for a great number of consumer products (food, above all);

6) establishment of a social safety net to protect the working public; and, finally

7) subsidies for the construction of public housing, in both rural and urban areas.

González and Lacruz put it like this:

Not enough importance is paid to social policies as possible transformers of Venezuelan society. . . . Social policy did not intend to create conditions favorable to labor and productivity; the relation between the state and the beneficiary was reduced to a client relationship, paternalistic and based on dependency . . . Its importance was not so much tied to the productive transformation of the country as to the obtaining of political support necessary to the continuance of the system.

With regard to education, let's remember the establishment of free education at all levels. With the arrival of democracy, the Constitution approved in 1960 established that all Venezuelans have the right to education. It assigned to the state the responsibility of opening schools and educational services to assure free access to education. The result of this was that there was an increase in the rate of elementary school graduation from 7% in the mid 1950s to 20% shortly after the initiation of the democratic period in 1958. By 1983 the percentage of graduates had risen to 83%, and by 1989 to 85%.[96]

This was mirrored by an increase in university education. Between 1958 and 1998 the number of university students increased substantially. In 1950, there were only 6,900; in 1958, 11,000; in 1981, 331,000; in 1990, 513,000; and in 2001, 770,000.[97] Education costs as a percentage of government spending increased from 18% in 1965 to 21% in 1988. However, this percentage had begun to decline in 1983 as a result of the economic crisis.[98] On the other end of the educational scale, according to official figures, the illiteracy rate was 48.8% in 1950; 34.8% in 1960; 22.9% in 1971; 14% in 1981; 9.3% in 1991; and 6.4% in 2001.[99]

In the area of health, the trends were similar: improvement in sanitary conditions and the expansion of medical care into most sectors of the country resulted in a constant diminishment of infant mortality. (Infant mortality is an important indicator of general health, given that failure of health services most strongly affects infants, who suffer the most rapid consequences.) Venezuela's increase in health services in 1980 was one of the most rapid of the major countries in the region; at that time Venezuela's hospitals had 2.7 beds per 1000 population.[100] However, it's well known that during this period the healthcare system was primarily treatment, not prevention, oriented, and consisted of both a public and a private sector, which were both expanding; and the government sector did not have the authority to dictate health policy despite the vertical, centralized structure of the state.[101]

The social safety net also grew massively during the first decades of democracy, being catalyzed in 1966 with the new Social Security Law. This law established that the social safety net should cover the entire working population, and increased the types of risks covered by the system to include long-range problems (disability, old age, surviving minors). In this manner, a social security system took form that had two principal components: in the first place the foundation of a medical assistance system that paid attention to insured workers and their families; in the second place payment of pensions (for disability, etc.) and retirement. The expansion of this sector can be measured by the number of those receiving assistance, from 640,000 in 1967 to 2.5 million in 1989.[102]

As regards housing, in addition to providing services, the democratic state advanced a policy of construction for the benefit of the lower and middle classes, replacing shanties and slums with government housing projects. As indicated by national census counts, since 1961 the number of shanties has decreased: 37.18% in 1961; 23.48% in 1971; 15.78% in 1981; 12.56% in 1990; and 9.13% in 2001. There are similar indicators as regards provision of utility services. In 1961, dwelling places with electricity comprised 58.16% of the total, while in 1981 the figure was 76.59%. And in 1961, housing with running water accounted for 46.7% of the total, while in 1981 it had increased to 68.74% of the total.[103]

Despite all of these figures, which were proffered by the various governments as examples of the democratic advances in the country, the period after 1958 did not witness a structural diminution of poverty and inequality in Venezuela. As the researcher Juan Carlos Rey wrote in 1988, a year before the Caracazo uprising/repression:

> The efforts of our various governments . . . along various lines, such as education and health, have involved impressive sums and indisputable gains. However, even though they can cite objective figures and indexes that show that, in many individual aspects and as a whole, the well-being of the population in Venezuela has improved, what is certain is that there are many failures and that we have followed a development pattern that is top down and unequal. Far from having diminished socioeconomic inequalities, [this development pattern] has widened the gap between those who have the most and those who have the least.[104]

In 1989, the application of a package of neoliberal economic measures had devastating consequences. Inflation went above 100% per year and the poverty rate went from 55.1% in 1990 to 75.6% in 1996.[105] This period opened the door for the reappearance of the charismatic, authoritarian leadership style that characterized Venezuelan politics earlier in the twentieth century.

Bolivarian Social Policies: The Missions

Since the year 2003, the social policies the government developed under the Bolivarian Process have been called "missions," numbering 24 in all by the end of 2007, in such areas as nutrition, health, science and technology, sports, identification papers, housing and urban planning, and availability of land.[106] The objective here is to show a balance sheet for the most important missions, which are often used in international propaganda to show the supposed achievements of the Chávez government.

Before going further, we should make two observations. The first is that despite the positive impacts which the mission policies have had on the poorest levels of Venezuelan society, especially between 2004 and 2006, the missions are far from a structural solution to the problems they address. In the sectors of health, nutrition, and education, especially, the missions constitute, as we'll see, systems that are parallel to the already existing state systems; and even in conjunction with those systems they've never covered, even in their best moments, the entire territory of Venezuela. As well, the [funding of and concentration on the missions] has worsened the conditions of the public-service institutions of the state, built over a period of four decades— for example the public hospital network—and consequently has worsened the condition of those who depend on them.

To be more specific, there are two principal reasons for this. The first is the invigoration of the so-called Venezuelan culture of the campaign ("cultura Venezolana de campamento," in the words of Venezuelan novelist José Ignacio Cabrujas), in which temporary "extraordinary operations" that provide social assistance are carried out in a specified and limited territory. When it comes to funding, for example, a temporary portable clinic or a public hospital constructed by a previous administration, the Chávez government chooses the first option because of its political and propaganda potential. The missions, therefore, are a continuation of traditional Venezuelan political approaches to social problems.

The second thing to realize about the missions relates to their very origin. To illustrate this we'll limit ourselves to citing the words President Chávez delivered in a speech on November 12, 2004:

> You have to remember that, as a product of the [2002 attempted] coup and all the damage it caused, [such as] the high level of ungovernability, the economic crisis, [and] our own errors, there came a moment when we were [worried

about losing power]. There was an international investigator who came on the recommendation of a friend, spent two months here, and went to the palace to deliver a devastating message: "Mr. President, if the referendum [to recall Chávez] were held today, you would lose." That for me was a bombshell, because you know that many people will not tell you such things, and instead will soften them. . . .

That was when we began to work with the missions, designing the first [medical] and beginning to ask for help from Fidel. He told me: "Look, I have this idea: attack from below with all possible force"; and he told me, "If I know one thing, it's this: [you can] count on my complete support." And they [the Cubans] began to send doctors by the hundreds, an airlift, airplanes came and airplanes went in search of resources, here the economy improved, organizing the barrios, the communities . . . in the critical states. And we began to invent the missions. . . . And that avalanche of people saw us come out on top. . . . There's no magic here, it's politics, not magic, and see how we've come out.[107]

Educational Missions: Robinson & Rivas

The Bolivarian government puts its best foot forward with education indicators. The educational missions have as antecedents the promises made on education at the World Social Forum celebrated in Dakar in 2000 and the World Declaration on Higher Education made in Paris in 1998, both of which were subsequently included in the Chávez government's Economic and Social Development Plan for the Nation, 2001–2007. The lines of action that stemmed from these policy statements were the National Literacy Plan, 2003–2005, Bolivarian Secondary Education, Robinson Technical School, and other programs. However, the Literacy Plan, which didn't meet its goals, was replaced in June 2003 by the Simón Rodríguez Extraordinary National Literacy Plan, which later came to be known as the Robinson Mission, in honor of the pseudonym used by Simón Rodríguez, Simón Bolivar's teacher. Its goal is to eliminate illiteracy in the entire country. It began its activities with the aid of 74 Cuban advisors and a total of 50,000 volunteers.[108]

Considering that the acquisition of basic reading comprehension was not sufficient to guarantee the educational goals for the newly literate populace, the government created Robinson Mission II in October 2003, which had as its object the achievement of a sixth-grade level education by all participants in the literacy program, as well as to integrate the knowledge gained during the literacy process. In March 2004 the government created the Robinson Mission Foundation, and so the mission became the responsibility of the Minister of Education.

In October 2003, the government created the Presidential Commission for Community Participation in the Extraordinary Plan of the José Felix Ribas Mission, and on November 17 it legally sanctioned it. The Ribas Mission is directed toward helping young people and adults complete their secondary education so as to be able to enter the university system as freshmen. The Ribas mission statement is as follows: "[To create] new Bolivarian citizens capable of valuing themselves and their communities in order to live in democracy, in a participatory manner, actively and in keeping with Bolivarian ideals and concepts, with a holistic vision in harmony with the environment, in order to construct a society of coexistence, cooperation, solidarity, and justice, and therefore, of peace."[109] This implies, theoretically, three things: the incorporation of a populace excluded from the system of formal education; the completion by all Venezuelans of secondary education; and the democratization of education.

According to the human rights group PROVEA's annual report (October 2004–September 2005), the availability of educational establishments had increased significantly. For the five-year period 1994–1998, the increase was 8.9%, while the increase in the years 1998–2003 was 13.5%. Official figures also demonstrated positive outcomes, the most striking of which was a 58% increase in progression of students from grade 1 to grade 9. The development of the Robinson Mission was so successful that on October 28, 2005 UNESCO declared Venezuela a country free of illiteracy.[110] According to the 2008 report of the NGO World Campaign for Education, Venezuela had some of the best education indicators in Latin America.[111]

In parallel with these quantitative advances, there still exist concerns about the quality of the education in the country, and of the intent of the national government to use education as a tool of ideological indoctrination. But because there have been no rigorous independent investigations of these matters, we can only state that such concerns exist in civil society.

Housing Mission

In contrast with the gains achieved by its education missions, the government's housing policies have been a major failure. In September 2004, it decreed the creation of the Housing Mission that would later be called the Habitat Mission, which had as its objective, according to its self-definition, address of the issue of habitability, response to the problems of family and communities not only in the field of construction, but above all the development of the habitat and commencement of urban development that includes all essential services, from education to health.

Despite the different legislative measures that regulate Venezuelan housing in accord with international standards, the physical execution of housing policies has been inadequate. The UN Human Settlements Program has calculated that the housing deficit in Venezuela is almost three million homes [in a country with a population of 28 million], which includes housing in need of repair. This data has been validated by the Venezuelan government.[112] The Ministry of Housing estimates that at the beginning of 2007 the lack was 2.8 million dwellings: one million corresponding to new families; 800,000 to "ranchos" (huts/shanties) that need replacement; and another one million to houses located on steep slopes, flood zones, or other high-risk areas. This implies that nearly half of the population, 13 million people, are not enjoying the right to adequate housing; and that total is growing by more than 110,000 families annually.

Despite ten years of the government's failure to meet its own goals in this area, many officials continue to talk about the existence of a fictitious extraordinary government policy of housing construction. For example, on September 5, 2008, the then-Housing Minister Farruco Sesto stated that "during the administration of President Hugo Chávez, more houses have been constructed than during the previous thirty years."[113] He repeated this assertion days later: "The actions of the government have been better in the matter of housing than those [actions] in the previous 25 years. One can demonstrate this with statistics, with concrete data, with facts [deeds]." Nonetheless, a review of the government's own statistics demonstrates the contrary: The reports emanating from the Housing Ministry show that between 1999 and 2008 the initiatives of President Chávez resulted in the construction of 241,219 dwellings, an average of 26,000 per year. In contrast, the average in the 1990s was 64,000 per year.[114]

Questioning of the Bolivarian housing policies does not come solely from human rights organizations and anarchists. High government officials have also recognized the housing problems. In his speech on August 11, 2009 to the National Assembly, the Comptroller General of the Republic, Clodosvaldo Russián, alluded to the housing failures:

> The state, in the matter of housing, has not achieved the realization of unified [coherent] planning, coordination of execution, efficiency of results, and control in the [fair] adjudication [in delivery] to beneficiaries. The National Housing Plan is not a reflection of a holistic, structured planning process. This instrument should be sufficiently exhaustive as regards the real necessities of

housing and the situation of the plans under development, so that the national, regional, local, and community organizations that execute it not only efficiently carry forward the housing programs, but also act in a coordinated manner and so avoid repetition, unnecessary effort, misallocation of resources, and corruption.[115]

In his speech, the Comptroller General didn't skirt the matter of corruption regarding housing resources, which he referred to as one of the vices inherited from past administrations, and which has endured under the management of President Chávez:

It repeats itself: the lack of observance of bidding and competitive processes, in some cases under the shield of a declaration of emergency by authorities (governors) without the authority to do so. This conduct by those responsible is not only illegal and sanctionable, but it doesn't meet the obligations inherent in these processes, such as awarding contracts based on fitness, technical capacity, financing, proven experience on the part of the contractors, and just and reasonable market prices.

As well, the vigilance over and inspection of the execution of projects is deficient, which explains their frequent stoppages, the delays in meeting dates of delivery, the incompletion or defective nature of projects, the lack of enforcement of penalty clauses, the lateness in return or refusal of demands for the return of unused funds. The mechanisms of control in place do not guarantee that there will be no decisions to deliver dwellings to persons who do not need them, or to persons who have been illegal beneficiaries of housing decisions. The projects and proposals, in general, lack preliminary, verifiable technical studies, which translates into loss of time and resources—and in frustration—for the [affected] communities.

Nutrition Mission

Paralysis of the petroleum industry as well as other sectors occurred at the end of 2002 with the "petroleum strike" (see. pp. 112–114); one of its results was that it exposed the fragility of the food-supply system. In consequence, in March 2003 the government launched the Exceptional Plan of Economic and Social Development through which the supply of food and related products would fill the basic food basket. The objective of the plan was to guarantee the stable supply—growing and permanent—of the basic food basket, including, if there were shortages, products from the international market.

In April 2003, the government created the Mercal (Mercado de Alimentos), which is charged with the commercialization and marketing of food and other products of primary necessity. The products commercialized by Mercal are available in various places of sale: the "mercalitos" or "Mercal Bodegas" (Mercal stores/warehouses), the Mobile Bodegas, the Mercal Modules Types I & II , and the so-called "SuperMercales" and the "Megamercales," which are held under the open air.

Nonetheless, Mercal soon had a curious competitor, created by the national executive: the Producer and Distributor of Food (PDVAL), which is a dependency of the state petroleum company, PDVSA, and which fulfills in practice the same functions as Mercal. PDVAL began operations in January 2008,[116] and with its expansion has effectively debilitated Mercal's distribution chain.

During the years 2004 and 2005, Mercal set up dozens of food distribution centers with prices subsidized by the government. This effectively increased the consuming power of poor families, with the result that, by September 2008, it had increased the consumption of food by 16%.[117] However, the logistics of the popular markets were problematic. Mercal's clients formed long lines which often lasted for hours in order to acquire the products offered. As well, many of the open-air markets had a precarious structure, entirely dependent on the government—they were more of a policy guaranteeing food than an organic structure.

In the end, the implementation of chains of food distribution at subsidized prices is not a novelty implemented by the Chávez Administration. Since 1958, Venezuelan governments have created popular markets with intentions similar to that of Mercal. For example, in 1989 then-President Carlos Andrés Pérez formed the Fulfillment and Agricultural Services Corporation, a public company intended to commercialize the basic food basket and to provide services to agricultural networks supplying food. Another antecedent was the creation of the Strategic Foods Program in 1996 during Rafael Caldera's second administration.[118]

The decline of the Mercal Mission has been denounced by its own workers. In the National Union Encounter of Mercal Workers, held on July 2, 2009, those attending worked out a document that revealed the situation:

The Nutrition Mission is not complying with the goals foreseen in the National Simón Bolivar Plan. We've been having nine million to thirteen million inhabitants attending the Mercales at the national level. The little markets [mercalitos] are going down the same path, with interminable stoppages for reasons no one understands, and shortages in fundamentals in the basic food basket. This is not to say that we have a zeal for criticism for criticism's sake, but rather that we're concerned about the development of food policy in the country.[119]

The findings of the Mercal workers revealed irregularities in working conditions:

The health and safety working conditions are worrisome. There are many workers who suffer from work-induced health problems: hernias; vaginitis for lack of adequate sanitation; spinal displacement; displaced discs; carpal tunnel syndrome; etc. These are a product of carelessness and lack of preventive maintenance . . . and they result in mistreatment and humiliation. This includes resignation from employment. [These problems also include] the number of paralyzing injuries which require remediation via the Venezuelan Institute of Social Security. This creates an unsettled condition in the laboring masses. Mercal says that it doesn't have the resources [to comply with] the proposed Collective Work Agreement introduced by the Ministry of Labor and Social Security in 2005, that is to say, we've been four years now without a collective bargaining agreement.

The Comptroller General of the Republic, Clodovaldo Russián, also described the series of problems in the nutrition mission. He stated that bureaucracy and laziness undermined the purposes of the government in obtaining food safety/security for the public.[120] This is an indication of the failure of the governmental bureaucracy, a failure that impedes the fulfillment of the goals relating to the production and distribution of food for the citizenry.

After analyzing the actions of Mercal in the last few years, the Comptroller came to the conclusion that the levels of production, importation, and supply of milk, poultry, and sugar, in the referent period, were not sufficient to meet demand. Among other reasons, there was backsliding in most of the Venezuelan Agrarian Corporation's projects (CVA—Corporación Venezolana Agraria Lácteos) and The Socialist Milk of Dawn Company. In particular, failure to meet sugar benchmarks points out the problems with the sugar producers in the states of Cojedes, Monagras, Sucre, and Trujillo, under the responsibility of CVA Azúcar, S.A. as well as the Sugar Worker Ezequiel Zamora Agroindustral Complex in the state of Barinas, under the responsibility of CVA.

Another problem pointed out by Russián, regarding the state policies that guarantee the right to food, was the poor maintenance of food warehouses and what he called carelessness in the distribution chain for refrigerated foods, which puts at risk the stability of the state food-supply service. The irregularities detected in the distribution centers included problems with safety and hygiene in the supply chain and warehouses; lack of accountable control of entrances and exits; deficient planning/oversight in the buying and maintenance of inventories; and limited storage capacity. The comptroller's investigations found warehoused foods in various states of decomposition, oxidized and broken bottles, and spur-of-the-moment food orders that caused problems with rotation of stock, such as the traditional items for the Christmas season.

The supply centers and Type I Mercal modules, according to the comptroller, also had deficiencies in lighting and ventilation. The ceilings, at the time of the inspections, contained asbestos; the walls, ceilings and floors had leaks, cracks, erosion, and drainage problems; they were also made of materials that were not waterproof; and the windows in all of the inspected structures did not have screens to keep out insects. The refrigerated supply system was in no better shape. Some systems did not cool to the proper temperature; others didn't work at all; still others had dents, damage to their doors, and high levels of condensation in their interiors due to faulty seals. Some distribution centers entirely lacked refrigeration systems. With respect to health, hygiene and safety matters, the comptroller found that there were no health permits for the centers; personnel did not have health certificates; and local centers did not have smoke detectors and sprinkler systems.

The Barrio Within Mission: Primary Healthcare in the Barrio

Barrio Within (Barrio Adentro) is one of the government's signature missions, and has become the most important. Its objective is to guarantee access to healthcare to those excluded from the conventional health system. This is done through, in theory, an integral-health management model designed to improve the quality of life through having medical personnel [living] in the communities they serve, the creation of consulting services and people's clinics, and the transformation of public hospitals into "people's hospitals."

In May 2006, Barrio Within employed 13,000 Cuban doctors, 1,247 Venezuelan doctors, 3,602 Cuban dentists, 1,103 Venezuelan dentists, and 2,596 Venezuelan nurses. The Venezuelan doctors received a salary of one million Bolivars (about $450 US) per month; the Cubans received four hundred thousand Bolivars (about $180 US); and neither had any type of contract with the Ministry of Health.[121]

In September 2005, according to the figures from the Venezuelan NGO human rights groups that monitor the situation, Barrio Within had increased the amount of coverage it provided in its primary care network. The rights groups noted that Barrio Within was projected to have 8,573 Barrio Within I (primary care) modules, 30 diagnostic centers, and 30 rehabilitation centers, the last two known as Barrio Within II.

However, the reports from the ONGs expressed concern about the inequality in the number of doctors per thousand inhabitants in different regions of the country. The greatest disparity was between the state of Táchira, which had one doctor for every 24,667 inhabitants, and the capital district that had one for every 1,780.[122]

The year 2007 saw a loss of impetus for the Barrio Within mission. In that year, the mission didn't meet its own goals. Three years earlier, when it was initiated, Barrio Within was projected to have 8,573 primary care modules; in 2007 just over half that number had been constructed: 4,618.

The human rights group PROVEA's report stated that there were two co-existing healthcare systems: the traditional one that both served ambulatory patients and provided hospitals, and Barrio Within. This was "not only an institutional parallelism, but also a parallel financial system stacked in favor of Barrio Within. In consequence, the healthcare system is fragmented, disarticulated, with structural problems that have not been addressed, and which [adversely] affect the guarantees of universal access and also the quality of the services provided by the traditional networks of healthcare provision."[123]

In practice, this meant that Venezuela's people could go to a local clinic for a headache, broken bone, or stomach ache. But for more complex procedures, such as operations or births, they had to go to an underfunded, understaffed hospital. For example, during the ten years of the Bolivarian Revolution, poor Venezuelan women often gave birth in inhuman conditions, a situation highlighted in 2009 when a public awareness campaign revealed cases of babies who died from lack of medical attention.

A related matter is the number of women who die from back-alley abortions.* According to figures provided by Alba Carosio, the director of the Center for Women's Studies at the Central University of Venezuela, 16% of pregnancies in Venezuela end in clandestine abortions. According to Asia Villegas, a doctor who has held a number of posts in the Ministry of Health during the Chávez administration, "It's necessary to lift the sheet of hypocrisy covering the taboo of abortion. Those who can afford it have abortions in safe conditions; the poor do not have access to this service, and many die because of having abortions in unsafe conditions."[124] The same newspaper story that carried Villegas' words reported that approximately 150 Venezuelan women

---

* Translator's Note: Venezuela, despite its socialist reputation, is still very much in the grip of Catholic "morality." The government does not provide free abortion services.

are admitted to hospitals daily as a result of spontaneous or back-alley abortions—and this doesn't include those treated in private clinics.

Marino Alvarado, Coordinator General of the human rights group PROVEA, said in an interview regarding health policies of the Chávez government:

> If one reads the documents on health matters, their content is good: they say it should be free; they're saying it's the responsibility of the state; they say the emphasis should be on primary care and prevention rather than later treatment. The great problem is the execution of the policies. There's no short-term, medium-term, or long-term vision. They're constantly doing things on the fly. If there's one area where the government could advance, taking into account the existing resources and control over the institutions, it's health.[125]

Alvarado adds:

> It's not that [public] health is in crisis under the Chávez government: It was already in decline with President [Rafael] Caldera [Chávez's immediate predecessor] and well before that. But when one speaks of a "revolution," that implies the transformation of reality. And one of the realities that must be transformed is attention to public health, which is directly tied to the quality of life of the people. There, [Chávez's] "revolution" has been a great failure. If one compares the present situation with that under Caldera, nothing has changed significantly.

Alvarado mentions that PROVEA has supported the implementation of Barrio Within since its inception, but doesn't hesitate to point out its limitations:

> Since the present government proposed Barrio Within, PROVEA has supported it; but it doesn't appear to be an adequate program. We say, in the moment of greatest polarization in the country, that the nationality of the doctors doesn't matter to us, but rather that they be where the poor people reside. However, Barrio Within has been manipulated to not only engage in health care but also in political proselytization. The government promised to construct thousands of health modules in the country, but has only constructed half of them. As well, in the last year these have progressively deteriorated. And before consolidating this phase [of the project], constructing modules and making sure that they function correctly, they came up with what they call Barrio Within II, which consists of diagnostic modules, which do function well. The problem is that without consolidating the first level they're already jumping to a second, with a great amount of propaganda about the diagnostic clinics–while there are still very few in the country. But when they [government officials] appear on radio, TV, and other media outlets, they give the impression that we

have a health system that provides integral attention to the entire population, something which isn't true. Besides, a lot of [the health services] are located in Caracas. But it's necessary to emphasize the positive in the government's policy of providing free health care. All of these services are free, giving the public access to medicine and exams whose costs are prohibitive in the private sector. For us, the problem is the limited coverage [of the government's health-care system].

In its 2008 annual report, issued as I write these lines, PROVEA provides an analysis of healthcare policies over the previous decade in Venezuela. In the case of Barrio Within, there has been a slowing, and in fact a regression. The number of Cuban doctors has decreased from 13,000 to 8,500. There have also been cases of health modules closing or failing to supply adequate numbers of doctors as well as cleaning materials.[126] This situation was acknowledged by President Chávez himself in a speech at the National Assembly on July 25, 2009, commemorating the tenth anniversary of the election of the members of the Constituent Assembly that drew up the Constitution of 1999. Chávez said: "The Barrio Within mission . . . I have no doubt . . . has gone below the level of efficiency it always had. We're studying the matter, the reasons, the causes . . ."

One of the indications of the limitations of the Barrio Within mission is that no high- or mid-level government officials use its services. As an example, Jorge Rodríguez, former director of the National Electoral Council, had an automobile accident in August 2006. Rather than going to one of the Barrio Within's diagnostic and rehabilitation clinics, he decided to go to a private clinic for treatment.[127] The curious thing is that during his campaign to become mayor of Caracas, Rodríguez declared that "The guarantee of healthcare for all Venezuelans is one of the ethical and moral gains that the Bolivarian Revolution has won, and we have to defend it with the vote. The Barrio Within system is an achievement that we have to defend by voting for the Chávez candidates, for the candidates of the PSUV."[128]

While the Barrio Within medical system might be one of the "ethical and moral gains of the Bolivarian Revolution," the bureaucrats who administer that "revolution" go to private clinics for their healthcare.

Public Hospitals: Testimony from the Front Line

Johan Rivas (previously mentioned on pp. 52–53) has worked since 1997 in the Dr. José Ignacio Baldó Hospital Complex. The hospital was built in

1940 and became known continent wide for its treatment of tuberculosis and other respiratory illnesses. Rivas, like many other young people in Venezuela at the end of the 1980s, participated in the student movement and protested in the streets against the neoliberal policies—among them one that would have privatized the university system—of then-President Carlos Andrés Pérez. In 1998, Rivas joined the young volunteers who supported the candidacy of Hugo Chávez. So, he's part of the generation whose political militance reached maturity with the arrival in power of the Bolivarian Movement. In 2004, Rivas began to participate in the defense of the rights of health workers, and at the same time joined the Revolutionary Marxist Current. Rivas later broke ties with it and helped to organize the Revolutionary Socialist Collective (CSR), in which he was participating at the time I interviewed him regarding the condition of his hospital and its workers:

> Situations [contradictions] have been accumulating. The latest is that we're operating in a context of [proclaimed] revolution, participatory democracy, etc., and at the same time the problems of the past drag us down, and in fact are worsening. The health service provided to the community is not ideal, and is in fact precarious. Polarization has reached the stage where the government is politicizing its public health measures. Just as the traditional healthcare system is a refuge for the [rightist] political opposition–most of its managers are tied to the opposition parties—the government has developed its own platform, Barrio Within. It's certainly true that at the start [Barrio Within] had a great social impact, one that has seriously [and negatively] affected much of the traditional [healthcare] system.

Rivas described the deterioration of the hospital service while the government focused its efforts and resources on Barrio Within:

> The traditional healthcare system has collapsed since [the beginning of] Barrio Within. At present, [Barrio Within] is not providing the coverage that it did [in its early stages], and many people are returning to the traditional system, which doesn't have the capacity to respond [adequately]. And this has generated a profound crisis. The only truly new thing in Barrio Within is the intent to implement a policy open to the communities. But it has the same bureaucratic structure as the traditional system, a system constructed from the top down where there's no true participation of those below. [It's a system in which] the communities only advise, not decide, in which the workers have no say in the decisions, and public health policies are dictated from the seats of power, not developed in the concrete reality of individual communities.

All of this has brought about a gigantic collapse that I see today in "El Algo-donal" [informal name of the hospital in which Rivas works], which now has an operating capacity of only 30 per cent. Services that are very important to the community, such as [the treatment of] tuberculosis and other respiratory ill-nesses, have worsened. And this has created a climate of demotivation among the hospital's workers, and [has also caused] talent to flee. As for policies, the hospital continues to be managed according to the old policies, even when its directives are couched in the language of revolution. The hospital's practices are aberrant, and continue to be the same as always:[dependent] clients, bu-reaucracy, and corruption.

We also asked Rivas about conditions of workers with signed contracts:

That situation is also critical. One must recognize that in the last few years there have been economic improvements [for the workers], but these have been more crumbs than [loaves]. Health workers, in the case of the common laborers, have worked for the last 15 years without a collective bargaining agreement. The other workers have worked for five years without such an agreement. The government has not had a policy [designed] to improve the quality of life for health workers. What it has done is to make some pacts with unions which support its policies. It hasn't increased the level of profes-sionalization of the workers. Those who have become more professional have done it more on their own than with the help of the state. As well, working conditions are abominable. If The National Institute of Labor Prevention [of accidents, etc.], Health and Safety made an inspection, the hospital would have to—technically—close.

Rivas's critical stance is interesting due to the fact that, because of his youth, most of his political experience has been within the Bolivarian Move-ment. But after directly experiencing the contradictions in that movement, he's been developing his own ideas, and those ideas have caused him to distance himself from the bureaucracy in power. Later in our interview he provided an inventory of the practices of the past which continue under the Chávez government:

The first is the cult of personality, which is part of Venezuelan politics. This *caudillismo* [cult of the strong man] has to do with everything rotating around a leader. It appears to us that this contradicts the postulates of socialism, and that it has much to do with the politics of the past. And these reproduce them-selves in the bureaucracy, corruption, the [dependent] client practices which continue today as in the past, and which have not permitted a fundamental change in state structures.

The other element is [the cult of the political] party, in which everything is based on the party. That is to say, if in the past you weren't aligned with Democratic Action or COPEI, you wouldn't benefit from the policies of the state. Today, things continue practically the same. Unless you're aligned with the PSUV or Chávez's political apparatus, you have practically no access to public policy. And this appears to us to refute the postulates of socialism. It contradicts what one hopes for from a revolution . . .

[Popular] participation [in decision-making] is not real, but bureaucratic, done with elements that supposedly grow from the base, but that end up being manipulated by centralizing elements that are tied to the leaders of political parties. Then participation remains a sham, in which the people advise but don't decide.

Because of their critiques, Johan Rivas and the CSR have been labeled "counter-revolutionary" and "allies of imperialism" dozens of times by different sectors of the Bolivarian Movement. The heart of their critiques—the roadblocks in the way of autonomous social movements—will be the subject of the final part of this book.

7. Roberto Briceño-León and Olga Ávila Fuenmayor, *Violencia en Venezuela. Informe del Observatorio Venezolano de Violencia.* Laboratorio de Ciencias Sociales: Caracas, 2007.

8. Ana María Sanjuán, "La revolución bolivariana en riesgo, la democratización social en cuestión." Revista Venezolana de Economía y Ciencias Sociales, Vol. 14, No. 3, September-December 2008.

9. Ibid.

10. Venezolana de Televisión, July 2008, "Indice de homicidios bajó 8% durante primer trimestre en 2008." (Link no longer available)

11. María Sanjuán, op. cit.

12. Ibid.

13. Briceño-León and Ávila Fuenmayor, op. cit.

14. *Informe anual octubre 2007-septiembre 2008 sobre la situación de los derechos humanos en Venezuela.* PROVEA: Caracas, 2008.

15. Alfredo Olivo, "Caracas: ¿La ciudad más peligrosa del mundo?" YVKE Mundial, July 2009. (Link no longer available)

16. Search results on August 1, 2009 on the YVKE web site. (Link no longer available)

17. Briceño-León and Ávila Fuenmayor, op. cit.

18. Agencia Bolivariana de Noticias, "El Nuevo País criticó incremento de 'malls' Basta que Chávez lo diga para estar en contra" (December 2008) (Link no longer available; agency has been renamed Agencia Venezolana de Noticias: http://www.avn.info.ve/)

19. *Producto*, "Las plazas contemporáneas," No. 248, July 2004.

20. Roberto Briceño-León and Olga Ávila Fuenmayor, *Por temor perdemos la ciudad. Inseguridad y Violencia en Venezuela. Informe.* Editorial Alfa, 2009.

21. Pedro García Otero, *El Universal*, July 17, 2006, pp.2–4. "Inseguridad priva a los niños de disfrutar de las plazas."

22. Jesús Machado and José Gregorio Guerra, "Violencia en la escuela" (June 2009) (Link no longer available)

23. Luís Gutiérrez, "Planteles fijan condiciones respecto al uso de morrales." *El Tiempo*, February 2006. http://www.eltiempo.com.ve/noticias/default.asp?id=65046

24. An example: "Hospital de Lídice ya funciona normalmente y es resguardado por 25 efectivos policiales" (May 2009) http://www.radiomundial.com.ve/yvke/noticia.php?24640

25. Federación Médica Venezolana, "Resumen Domingo 9/11/2008" (November 2008) (Link no longer available)

26. PROVEA (2008), op. cit.

27. Observatorio Venezolano de Prisiones, "Informe 2008. Situación del Sistema Penitenciario Venezolano" (July 2009) See also the 2009 report at http://www.ovprisiones.org/pdf/INFOVP2009.pdf

28. Ramón Hernández, *El Nacional*, November 12, 2000. "Simón Sáez Mérida: El Gobierno de Chávez es la continuación de la Agenda Venezuela."

29. *Aló Presidente*, No. 158, August 2003. http://alopresidente.gob.ve

30. *Informe Anual octubre 1999 septiembre 2000 sobre la situación de los Derechos Humanos en Venezuela.* PROVEA: Caracas, 2000.

31. Red de Apoyo por la Justicia y la Paz, "Informe sobre la práctica de la tortura en Venezuela 2003-2007" (May 2008) http://www.redapoyo.org

32. Ultimas Noticias, June 27, 2009, p. 28. "20 torturados por año atiende la Red de Apoyo."

33. PROVEA (2000), op. cit.
34. *Informe Anual octubre 2007 septiembre 2008 sobre la situación de los Derechos Humanos en Venezuela*. PROVEA: Caracas, 2008.
35. *Ultimas Noticias*, May 23, 2009, p. 28. "Más de 10 mil violaciones a Ddhh [human rights] procesa la Fiscalía."
36. *El Universal*, June 2, 2009. "El Aissami: 20% de los delitos son cometidos por funcionarios policiales"
37. Gustavo Rodríguez, *El Universal*, July 13, 2009. "La PM tiene bajo investigación a 1.800 policias por delitos."
38. Eligio Rojas, *Ultimas Noticias*, October 1, 2008, p.34. "Pablo Fernández recomienda enlistar a funcionarios hampones."
39. Agencia Bolivariana de Noticias, "Luis Reyes Reyes: Discurso de Chávez de 4F anunciaba insurrección de 27N" (February 2007) (Link no longer available; agency has been renamed Agencia Venezolana de Noticias: http://www.avn.info.ve/)
40. Comité de Víctimas contra la Impunidad, *El Libertario*, No. 55, January 2009.
41. Jorge Chávez, *Ultimas Noticias*, July 13, 2008. "Manos manchadas de sangre roja rojita."
42. Ibid.
43. Ibid.
44. See http://www.gobiernoenlinea.gob.ve/venezuela/perfil_apure.html
45. PROVEA; "Las estrategías de la impunidad. Nueve años de lucha por la justicia en El Amparo." PROVEA: Caracas, 1997.
46. Ibid.
47. PROVEA, "Masacre de El Amparo, 20 años de impunidad. PROVEA: Caracas, 2009.
48. *El Libertario*, No. 54, September-October 2008. "Rodríguez Chacín: Ministro del Poder Popular par la Impunidad."
49. "Emmanuel" is the name of kidnapped Colombian Politician Clara Rojas' child; her son was born while she was held captive by the FARC (the marxist-leninist Fuerzas Armadas Revolutionarias Colombianas). Operation Emmanuel succeeded in obtaining Rojas' release.)
50. Beatriz Caripa, *Ultimas Noticias*, July 7, 2009, p. 22. "Masa laboral del Estado ha crecido 220%."
51. Instituto Nacional de Estadística. http://www.ine.gov.ve/
52. PROVEA (2000), op. cit.
53. Agencia Bolivariana de Noticias, "Salario mínimo venezolano duplica al rest to Latinoamérica" (March 2009) (Link no longer available; agency has been renamed Agencia Venezolana de Noticias: http://www.avn.info.ve/)
54. Laclase.info, "Venezuela ha sido el país con más alta inflación durante los últimos 3 años en América Latina" (March 2009)
55. Domingo F. Maza Zavala, *Nueva Economía*, No. 28, October 2008. "Diagnóstico Crítico de la economía venezolana en el periodo 1982–2007."
56. *Ultimas Noticias*, March 28, 2009, p. 12. "El gobierno tiene 71.2% de aprobación segun Ivad."
57. Miguel Angel Santos, op. cit.
58. Agencia Bolivariana de Noticias, "Ministra Iglesias instó a los trabajadores a crear sindicatos" (April 2009)
59. Miriam Blanco, *Ultimas Noticias*, April 27, 2008, p. 48. "Sindicatos buscan la unidad."
60. *El Nuevo Sindicalismo*, "La arremetida contra los trabajadores." Caracas, 2009.
61. Armando Vergueiro, *El Libertario*, No. 47, May-June 2006. "UNT: Historieta sindicalera de la Quinta República."
62. Opción Obrera, "La UNT, crisis desde su nacimiento" (April 2008)
63. PROVEA (2007), op. cit.
64. Opción Obrera, op. cit.
65. Juventud de Izquierda Revolucionaria, "Defendamos la independencia de los sindicatos" (Link no longer available)
66. YVKE Mundial, "Chávez advirtió que no permitirá la extorsión por parte de algunos sindicalistas" (March 2009) http://www.radiomundial.com.ve/yvke/noticia.php?20910
67. Laclase.info, "Las palabras del presidente Chávez son una declaración de guerra contra los trabajadores" (March 2009) (http://laclase.info/ Page no longer available)
68. Sandy Martínez and Johan Rivas, "¿Como se encuentra el Movimiento Sindical en Venezuela hoy?" (March 2003) http://www.aporrea.org/trabajadores/a74116.html
69. PROVEA (2008), op. cit.
70. E-mail from Alfredo Vásquez of the Vicarío de Derechos Humanos de Caracas, June 26, 2009.
71. Ibid.
72. Ibid.
73. G. Gómez and G. Richards, "Orlando Chirino en el congreso de la UNT: Queremos una central obrera que defienda el proceso revolucionario" (August 2003) http://www.aporrea.org/actualidad/n8917.html
74. Armando Vertgueiro, op. cit.
75. For example see http://www.aporrea.org/trabajadores/a50875.html
76. Lexys Rendón, *El Libertario*, No. 56, May–June 2009. "Entrevista a Orlando Chirinos."
77. "Sindicatos de la UNT incorporados de lleno a la Campaña de Santa Inés" (July 2004) http://www.aporrea.org/trabajadores/n18515.html
78. Kamanchec Torin Conde, "8 razones por las cuales los petroleros estamos arrechos" (August 2009) http://laclase.info/
79. Prensa Web YVKE, "Chávez advirtió que no permitirá la extorsión por parte de algunos sindicalistas" (March 2009) http://www.aporrea.org/actualidad/n130237.html
80. Lexys Rendón, op. cit.
81. Agencia Bolivariana de Noticias, "Chávez instó a crear consejos de trabajadores del poder popular" (Link no longer available; agency has been renamed Agencia Venezolana de Noticias: http://www.avn.info.ve/)
82. Lexys Rendón, op. cit.
83. Ramón Fernández Durán, *Capitalismo global, resistencias sociales y estrategias del poder. En globalización capitalista, luchas y resistencias*. Virus Editorial: Barcelona, 2001.
84. PROVEA (2007), op. cit.
85. Topo Obrero Caracas, "Flexibilización laboral¿una realidad del capitalismo?" (November 2008) http://bellaciao.org/es/spip.php?article5564
86. Partido Comunista Internacional, "Socialismo de papel" (January 2006) http://www.aporrea.org/actualidad/a19088.html

87. Agencia Bolivariana de Noticias, "Venezuela exportará el Vergatario luego de abastecer el mercado interno" (May 2009) (Link no longer available; agency has been renamed Agencia Venezolana de Noticias: http://www.avn.info.ve/)

88. Levy Revilla Toyo, "Situación general de la fábrica de celulares Vetelca" (August 2009) http://www.aporrea.org(poderpopular/a84042.html

89. Agencia Bolivariana de Noticias/YVKE Mundial, "Vetelca ensambló primer celular 'Vergatario'este primero de mayo" (May 2009) http://www.radiomundial.com.ve/yvke/noticia.php?23836

90. Agencia Bolivariana de Noticias/YVKE Mundial, "Hay que formar trabajadores integrales para fortalecer fábricas socialistas" (August 2009) http://www.radiomundial.com.ve/yvke/noticia.php?30126

91. Andreina Blanco, *Ultimas Noticias*, August 7, 2009. "Vetelca niega botazón de personal."

92. Eva Riera, *Ultimas Noticias*, August 19, 2009, p. 20. "Salen 30 trabajadores más de Vetelca."

93. YVKE Mundial, "Vetelca se encuentra completamente operativa" (August 2009) http://www.radiomundial.com.ve/yvke/noticia.php?29983

94. Diagonalweb, "Venezuela está rompiendo el modelo de EEUU" (2nd ed., Marcy 15, 2006) http://www.diagonalperiodico.net/

95. Lisette Gonzalez and Tito Lacruz, *Politica social en Venezuela*. Instituto de Investigaciones Económicas y Sociales UCAB: Caracas, 2008.

96. Fernando Reimers, "Educación y democracia." *Revista latinoamericana de desarrollo educativo*, No. 116.

97. Victor Morales, Eduardo Rubio and Neptalí Alvarez, "La educación superior en Venezuela" (IESALC-UNESCO, 2003) http://unesdoc.unesco.org/images/0013/001315/131594s.pdf

98. Reimers, op. cit.

99. González and Lacruz, op. cit.

100. Teresa Gamboa Cáceres, "La Salud Pública Venezolana: entre el compromiso social y la economía de mercado" (2000) http://unpan1.un.org/intradoc/groups/public/documents/CLAD/clad0038527.pdf

101. Yolanda D'Elia, Tito Lacruz and Thais Maingon, *Los modelos de política social en Venezuela: Universalidad vs. Asistencialismo*. Instituto Latinoamericano de Investigaciones Sociales: Caracas, 2006.

102. González and Lacruz, op. cit.

103. Enrique Rodríguez, *Politica social actual: una visión desde el gobierno. En Balance y perspectivas de la política social en Venezuela*. Instituto Latinoamericano de Investigaciones Sociales: Caracas, 2006.

104. Juan Carlos Rey, "Democracia, desarrollo y redistribución en Venezuela." *Pensamiento Iberoamericano, Transición y perspectivas de la democracia en Iberoamérica*, No. 14, July–December 1988.

105. Enrique Rodríguez, op. cit.

106. González and Lacruz, op. cit.

107. See http://www.aporrea.org/audio/2004/12/intervencin_del_presidente_en_la_reunin_de_alta_nivel_viernes_12_nov_04.pdf

108. González and Lacruz, op. cit.

109. Ibid.

110. PROVEA, *Informe Anual octubre 2004 - septiembre 2005 sobre la situación de los Derechos Humanos en Venezuela*. PROVEA: Caracas, 2005.

111. PROVEA (2008), op. cit.

112. *Memoria y Cuenta*. Ministerio del Estado para la Vivienda: Caracas, 2005.

113. Agencia Bolivariana de Noticias, "Gobierno aplica sólidas estrategias para garantizar viviendas dignas para todos" (September 2008) (Link no longer available; agency has been renamed Agencia Venezolana de Noticias: http://www.avn.info.ve/)

114. PROVEA (2008), op. cit.

115. "Discurso del Contralor, informe de gestión 2008" (August 2009) http://www.derechos.org.ve/proveaweb/wp-content/uploads/10-vivienda.pdf

116. Ministerio del Poder Popular para la Comunicación e Información, "Nace Pdval como instrumento para la batalla por la soberanía alimentaria" (January 2008) http://www.minci.gob.ve/

117. PROVEA (2008), op. cit.

118. González and Lacruz, op. cit.

119. Sindicato Único Nacional de Trabajadores Bolivarianos de Mercal, "Conclusiones del encuentro nacional sindical de trabjadores de Mercal (July 2009) http://www.aporrea.org/actualidad/n137811.html

120. "Discurso del Contralor, informe de gestión 2008," op. cit.

121. González and Lacruz, op. cit.

122. PROVEA (2005), op. cit.

123. PROVEA (2007), op. cit.

124. Jorge González, "Las pobres no tienen acceso al aborto seguro." *Ultimas Noticias*, August 1, 2009, p. 8.

125. "Entrevista a Marino Alvarado: 'La revolución bolivariana ha tenido un gran fracaso en sector salud.'" *El Libertario*, No. 53, May–June 2008.

126. PROVEA (2008), op. cit.

127. *Ultimas Noticias*, August 8, 2006. "Jorge Rodríguez demandará a clinica Ávila."

128. "Barrio Adentro es un logro de la revolución que hay que defender con el voto" (November 2008) http://www.abrebrecha.com/articulos.php?id=7504

CHAPTER 3
The Devil's Excrement

According to the web site of PDVSA, Venezuela is fifth in the world in proven reserves of oil and natural gas; seventh in the production of petroleum; fifth in refinery capacity; and eighth in sales. [129]

Venezuela was involved in petroleum extraction almost from the dawn of the industry. Only twenty years after the discovery of Drake's Well in Pennsylvania, the Compañia Nacional Minera Petrolera del Táchira was formed in the Venezuelan state of Táchira. Its owner, Manuel Pulido, obtained from the regional government the concession for the exploration and extraction of petroleum from the Alquitrana field a short distance from the Colombian frontier. However, this pioneering effort had limited scope. Its small refinery produced kerosene, which was in demand in the region as a substitute for firewood and also as a replacement for whale oil, which was used in lamps. The families involved in this venture later traveled to Pennsylvania to study the extraction and refining process. There, they acquired better equipment and sailed with it to the port of Maracaibo, before making the long journey overland, with mules hauling the gear, to the petroleum fields.[130]

Foreign involvement in the exploitation of hydrocarbons and analogous materials began in 1893 when R.H. Hamilton and J.A. Phillips obtained an asphalt concession at the other end of the country in Guanaco in Sucre state. This concession was transferred to the Bermudez Company, based in the U.S., which became embroiled in a dispute with the government of Cirpriano Castro, to the point of financing an armed insurrectionary movement called "Liberating Revolution," which was defeated in the Battle of La Victoria in 1902.

Despite this, the process of delivering concessions to foreign businesses began under Castro. This policy was continued by his successor, Juan Vicente Gómez (1908–1935). The first three decades of the twentieth century saw roughly 75 million acres delivered as petroleum concessions to foreign companies. Astoundingly, this is over a quarter of Venezuela's national territory.[131] Gomez delivered, on average, 323 concessions annually during his 27-year reign.[132]

This voracity for (extraction) concessions was ignited by the first truly important discovery of petroleum in the country, the so-called Zumaque I find in the country around Mene Grande in Zulia State, near the eastern shore of Lake Maracaibo. However, the outbreak of World War I delayed the expected development of the petroleum industry for several years, until it was definitively reinitiated in 1922 with the drilling of the Los Barrosos 2 ("The Muddy Ones 2") well near Cabimas, also in Zulia State. During its first ten days, the well demonstrated its potential by throwing a torrent of oil into the air; it's estimated that the torrent reached a height of 100 meters (approx. 330 feet), and it could be seen from 20 kilometers (approx. 13 miles) away.[133] Beginning with the Mene Grande find, the amount of petroleum activity in Venezuela grew to such magnitude that within 15 years production reached 375,000 barrels of crude oil per day, making Venezuela the second largest oil producer in the world.[134]

To recount a bit of history, after the War of Independence against Spain, which ended in 1826, four years prior to the death of Bolivar, Venezuela found itself in a difficult political and economic situation. It was very dependent on agricultural exports, especially of coffee and cocoa beans. In 1920, per capita income was $250 annually (approx. $2750 in 2010 dollars), and the population was less than three million, with 75% of the people living in rural areas. The illiteracy rate was 70%, and the people were scourged by malaria, tuberculosis, and other diseases. The economist Maza Zavala states that the definitive start of the "era of petroleum in Venezuela" was in 1927, because that was the year in which extracted materials (minerals, petroleum) displaced agricultural materials as Venezuela's number one export.[135]

Between independence in 1826 and the elevation of Juan Vicente Gómez in 1908, the political situation was unstable. It was characterized by bitter struggles for power among regional caudillos. During that 78-year period, Venezuela had 34 different governments. On average, a new regime took power every two years and four months.[136]

At its beginning, the development of the petroleum industry in Venezuela was not integrated into the national economy. Rather, it was an "enclave," owned and operated by foreign economic interests for their own benefit. It was a technically sophisticated operation located in a rural area totally lacking in infrastructure.

A Country Transformed by Petroleum

The "black gold" manna transformed Venezuelan society. This can be seen in the effect it had on local economics. Prior to the exploitation of petroleum, the primary source of wealth was agricultural exports. With the oil economy, the primary source of wealth became the sale of imported goods. Venezuelan business interests created rudimentary networks distributing foreign merchandise. (Previously, for the most part these interests had sold, within Venezuela, domestic goods.) The financial system was also transformed, with the banks being controlled by both Venezuelan and foreign capital. These banks focused on financing commercial development, such as construction and services in urban areas.

The exploitation of petroleum spurred the migration of agricultural workers from areas such as Táchira, Mérida, Trujillo, Falcón, Nueva Esparta and Delta Amacuro to Zulia State, where they searched for work in the oil fields. The historian Ramón J. Velásquez, referring to this process, states that the development of petroleum had displaced civil war as a means of change: "The campesinos came to understand the value of a wage: electric lights at night, boots to protect their callused feet that had previously worn sandals, doctors in place of 'healers,' shamans, and miraculous religious cures. The news of the change arrived in the villages and fields with the letters from those who had already migrated, and stoked the imaginations of their brothers and friends, who would likewise abandon their native lands. Thus began the depopulation of the countryside."[137] This slow but profound transformation provided the background for many of the best Venezuelan novels, such as *Sobre la misma tierra* ("Upon the Same Earth "), by Rómulo Gallegos (1943); *Mené*, by Ramón Díaz Sánchez (1936); and *Casas Muertas* (Dead Houses) and *Oficina no. 1* ("Office Number One"), by Miguel Otero Silva (1955 and 1961).

Casas Muertas recounts the history of the village of Ortiz, a symbol of the rural countryside in the nineteenth century, a countryside devastated by the civil wars instigated by the regional caudillos, and whose people were decimated by epidemics. The final survivors of these horrors left the dusty streets of Ortiz heading toward what they thought was their salvation: the petroleum fields. "Black and powerful blood that pours forth in sheets, far from the villages in rubble that they [the workers] are now leaving, far from the skinny cattle and the miserable ashes. Petroleum was the violent stridency of machines, food for the cooking pots, money, liquor—another thing altogether. Some migrated because of hope, others because of greed, most because of necessity." [138]

If we've spent a little time recounting this transition in Venezuela from an agricultural to a petroleum economy, it's because it involved a multi-faceted cultural process which is necessary to understanding the Venezuela of today, and to understanding the peculiarities of the country in respect to other Latin American countries.

"Sowing Petroleum"

From the beginning, the petroleum industry in Venezuela has been a global phenomenon, in which there are three principal actors: the proprietors of the resource, the investors that exploit it, and the consumers who use it. The proprietors want just compensation for the exploitation of a nonrenewable resource; the investors want profits for money invested; and consumers want guarantees of a safe supply at reasonable and stable prices. Throughout the history of the petroleum industry in Venezuela, conflicts and tensions between these three actors, especially between the first two, have always been present.

To sum up the history of the industry to 1976, when it became a state enterprise, it's useful to remember the actions of several key players in its development. The first is Gumersindo Torres (1875–1947), who was named a minister twice by long-term dictator Juan Vicente Gómez and was the author of the country's first Hydrocarbon Law, which was intended to maximize the income of the Venezuelan state. It contained a detailed compendium of norms and procedures, from exploration, to the drilling of wells, to the measurement of the oil in storage tanks. This law was intended to conserve this nonrenewable resource, establishing the basis for what would later be the Ministry of Mines and Hydrocarbons. Those holding the petroleum concessions opposed the initiatives promoted by Torres, calling the measures "unconstitutional, impractical, and interventionist." They demanded that the government overturn the law, and they exerted enough pressure that they achieved their objective.

Years later, attorney Juan Pablo Pérez Alfonzo, as Minister of Public Works in the so-called Triennial Accommodation (1945–1948) advanced "no more concessions" policies, owing to the fact that he considered transnational corporations "arbitrary, unilateral, and voracious." He proposed that taxes on those enterprises be raised as high as possible; that Venezuela compete directly and independently, without intermediaries, in the world market; that a system of refineries and service stations be developed by the state to complement industrialization and the merchandising of petroleum; that natural gas be utilized as part of a vast national petrochemical industry; and that a cartel of petroleum-producing countries be formed. Because of this, Pérez Alfonso is considered the father of OPEC, which was founded on September 14, 1960. (Prior to that, Pérez Alfonzo had instigated an increase in energy taxes in 1947, to the level of 50/50 profits to the corporations versus profits [taxes] to the state). In 1963 he retired from public life, but he continued to investigate and publicize the harmful effects of Venezuela's dependence upon the export of petroleum, which he called "the excrement of the devil."

The writer Arturo Uslar Pietri (1906–2001) held a contrary opinion to that of Pérez Alfonzo. Uslar believed that Venezuela should take advantage of the technology, knowledge, and financial power of transnational oil companies in order to develop the country's resources.[139] Needless to say, this vision was diametrically opposed to that which envisioned nationalization and unilateral control of the petroleum industry by the state.

Even though Pérez Alfonzo and Uslar Pietri held very different views about control of Venezuela's petroleum resources, they were in agreement about what needed to be done with the income from those resources. As Uslar Pietri put it, there was "a necessity to invest the riches produced by the destructive system of extraction into creating agricultural riches: 'sowing petroleum.'"[140]

One of Uslar Pietri's disciples, Miguel Ángel Burelli Rivas, put in concrete terms the meaning of "sowing petroleum": "Constructing schools, shops, factories, roads, clinics where they're needed and to prepare above all else from the very beginning a post-petroleum mentality. We cannot permit a spirit of dependency to spread to the soul of the nation, because we would soon see that a society used to working would instead become used to having the government administer the public wealth, with the attendant incompetence, sloth, and dishonesty." [141]

The Nationalist Bolivarian Model

If he was best known for his novels and short story collections, such as *Las lanzas coloradas* ("The Red Lances") (1931), *El camino del Dorado* ("The Way of the Golden") (1947) and *Oficio de Difuntos* ("Office of the Dead") (1976), Uslar Pietri's appearances in television series, such as *Valores Huma-*

nos ("Human Values") and *Cuéntame a Venezuela* ("Tell Me About Venezuela"), and his long career as a politician and journalist were also significant. He was born in Caracas in 1906 and received his law degree in 1927. He came from a privileged family background, as he was the nephew of the doctor and general Juan Pietri, who was the dictator Juan Vicente Gómez's vice president. In the year he received his law degree, there was a student revolt against the dictator Vicente Gómez. At a time when many student leaders were imprisoned, Uslar began his career as a diplomatic official in Paris. He returned to Venezuela after the death of the dictator in 1935, and occupied various posts in the government of Eleazar López Contreras, which continued persecuting Venezuela's leftist organizations.

Uslar Pietri also served, from the beginning, as a cabinet minister in the government of Isaías Medina Angarita, a military man who assumed power in 1941. Even though he had legalized opposition and leftist political organizations, Medina was overthrown by a coup d'etat in 1945; and Uslar Pietri was sent into exile in the United States. In 1948, the government that had taken power in 1945 with the coup was in turn overthrown by the same military men who had installed it. Two years later, Uslar Pietri returned to Venezuela during the government of Marcos Pérez Jiménez, another military dictator, and undertook educational activities until the fall of Pérez in 1958, a year which marked the culmination of the struggle for democracy in Venezuela, a struggle which had commenced under Juan Vicente Gómez in 1925.

When the second national presidential election was held in 1963, a number of factions promoted the idea of a unity candidate to defeat the Democratic Action party (AD) of then-president Rómulo Betancourt. The proposed unity candidate was Uslar Pietri, but he was unacceptable to some members of the coalition, owing in part to accusations by leftist organizations—some of which were conducting guerrilla warfare in the mountains—that the novelist represented the financial oligarchies.

After the elections, in which he came in fourth place with 16% of the vote, Uslar Pietri founded the center-right party, National Democratic Front, in which he participated for three years. During the following presidential election campaign, in 1969, Uslar Prieti acted as an intermediary between President Rafael Caldera and the budding insurgencies of groups such as the Movement of the Revolutionary Left and the Party of the Venezuelan Revolution, in an effort to get the insurgents to abandon armed struggle. Simultaneously, he acted as the editor of the daily paper, *El Nacional*. In the government of Carlos Andrés Pérez, starting in 1974, Uslar Pietri was a Venezuelan representative to UNESCO. Returning to the country in 1979, he concentrated on his writing and educational efforts, leaving behind political activity until his death in 2001. However, during those years his views on Venezuelan life were amply diffused in the Venezuelan media. He was part of a group of intellectuals know as "Los notables," whose influence was considered a moral counterweight to that of the traditional political parties.

This was Arturo Uslar Pietri, one of the most well known defenders of the participation of foreign capital in the Venezuelan petroleum industry. As noted above, the contrary thesis, arguing for total control of the industry by the Venezuelan state, was advanced by Democratic Action militant Juan Pablo Pérez Alfonzo, and was put into practice at the end of 1975 (with the nationalization of the industry, which was put in effect in 1976). These two actors, along with other outstanding intellectuals of the epoch, such as Alberto Adriani (1898–1936) and Salvador de la Plaza (1896–1970), alerted Venezuela to the social, cultural, and environmental consequences of dependency upon hydrocarbon exportation. But in economic terms, their positions were opposite: Uslar Pietri advocated the path of neoliberalism, while Pérez Alfonso was a determined nationalist, a defender of state sovereignty. If we project the positions of Uslar Pietri and Pérez Alfonso to the present, whose approach is closest *in practice* to that of the so-called Bolivarian Process?

In a speech on October 18, 2005 President Hugo Chávez referred to one of these two men in the following terms: ". . . I respect him, all Venezuelans respect him as an intellectual, as an honest politician, and as one who was very nationalist. He was of the upper class, but was of the type we need from that class: a nationalist who thought first of the nation and who would not kneel before the imperial interests of any world power." This does not refer to Pérez Alfonso, the "nationalist anti-imperialist," but rather to Arturo Uslar Pietri.

Like all the democratically elected presidents before him, Chávez speaks about the necessity of "sowing petroleum," referring in elegiac terms to the author of *Las lanzas coloradas*.[142] In fact, "Sowing Petroleum" is the name of an ambitious energy-expansion program that began in 2005, scheduled to unfold over the following 25 years.[143] It could be argued that President Chávez intends to reclaim, to re-emphasize, the need to use the income from the sale of crude oil for the benefit of society. But is it possible to separate the nationalist politics of "sowing petroleum" from the participation of the great transnational energy companies? Are we seeing a model that joins the vision of Uslar Pietri with that of the nationalist Perez Alfonso? Is this the goal of the "socialism of the twenty-first century" that is unfolding in Venezuela?

A Capsule History of PDVSA

Petroleos de Venezuela, Sociedad Anónima (PDVSA—"sociedad anónima, or "s.a.," is equivalent to "inc."), the Venezuelan state oil company, began operating on January 1, 1976, after the nationalization of the industry the previous year by the Democratic Action government of then-President Carlos Andrés Pérez. From the initiation of its operations until 1999, PDVSA had a monopoly on the sale, marketing, and transport of all Venezuelan petroleum products and petroleum derivatives. Following nationalization, the transnational oil companies that up until that time had owned the oil industry in Venezuela were indemnified in what many petroleum-industry analysts considered excessive amounts.

The transnationals, however, did not totally withdraw from Venezuela, as they obtained "technical assistance" contracts from PDVSA and agreements regarding the marketing of Venezuela's petroleum products. As well, in the years 1976–1990, some transnational companies, including Halliburton, obtained well-paying service contracts from PDVSA. In 1996, the government of Rafael Caldera signed shared-profits agreements with several multinational corporations for the exploration and exploitation of hydrocarbons in Venezuela. These companies included Dupont, Amoco, and BP. The Venezuelan government, however, retained formal ownership under all of these agreements.

During the 1990s, politicians, academics, and journalists began discussing the "necessity" of increasing petroleum revenues by allowing the participation of foreign capital in the petroleum industry. But it wasn't until after the election of Hugo Chávez that the Venezuelan government signed the first "mixed enterprise" agreements under which transnationals such as British Petroleum, Chevron, and Repsol YPF became part owners (up to 49%), along with the Venezuelan state, in various hydrocarbon companies.

During the pre-Chávez era, PDVSA had close relationships with the two primary political parties, the social democratic Democratic Action (AD) and the social christian COPEI. These two parties appointed their members to key posts within PDVSA and also controlled the unions in the petroleum industry. But PDVSA also developed within itself a technocratic culture, and the highly paid professional specialists in PDVSA ended up becoming a social class unto themselves. They made their own rules and managed the company outside of the direct control of the government of the day.

It was for this reason that the bureaucratic reordering that took place after Chávez's election had little effect on PDVSA and, of course, the principal industry in Venezuela: petroleum. Chávez couldn't control and use PDVSA as he did the rest of the state institutions, and there was antagonism between the Chávez regime and the AD/COPEI/technocratic hierarchy in PDVSA.

In December 2002, the PDVSA workers—especially those in medium-level and high-level posts—called an indefinite strike, citing as the reason President Chávez's discharge of a group of PDVSA managers on television, without previous notification. As a result of the strike, gasoline imports into the country dried up until the Chávez government was rescued by shipping and communications magnate Wilmer Ruperti, who re-established gasoline imports into the country.

After the PDVSA strike was broken, Chávez fired 18,000 PDVSA workers, approximately 40% of the PDVSA work force.

Mixed Enterprises: A Model for Globalization

The first landmark in the legal accommodation to the tendencies of economic globalization was the promulgation on September 23, 1999 of the Organic Law of Gaseous Hydrocarbons, whose two most important objectives were to stimulate the search for gas deposits and to allow gas activities to be undertaken by private entities, be they Venezuelan or foreign, with or without the participation of the state. This served to screen transnational investment in the sector. A second step in this direction was the approval of a new constitution on December 20 of the same year. The Constitution of the Bolivarian Republic of Venezuela established, in its Article 301, that "The state reserves to itself the use of commercial policy to defend economic activities of public and private national enterprises. Rules more beneficial to foreign persons, businesses, or other organisms than rules established for domestic [persons, businesses, or other organisms] shall not be established." The final sentence of the article is key: "Foreign investment is subject to the same conditions as domestic investment."[144]

The legal architecture favorable to globalization doesn't end there. The proposal to reform the Constitution, presented by President Chávez himself in August 2007, was intended, in part, to give constitutional cover to mixed enterprises—which had in fact been operating in the country as associations between PDVSA and companies such as Repsol YPF, Chevron, BP, and others. The proposed change to Article 112 established that the state "will encourage and develop distinct forms of enterprises and economic units of social property, as much direct or community as indirect or state, as also businesses and economic units of production and/or social distribution, and these can be mixed enterprises between the state, private sector, and community power, creating the best conditions for the collective and cooperative construction of a socialist economy."

The proposal for article 113 states, "When one deals with the exploitation of natural resources or any other strategic goods in the dominion of the nation, or of the provision of vital public services, the state will reserve to itself the exploitation or execution of these things, directly or through enterprises that it owns, without prejudicing the establishment of directly social enterprises, mixed enterprises and/or socialist units of production, that assure economic and social sovereignty, respect the control of the state, and comply with the social duties placed upon them." Article 155, regarding the proposal made by President Chávez himself, states that "mixed property is that combined between the public sector, the social sector, the collective sector, and the private sector in distinct combinations, in order to take advantage of resources or execution of activities, always subject to absolute respect for the economic and social sovereignty of the nation."[145] It's necessary to stress that this initiative from the president left Article 301 intact.

This does not sit well with many erstwhile Chávez supporters. Victor Poleo, a petroleum engineer, was one of the Venezuelans enthused by the dismantling of the traditional state bureaucracy beginning in 1998 with the election of Hugo Chávez. He was the director of the Ministry of Energy and Mines' electricity sector between 1999 and 2001, and he's a member of the Grupo Soberanía (Sovereignty Group), a coalition of leftists with ties to the petroleum industry, whose members took actions in defense of the state petroleum enterprise PDVSA during the "petroleum strike" in 2002.

In April 2007, Poleo delivered a report to the Venezuelan Communist Party (PCV) titled *La Agenda Energética Bolivariana materializa los intereses del Imperio y del Capital Energética Global* ("The Bolivarian Energy Policy Serves ['Realizes'] the Interests of Imperialism and of the Global Energy Companies").[146] The report contextualized in relatively few words the genesis of the world petroleum industry, its importance, and its prospects in regard to the development of alternative energy sources. The report states: "Politics in Venezuela *is* energy politics, that is to say, hidden within energy policy is the relation of Venezuela with Energy Capital, be it that of sovereignty or subservience. By extension, the nature of energy policy in Venezuela determines the nature and size of class struggle [in the country]." It goes on to outline "a combination of decisions forged in Washington that characterize the pro-imperialist nature of the Bolivarian Energy Agenda." Poleo names those responsible for the execution of these decisions in Venezuela: high officials at the time such as Alí Rodríguez Araque (president of PDVSA), Bernard Mommer (Vice-Minister of Hydrocarbons), and Bernardo Álvarez (Venezuelan Ambassador to the United States).

Poleo's document denounces the creation of mixed enterprises to exploit energy exploration and production in Venezuela, such as those that created in March 2006, when the Venezuelan government signed 32 contracts with transnational companies, and in which PDVSA maintained majority control. [This is in contrast to the post-1975 arrangement, in which the Venezuelan government maintained sole ownership of the oil industry.] In an interview, Poleo waxed ironic about the change in status: "We've gone from the model of the maid to the model of the concubine. The maid who provided services [the transnationals], and who we accused for years of swindling us, has now become our partner. Now we share, with international petroleum capital, ownership of the subsoil resources. And the profits from them. This is a surprising scheme."[147] The interviewer then asked Poleo, "Are we in reality throwing aside nationalization?" The former energy official responded: "Yes, but it's disguised as nationalization." In the report delivered to the PCV, Poleo points out that "the political revolutionary project bases its survival upon the income from petroleum, but this false concept is at best a pyrrhic national victory [leaving the appearance of sovereignty, but in reality placing control in foreign hands]." [148]

Effectively, this type of business policy based upon the establishment of mixed enterprises (with 51% to 60% in the hands of the Venezuelan government and 40% to 49% in the hands of foreign businesses, such as Chevron, British Petroleum, and Repsol YPF) is promoted to the world as "energy sovereignty"—a euphemism worthy of the label "double think"—and which serves to induce confusion regarding Venezuela in the international anticapitalist social movements. As an example, the web site Iconoclasistas, which defines itself as a "counter-hegemonic laboratory of freely circulating communication and resources" features a map of Latin America labeled "resistance to capitalism." Its entry on Venezuela states that "Petroleum was nationalized by President Chávez."[149]

Many different social movements and organizations on the Venezuelan left, including anarchist groups and organizations, questioned the establishment of mixed enterprises. In the reform proposal of 2007, covering 33 articles in the Venezuelan Constitution, a proposal impelled by President Chávez himself, mixed enterprises were classified as constitutional. A coalition of leftist/antiauthoritarian organizations, dubbed The Insurgents, criticized this "reform" for motives quite different from those proclaimed by the social-democratic and rightist opposition. According to an Insurgent manifesto issued before the constitutional referendum, and endorsed by dozens of anarchist, Communist, and other leftist groups and individuals:

> The principal objective pursued by big capital with this "reform" is the classification of mixed enterprises as constitutional. That implies the bestowing of sovereignty on the transnationals and on foreign governments, not only in the area of petroleum, but also in mining and in all public services. . . . This is the essence of the "reform," and explains the rapidity with which this proposal has been brought before the public, to legitimize this new political swindle via the electoral process. Once it has achieved its primary objective, global capitalism will deliver to the Bolivarian government a series of complementary changes that will assure the deepening and stability of this new model. From this moment, mixed state/capital property will become the economic basis of the entire society, not only in the petroleum industry, but in all branches of the economy.

From the Nationalization of Petroleum to Mixed Enterprises

What was the route from the nationalization of the petroleum industry in 1976 to the establishment of mixed enterprises thirty years later? Juan Pablo Pérez Alfonso had predicted that owing to the conditions under which nationalization was established in 1976, the transnationals would return to the country in a few years. At the beginning of the 1990s, the state petroleum agency PDVSA started to argue that it was necessary to implement a new strategy of "openness" toward private initiatives where they were legally permitted.

So it was that in 1992 a program of reactivating the so-called closed petroleum fields was established, in which private companies received 20-year agreements which allowed them to resume production in these areas and sell the oil obtained to PDVSA, while paying taxes upon their profits. In the period 1992–1997, 33 such agreements were signed.[150] For the leftist Venezuelan economist Mazhar Al-Shereidah, the basis of this "opening" was the formula that the Caldera-Giusti (President of Venezuela/President of PDVSA) administration had established to rejoin and reconcile those who had been temporarily separated: the state and the companies that had formerly held the oil concessions.[151] With the arrival in power of President Chávez in 1998, this practice continued, with the establishment of more agreements with private concerns, all transnationals. In 2005 there were 32 operating agreements, five licenses authorizing exploitation of natural gas, three licenses for exploration of offshore natural gas, three strategic associations, and three zones assigned for exploration under the system of shared profits. Some of the transnational firms involved were British Petroleum, Chevron, Statoil, Repsol YPF, Total Oil, Conoco-Phillips, and Exxon-Mobil.[152]

In 1992, intense social mobilizations in Venezuela resulted in the political disablement of President Carlos Andrés Pérez. One of the charges made by the left was that PDVSA was being privatized via the operating agreements and the official pronouncements about the "opening." This popular pressure, coming from many directions, originated when the Venezuelan Congress undertook a discussion of the commercial policies being implemented within PDVSA.[153] A deputy of the emerging party, La Causa Radical (La Causa R), who had the prestige of having participated in the guerrilla struggle during the 1960s under the pseudonym "Comandante Fausto," was one of the major critics of the association of the Venezuelan state with international private capital:

> The analysis of the contracts put before Congress reveals certain constants within them; these reveal that the apparent incoherence is more a matter of appearance than of reality. It appears that there's an ever-clearer plan that aims toward a particular end: the transference of productive activities to foreign investors. Certainly, PDVSA continues to be the principal producer within the country, but seen in the perspective of the next 40 years, its relative role will be reduced without the compensation of an increase in productivity of other national assets. (We speak of 40 years, since this is the duration of the [mixed-economy] contracts, as in the times of Gómez.) This is the essence of the problem. And it is, in turn, the point from which we can see the form of the confrontation which, we have no doubt, will become clearer every day to Venezuelans. [154]

The deputy who spoke these words was Alí Rodríguez Araque, who ten years later, with the changeover in the bureaucracy, became the president of PDVSA. As president of PDVSA, he said that the only problem with putting the new scheme into practice was that it did not include the inclusion of 100% of the old operating agreements: "The only [company] that was contentious was Exxon; all of the other enterprises negotiated peacefully and arrived at accords. They're satisfied and continue to operate in Venezuela." [155] In an interview on the state radio chain, Radio Nacional de Venezuela, he dispelled rumors about the possible discomfort of the foreign enterprises:

It would be good if you'd interview some of the representatives of the companies that now participate in the mixed enterprises such as the petroleum area in Orinoco to see how they feel . . . There are now investing in Venezuela not only the companies that installed themselves during the "opening," but many other companies from many nationalities have come, in a strategy that is absolutely correct: on the one hand diversification of investors, and on the other diversification of markets. [156]

Unlike Rodríguez, not all of the old g'uerrillas from the armed struggle in Venezuela hold high office in the Bolivarian government, and neither have they aligned themselves with the contradiction between words and actions which appears to characterize the petroleum policies of President Chávez. An example is provided by Douglas Bravo, in 1965 a director of the PRV, who along with his organization, Third Way, and other social activists, on January 17, 2008 argued before the Venezuelan high court that the legal form of the mixed enterprises was unconstitutional. Bravo stated: "The mixed enterprises represent a fifty-fifty [arrangement] in practice, and are part of the new model of domination that imperialism is imposing on the countries [of Latin America]."[157]

In June 2008, a communique from Bravo's group reiterated its rejection of the mixed-enterprise model as one of their primary reasons for confronting the so-called Bolivarian Process:

Our petroleum industry is passing from a basis of "simple service contracts," in which the state pays for services rendered, while maintaining its status as the absolute owner of all hydrocarbons produced, to a basis in which the foreign companies have become partners of PDVSA, and in consequence PDVSA had to cede to them "the part corresponding to the association." According to the standard contract that regulates mixed enterprises, private capital is the owner of 40% of the capital comprising the enterprise, and therefore are also the owners of 40% of the dividends or earnings that come from the hydrocarbons that are produced. In addition, in all decisions of the enterprise that require the agreement of 75% of the capital held, the opinion of the private owners will determine the outcome, that is to say, our petroleum policies are in the hands of the multinationals.[158]

The same reasoning formed the basis months before for the rejection of the constitutional "reform" proposal advanced by President Chávez.

The proposed articles—112, 113, and 115—give constitutional status to property mixed between the state and the private sector regarding the exploitation of natural resources. In this manner multinational capital consolidates its position as the owner of strategic natural resources and the provider of essential public services, a situation which was initiated on March 31, 2006 with the approval by the National Assembly of the standard contract for the FORMATION OF MIXED ENTERPRISES [capital letters in the original] for the exploitation of hydrocarbons, a model which will now be extended to the exploitation of uranium, iron, coal, water, plutonium, gold and other natural resources. In addition, the public services of education, health, housing, social security, telephone, transportation, etc., will be privatized.[159]

For its part, anarchist opinion cites as a precedent of the mixed enterprises the "Magna Carta" emanating from the constituent process of 1999, which was in tune with the "necessity" for globalization of the economy in order to deliver benefits such as the free circulation of capital and economic investments free of obstacles and borders:

February 27, 1989—the social explosion known as the Caracazo—constituted a firebreak for the restructuring of world power. The eruption of passions and irrationality confronted the nascent architecture of the free circulation of capital. [The necessity of systemic relegitimazation had governability as a precondition, something which had been clearly expressed in the so-called Washington Consensus.] A new form of subordination and discipline had to be infused through the branches of the social structure and internalized by the citizens: the setting in of "petroleum socialism," the presently existing Chavista populism. Obscured by leftist rhetoric, the Constitution of 1999 bundled the territory of Venezuela with the needs of the moment, delivering to foreign investors, in Article 301, the same rights and conditions ceded to domestic capital. This article definitively reversed the process of nationalizing the petroleum industry that had begun in 1974. The rest of the 349 articles [in the Constitution], including the exalted ones about social benefits, were a necessary artifice. In the Constitutional reform proposal the [mixed-enterprise] model became further embedded.[160]

These are the opinions of some non-Chavista revolutionary anti-capitalists. There are also more conservative opponents, and they have a much greater capacity to spread their messages via the communications media, advocating for the total control by private capital of energy extraction in Venezuela. Months after the failed coup d'etat in 2002, grouped together as the Democratic Coordinatorship, these conservative opponents promulgated a number of proposals about management of the country. In its National Project document, the conservatives euphemistically [and outrageously] described [the state's] association with private capital as "citizen participation":

> First of all it's necessary to emphasize that citizen participation does NOT [capitals in original] signify a definitive privatization of our primary natural resource or of PDVSA. According to the Organic Law of Liquid Hydrocarbons, of November 13, 2000, according to the Official Gazette #27076 in its Article 22, [the state] can reserve to itself participation of over 50%. The state clearly can maintain control with 51%. Well then, can the industry continue to be a state enterprise with 51% [ownership by the state]? Obviously YES [capitals in original]. Then what can be done with the remaining 49%? In this 49% there is sufficient space for citizen participation.[161]

Pablo Hernández Parra, a former guerrilla and an investigator of the energy industry, upon comparing the two approaches, stated: "There is no difference, neither at the base nor in form, between the privatizing proposals of the Democratic Coordinatorship–which directed the [attempted] coup d'etat [in 2002] and the sabotage of petroleum production [also in 2002]—and the present policy of 'full petroleum sovereignty' put into practice by this [Chávez's] government."[162]

Chevron's Diplomacy in Bolivarian Times

If one reviews certain leftist literature—including, in good measure, that of the environmental and anti-globalization movements—regarding the politics of the worldwide expansion of the energy conglomerates, the absence of information about the transnationals' operations in Venezuela is striking. And it can lead to misperceptions. To paraphrase Camus in *Algerian Chronicles*, good politics are well informed politics. And then there are those who do not want to, or cannot, interpret certain things. The Multinational Observer of Latin America reports that the amount of news and analysis about Venezuela is the fifth lowest of the 26 countries it monitors.

Another example is the 2005 Oilwatch report, "Chevron, the right hand of the empire: A report on Chevron, Texaco, Caltex and Unocal," which attempts to document the worldwide impact of Chevron-Texaco. In the report's 256 pages, there are exactly two paragraphs about Venezuela. This investigative report, produced by the Oilwatch Network of Petroleum Alerts, was delivered to this author at the Pan-Amazon Meeting of Communities Affected by the Petroleum Industry, which took place in Quito, Ecuador in November 2005, by the authors of the report, who were also the organizers of the event. During the conference, one of the coordinators of Ecological Action—the local member-group of Oilwatch—told me of her enthusiasm for the trans-formations which, in her view, had occurred in Venezuela. After I told her about the reversal of the nationalization process and the aggressive expansion of foreign energy companies in Venezuela, I was puzzled by her muted response to that information. Then I understood the omission in the report: in the entire world, the expansion and practices of companies such as Chevron are questionable—except in Venezuela.

The absence of data on the presence and impact of Chevron in Venezuela sharply contrasts with the very active role it has taken in extracting energy from the country. The ascendency of the company is of such a magnitude that it has international diplomatic reach. It overcomes antagonisms which, on the surface, appear irreconcilable, such as that between Hugo Chávez and his Colombian counterpart, Álvaro Uribe Vélez.

In September 2001, Chevron and Texaco concluded their merger, in the process becoming the fourth largest oil company in the world and the number one contributor to political parties in the United States.[163] Five months after the merger, the president of Chevron's Division of Exploration and Production in Latin America, Alí Moshiri, held a conference in Houston, Texas, in order to explain the potential for expansion of the company in South America: "We are the largest private foreign producer in Venezuela in terms of daily oil production. We operate the largest natural gas fields in Colombia."[164]

In that speech, titled "Latin America Upstream: Progress and Pitfalls," Moshiri outlined an optimistic vision of business development in the region: "[T]he potential of Latin America is hard to overstate. It could one day exceed that of the former Soviet Union." He pointed out that "[P]rogress can only continue through a commitment to open markets and continued liberalization," and then continued rapidly reviewing the inconveniences that, in his judgment, had to be overcome: "In Latin America, cross-border transactions have always been hampered by red tape and by regional trade agreements that amount to managed trade."

For the director of this transnational, the objective was clear: to exercise, intelligently and discreetly, business diplomacy. Moshiri already had in mind a gas pipeline between Colombia and Venezuela, and drew his conclusion: "While the Bolivia-Brazil pipeline stands as a shining success, other projects of tremendous promise have been stalled at the border by a narrow view of the national interest. . . . [C]onsider the Venezuela-Colombia pipeline, a natural linkage between gas-rich Northern Colombia and the power markets of Venezuela. For all its promise, this obvious matching of supplier and customer cannot seem to cross over a common border."

This seemed to be a major challenge, since President Chávez appeared to be heading in a direction contrary to that of Uribe. However, greenback diplomacy did its work quickly. In only five months, on July 23, 2002, PDVSA-Gas, Ecopetrol, and ChevronTexaco concluded a joint study on the laying of a gas pipeline between the gas fields in La Guajira in Colombia and Maracaibo. A press release circulated on that date by PDVSA-Gas demonstrated that from the legal, economic, and technical viewpoints such a pipeline was feasible.[165] Only a year before, the trio [Colombia, Venezuela, and Panama] had signed a memorandum of understanding to evaluate the feasibility of such a pipeline—and 365 days later they had their result.

On December 15, 2003, Colombian president Álvaro Uribe Vélez announced in Bógota the construction of a Colombia-Venezuela-Panama gas pipeline, thanks to a contract between the Empresa Colombiana de Petróleos and ChevronTexaco. Uribe said, "It pleases me that after a difficult process, through the intervention of all of the institutions, such as Comptroller General of the Republic and the Council of State, we've been able to sign the contract extension with ChevronTexaco. This clarifies the gas-availability panorama in the country and also clarifies the vision of having a gas pipeline between Venezuela, Colombia, and Panama. Without this [contract extension with ChevronTexaco], it's almost impossible to think of this project."[166]

The project went forward despite Venezuela's having twenty times more gas reserves (147 trillion cubic feet) than Colombia. The reason for the pipeline was that most Venezuelan gas production was centered in Anzoátegui, at the eastern extreme of the country, and there were no gas pipelines to carry the gas to the western part of Venezuela, which was the part demanding gas. And the gas fields in Anzoátegui are much farther from western Venezuela than the Colombian fields in La Guajira. The Zuliana fields near Lake Maracaibo could not meet the demand, and the deficit between supply and demand was 430 million cubic feet per day. Hence the Venezuela-Colombia-Panama gas pipeline.

While Venezuela advanced internal gas interconnections, it was expected that part of the unmet demand would be met via Colombian gas from the Guajira fields operated by ChevronTexaco. So, Venezuela contracted for 200 million cubic feet of gas per day starting in 2005, for a period of at least seven years. This was the pilot project for future joint ventures between Colombia and Venezuela. For Colombia it represented an income of $50 million to $70 million U.S. dollars annually.

In the medium term, according to the negotiations highlighted by President Chávez, after the internal interconnections in the national gas net were

VENEZUELA ◆ 95

completed, the red star of the Venezuelan economy would have a new outlet direct to the Pacific Ocean, an outlet that would allow the search for new markets: "We will continue to sell oil and other petroleum products to the U.S.A. and to the countries of the Caribbean and South America, but there is another market that remains distant because of lack of connections [pipelines and related infrastructure], the Asian market."(167) In his discourse the President focused on major participation by Venezuela in the Asian energy market, leaving to one side ideological considerations: "One must imagine a Venezuelan supertanker crossing the Caribbean and Atlantic, rounding the horn of Africa, and then completing the trip to far-off China. This is a very long route, but via Colombia? No. Via Colombia it would be a direct shot." This pronouncement was made at a press conference on July 14, 2004, at which the presidents of both Colombia and Venezuela spoke about the progress of the pipeline.

In another official news release about the binational meeting, distributed through official Venezuelan press channels, these words of Álvaro Uribe appeared: "We will be with [Panamanian] President Torrijos to formalize the entry of the countries into Plan Panama Puebla, and we'll sign an act for the integration of this gas pipeline, the construction of interconnecting electric lines, and the advance of highway construction."(168) Uribe then emphasized the importance of the Asian and the U.S. West Coast markets. The official press release also stated that "the Plan Panama Puebla is an instrument of cooperation that seeks to integrate the seven countries of Central America with southern Mexico in order to further the development of the region."

As the PDVSA web site indicated on July 8, 2006, construction had begun on the pipeline "Antonio Ricuarte" along the Maraciabo-Punta Bellenas route from La Guajira in Colombia to Zulia state in Venezuela.(169)

A year later, relations between the two countries came to their worst moment since the arrival of Hugo Chávez in the presidential palace. On August 5, 2007, the Venezuelan president promised to mediate in negotiations on a humanitarian accord between the Colombian government and the marxist guerrilla group, the FARC (Fuerzas Armadas Revolucionarias de Colombia—Revolutionary Armed Forces of Colombia). Days later, Chávez met in Caracas with family members of prisoners of the FARC and sent a message to its leader, Manuel Marulanda. After various attempts at negotiation, on November 22 Colombian president Uribe decided unilaterally that the mediation efforts of the Venezuelan president were at an end. Chávez protested: "I feel betrayed," and a day later announced that relations between the two countries were "frozen"; he also called his Colombian counterpart a "liar."[170] On November 27 he responded to signals from Uribe about heading up a regional project. He didn't mince words:

Uribe, the mouthpiece of U.S. Imperialism, has spoken, and he's spoken from the guts. I'm happy that President Uribe has finally said who he is. He obliged us to pull off his mask, because he didn't want to speak. He hid behind communiques and we had to shake him hard to force him to speak. When he did speak he let down the mask and then accused me of having an expansionist program. Me, with an expansionist program, President Uribe? The [U.S.] empire is what has an expansionist program, and you are a servile instrument of the North American empire's expansionist program in Latin America! You are a poor peon of the empire! What a shame![171]

A day later Chavez made a declaration that appeared to define future relations between the two neighboring countries: "While President Uribe is president of Colombia, I will have no type of relations with him or with the government of Colombia. I can't do it [and retain] dignity."[172] In succeeding speeches where Chávez made reference to Uribe, he sustained his accusation of Uribe's being an ally of imperialism: "Coward, liar, sower of discord, manipulator! . . . Uribe serves [as president] in order to be head of the mafia. Vito Corleone! Don Vito Corleone comes up short against men such as Álvaro Uribe. I believe that Uribe will shortly become very familiar with Bush. Let's see who he cozies up to now in order to continue his work of being a little imperial peon. How sad this Colombian president is." Chavez also underlined the "strong connections [of Uribe] with the [right-wing paramilitaries in Colombia]. Only the gringos protect him, and they have him on a leash because he's their peon."[173]

In March 2008, after an incursion by the Colombian army into Ecuador, in order to destroy a FARC camp, killing FARC spokesman Paul Reyes in the process, the Venezuelan president gave a televised order that heated up the polemic: "Mister Minister of Defense, move ten battalions to the Colombian border, battalions with tanks." Chávez called the death of the FARC spokesman a "cowardly murder" and called for a moment of silence in memory of Reyes, adding that Colombia aspired to be the "Israel of Latin America."[174]

Chávez's accusations against Álvaro Uribe were not minor. He charged that Uribe was an executor of U.S. policy in the region, that he promoted paramilitarism, that he was a war-monger and statist with little regard for the truth—"a little imperial peon," to put it briefly. If there was any regime incompatible with the construction of Bolivarian socialism in Venezuela, it was the one that shared 2,216 kilometers of border with Venezuela.

But had ChevronTexaco's attempts to transcend the two nations' "narrow vision of national interests" failed?

Three months after this affair, according to a note from the Venezuelan state press, President Chávez said that it was necessary to renew relations with Colombia.[175]) On July 11, 2008, Chávez and Uribe had their first meeting after their falling out. Their press conference opened with words from the leader of the Bolivarian Process: "We are destined, no, condemned, to always be together . . . [W]e have given instructions to our chancellor and ministers of Energy and Petroleum, Telecommunications, Finance, and Agriculture to take up all the matters which had been going forward, but that were stalled and are pending with Colombia." In his address, Chávez referred to the impasses that had almost caused a military confrontation between the two countries: "In a friendly call, [Álvaro Uribe] gave me an explanation that I have accepted. Later, he asked me: 'Why did you treat me in such a personal manner?' And I responded, 'It was because I felt very wounded personally!'"[176]

Yet only a few days previous to this conversation, the Venezuelan president had questioned his disciples about organizing a demonstration against the visit of "the little peon of the empire" to Venezuela—something that would have clearly been in accord with his position of a few months before. Chávez directed his remarks to the Venezuelan Communist Party, an organization integral to the Bolivarian movement. At the time, the PCV was putting forward candidates for the upcoming mayoral and governors' races in opposition to those of the PSUV, the party of President Chávez. Chávez said: "The PCV has organized a march to oppose the visit of the president of Colombia. I invited the president of Colombia [to visit] . . . [Y]ou can have your march, but I do not recall that the PCV called a march when Bill Clinton came here! Because you were supporting [former president Rafael] Caldera! There are truths that must be recalled in order to reflect and assess [one's position]," said the Venezuelan president. He also asked the PCV if they weren't "more Catholic than the pope."[177]

The economist Domingo Alberto Rangel, an AD deputy during the 1960s and a member of the MIR, states: "Greater Colombia is being re-established by ChevronTexaco. Is there now a more important Colombian-Venezuelan initiative than the Transcaribbean gas pipeline? This task of restoring the work of Simón Bolivar has been undertaken by Chevron."[178]

In March 2009, Panamanian president Martín Torrijos visited Caracas in order to continue the negotiations regarding the participation of his country in the Transcaribbean gas pipeline.[179] In April 2009, in a new business meeting between Chávez and Uribe, the Venezuelan president highlighted advances in energy integration: "Pay attention to how this pipeline is functioning. We're beating the record . . . Beginning in 2012 we'll be sending from here to there an estimated 150 million cubic feet, a quantity which will rise in the years to come."[180]

According to its web site, Chevron is currently involved in five important projects in Venezuela. In the west of the country, in Zulia State, they're partners with the Venezuelan state in the mixed enterprises Petroboscán and Petroindependiente, whose output consists of heavy and light crude, respectively. At the other end of the country, in Anzoátegui state, Chevron participates in the mixed enterprise Petropiar, which produces heavy crude and refines it into bulk synthetic petroleum. Chevron's offshore operations include projects in the sector called Cordón III. In the delta of the Orinoco River, they've been conceded Block No. 2 in the "Deltana Platform." At the same time, the government has invited Chevron to participate in the first rail line in the country to transport liquified natural gas. According to the company, "[A]ll of our operations are accompanied by sustainable employment projects for the community that permit growth in the areas where we work. We also make significant contributions to educational, health, social, and cultural programs."[181]

In 1996, when Chevron returned to the country following its departure in 1976 due to nationalization, the company established its operations office for all of Latin America in Caracas. In 2004, the transnational announced the investment of $400 million in its Venezuelan projects.[182] In many interviews, Chevron official Alí Moshiri has reiterated, time and time again, that Chevron's business in Venezuela is sailing forward with a tail wind. In November 2007, when asked about Chevron's operations in the country, he replied: "Our activities in Venezuela are moving forward extremely well. The mixed enterprises in which we participate are working, and the result has been very positive. It's therefore a question of attitude. We came here with the intention of working, and the cooperation of Chevron and PDVSA has been established for many years. Petropiar (formerly Ameriven) is functioning very well, it's been reorganizing and its activities are moving in the right direction." In the same interview, Moshiri also commented on the keen insight of the Bolivarian government regarding business development: "The gas industry never got started in Venezuela after nationalization. It's always been an oil country. The government of President Chávez is the first to develop natural gas; before this no one knew that Venezuela had gas . . . The government is on a good path . . . In the past, Venezuela never had competitive prices for gas because nobody had tried to export it."[183] At another moment, in a conference that took place at the University of Tulsa, Moshiri said: "President Chávez has his own agenda. Many people believe that we're there to help him. This is incorrect. We're there to do business. We have an embassy there, the government of the United States is there. We're doing business in compliance with the law." Victor Poleo, former director of the Ministry of Energy and Mines' electricity sector (1999–2001), has estimated during the years 2006 and 2007 businesses such as Chevron had income of between $30 billion and $40 billion from their operations in Venezuela.[184]

Gas Projects

The natural gas projects currently under development in Venezuela are designed to supply thermoelectric generation. The axis of gas production will be along the Orinoco-Apure line, a long relatively undeveloped and sparsely populated strip in the central part of the country. In 2004, Vice-Minister of Planning and Regional Development, Gilberto Buenaño, described the benefits to the zone of economic development: "In terms of the policies of territorial development, one of the most fundamental projects is the Orinoco-Apure axis, in which the plans and investments prefigure a social base that benefits almost two million people . . . The Orinoco-Apure axis is a part of the territory that traditionally has not been subdivided by a river, as a division between north and south; now it's an integrated region of approximately 300,000 square kilometers."[185] A report from Buenaño highlights the excellent climate and topography of the region for agriculture, as well as its mineral resources, and the petroleum-field bands of the Orinoco. However, within Venezuela the gas interconnection projects are located in the same places where extraction is taking place, so the petroleum-development zones are doubly affected.[186]

During the years 2005 to 2007, on an international level, the most significant project involving the Orinoco-Apure axis was the Great Gas Pipeline of the South (El Gran Gasoducto del Sur). It was to run 12,000 kilometers, from Venezuela through Brazil and Uruguay, terminating in Argentina, and it would have affected the Venezuelan-Guayanan and the Amazon Basin ecosystems.[187] In January 2006, following a trilateral meeting between presidents Lula da Silva (Brazil), Néstor Kirchner (Argentina), and Hugo Chávez, the Venezuelan president announced that they had decided to construct the largest gas pipeline the world had ever seen. In declarations to the press prior to the meeting, Chávez made plain his intention that the gas pipeline, whose construction time was estimated at five to seven years, would benefit the other countries in the region: "The gas pipeline has to be accompanied by development zones" in all of the countries, and so "would aid in saving the lives of many indigenous children who die every year in our South America."⁽¹⁸⁸⁾ Analysts estimated that a gas pipeline of such length would demand an investment of nearly $20 billion; for that reason negotiations had to resolve where to obtain such a sum and to accept or reject the idea of accepting aid from the Inter-American Development Bank and the Andean Development Corporation. The gas pipeline signified relief for Brazil and Argentina, which were importing gas from Bolivia to supply local demand. Chávez also stated that "in no way" was the project designed to impede Bolivia's gas business.[189]

As the negotiations progressed, President Chávez, during a visit to Sao Paulo on April 26, 2006, denounced the start of a campaign to impede the pipeline project by "hegemonic interests that do not want the integration of the region."[190] This was a curious pronouncement, given that the primary criticisms of the project came from Bolivia, indigenous organizations, and environmentalists.[191] On exactly the same date that Chávez made his pronouncement, the Bolivian Vice-Minister of Hydrocarbons, Julio Gómez, declared that the project was "craziness." Gómez said that solely because of the environmental impact of such a large project "the nations of the entire world will react unfavorably." However, Gómez also pointed out that the proposal did not originate with Hugo Chávez, nor with his government, nor with PDVSA; instead, he said that the private petroleum companies were responsible for the proposal: "There are negative antecedents that stem from the same petroleum companies; they intend to reduce the importance of the new negotiations over the export of Bolivian gas to Brazil."[192]

In March 2006, the Civic Association of Friends of the Gran Sabana and the Network of Orinoco Petroleum Alerts, Oilwatch stated, in a communique which was distributed internationally:

> [T]he construction of a long, huge pipeline, such as the one planned, and its complementary string of compression plants, would affect the integrity of all of the natural, pristine ecosystems through which it passes. It would require deforestation and earth-moving on a grand scale, such as road construction through virgin sites, and in the end would require permanent maintenance and vigilance . . . No bonanza based on the hydrocarbon depredation model, even when its pretended purpose is to pay a social debt, can be relied upon, especially when [a project] generates new social and environmental debts. Overcoming the alienating hegemony of the hydrocarbon model and those who usurp its power is a vital task for those who want to safeguard healthy democracies, economies, and societies.[193]

As well, the parents of the indigenous children who President Chávez was so concerned about have rejected the project. Italo Pizarro, president of the Indigenous Federation of Bolivar State, lamented in March 2006 that Venezuela made international deals on projects that affect indigenous communities in Bolivar State, and that it's precisely the local inhabitants who are the last to know the details of those projects. Pizarro explained that the indigenous communities had no precise information about the Great Gas Pipeline of the South, because "We haven't been consulted, and that has been the plan. . . . There are many communities that are very concerned, because the impact will be great."[194] The former mayor of the town of Gran Sabana and an indigenous leader in Bolivar State, Ricardo Delgado, has sounded the alarm that the crime that was about to be committed in the National Park was very grave, because before negotiating internationally [the Venezuelan government] had to consult with the indigenous population, as is spelled out in the Venezuelan Constitution:

> The Constitution established that [in such cases] there has to be a consultive referendum so that the people can participate and decide. . . . We're very concerned about the consequences to the environment of indigenous peoples and communities . . . [A] gas pipeline is extremely dangerous and we've already seen cases along the Regional Central Highway where a pipeline exploded and caused considerable damage. Imagine if this happened in the National Park near an indigenous community. . . . This project is a threat against the very life of the communities."[195]

Nonetheless, it was neither environmental nor indigenous criticisms that stopped the project. Rather, a halt to the gas pipeline was called in October 2008 after a presidential summit involving Brazil, Ecuador, Bolivia, and Venezuela. There would be no gas pipeline, said President Chávez, after which he explained that gas distribution would be done via tanker ships in order to integrate gas distribution. In declarations to the BBC, Franklin Rojas, director of the Venezuelan environmental group Provita, said that "regrettably" ecological considerations were not the principal reason the pipeline had been canceled: "economic and political considerations weighed much more heavily than social and environmental considerations."[196] After Petrobrás, the Brazilian state energy company, announced that it considered the gas pipeline unviable, negotiations became paralyzed, and they have not been resumed.

Integration with the World Market and IIRSA

Venezuelan researcher and environmental activist María Pilar García-Guadilla, upon analyzing the huge projects executed by the Bolivarian bureaucracy, established that despite the Chávez government's verbal attacks on the neoliberal capitalist model, that same model forms the underlying principle guiding the design of the economic policies that are the basis of development:

> [There exists] continuity in the development projects of the present government with those of former governments, which were labeled by President Chávez and his followers as neoliberal, capitalist, and destructive of the environment . . . If, as they say, President Chávez and various spokesmen of the Ministry of the Environment and Natural Resources reject capitalism and neoliberalism, the envisioned Bolivarian model of development—which would guide economic policies in the years 2001–2030—is a continuation and amplification of the current extractive model; this implies heavy environmental impacts and presupposes a rationale that is development oriented and orchestrated, and neoliberal in nature.[197]

This is evident when one compares Chávez's great development projects in the areas of energy production and transport with the policies emanating from IIRSA (Iniciativa para la Integración de la Infraestructura Regional Suramericana—Initiative for the Integration of Regional Infrastructure in South America). This proposal was made concrete at the Meeting of the Presidents of South America held in August 2000 in Brasilia. At the meeting, the presidents of the region agreed to joint actions to impel the process of political, social and economic integration in South America, including the modernization of regional infrastructure and specific actions to stimulate the integration and development of isolated subregions.[198] Venezuela is one of the twelve member countries in IIRSA, and the Initiative envisions 507 projects distributed among ten axes of development. Venezuela will participate as part of the "Andean Axis," along with Colombia, Ecuador, Bolivia and Peru. Venezuela will also take part in the "Guyanan Shield Axis" along with Brazil, Guyana, and Surinam.

After the meeting in Brasilia, in which the Initiative was announced in the "Brasilia Communique,"[199] it was backed by all of the most important South American presidents, including Hugo Chávez. The Communique is explicit regarding the motives of IIRSA: "The cohesion of South America . . . constitutes also an essential element in determining . . . [South America's] insertion into the world economy. The common challenges of globalization . . . will be best [calibrated by] the measure to which the region deepens its integration and continues, each time more efficiently, acting in solidarity in a coordinated manner regarding the grand themes of the international social and economic agenda." Later the Communique states that "the presidents of the countries of South America reaffirm their promise to strengthen the World Trade Organization and to perfect the international system of commerce." As well, it states that the "integration and development of the physical infrastructure are two lines of action that are complementary . . . [and have the] capacity to attract extra-regional capital and to generate multiplier effects inter-regionally." In addition, "because of its volume, the financing of integrative infrastructure projects must be shared by the [various] governments, by the private sector, and by international, multilateral financial institutions, among which are the International Development Bank, the Andean Corporation of Development, the Financial Fund for the Development of the River Plate Basin, and the World Bank."

The Communique also establishes the central place of energy resources:

> The presidents emphasized the role of energy, and of the networks of transport and communications, as the driving forces in the integration of the South American countries . . . In the energy sector, the integration and complementary role of the South American continent's resources . . . should be increased and improved, parallel with the preservation of the environment and the elimination of unjustifiable [trade] barriers . . .

Finally, the Communique affirms the participation of the private sector:

> "The presidents of South America strengthen their commitment to giving even greater priority to national, bilateral, and subregional initiatives already undertaken, with consideration of modernization and the development of the infrastructure network in the entire region, highlighting, in this regard, the fundamental role of the private sector."

As was outlined at the Alternative Social Forum (an anti-capitalist counter to the Sixth World Social Forum in Caracas in January 2006), the strategic vision of the IIRSA mega-project advances the belief that it's necessary to implement a new regionalism whose first objective is the conquest of new markets, making the capitalist economic vision primary. Despite the euphemisms, the initiative advances neoliberal structural reforms oriented toward augmenting competitiveness in the race to supply international demand. For Lusbi Portillo, the present coordinator of Homoetnatura, an organization involved in indigenous struggles in the Sierra de Perijá [a range on the Venezuelan/Colombian border] in Zulia State, IIRSA is a structural element in the political hegemony of the United States in the Americas and Caribbean. Specific elements are NAFTA, the Free Trade Area of the Americas (ALCA—Area de Libre Comercio para las Américas), the Plan Colombia, and the Plan Puebla Panama (PPP). In fact, for Portillo, IIRSA and ALCA are "two sides of the same coin":

> ALCA determines the judicial administration in the most concrete form and IIRSA determines the infrastructure . . . : to modernize and make real the regulatory systems and national institutions that standardize the use of the infrastructure. It harmonizes the policies, plans, and regulatory and institutional norms among the states. ALCA is not only a commercial agreement, but also supports a series of parallel projects whose disastrous effects can be very well illustrated by the much-questioned Plan Puebla Panama and IIRSA.[200]

In November 2003, President Chávez began a rhetorical offensive against ALCA during the inauguration of the Bolivarian Congress of the Peoples: "Nobody really knows what ALCA is or what it signifies, but the whole world wants to sign it. It appears that the document that all the countries will sign is an instrument of commercial trade that has been transparent neither in its organization nor in its hasty creation. . . . It is, in addition, another invention of neoliberalism, and in no way is a progressive alternative for the peoples of Latin America."[201] As a counter-proposal, in September 2004 Chávez outlined the Bolivarian Alternative for the Americas (ALBA—Alternativa Bolivariana de las Américas), as a purportedly alternative path to the integration of the region. [202]

During these years, the attack on the pretensions of ALCA and on the foreign policy of George Bush became the official discourse of the Bolivarian government, which made it appear that only these two forces were responsible for the expansionist policies and commercial accords of economic globalization. Thus, other similar, shameful projects were virtually ignored in the discussion titled "socialism of the 21st century."

One indicator of this can be seen by glancing at the pro-government web site APORREA (Asamblea Popular Revolucionaria Americana—American Popular Revolutionary Assembly). In July 2009 it added the term "IIRSA" to its internal search engine. A search for the term yielded 285 results. The same internal search engine yielded a result of 7,350 results for ALCA.

However, this focus on ALCA appeared to be exclusive to Venezuela. Further to the south, the Bolivian Forum on the Environment and Development (FOBOMADE—Foro Boliviano sobre Medio Ambiente y Desarrollo) understands that the integration of the planet for the benefit of global trade has several mechanisms:

> While reflecting upon ALCA, we forget many times that there are clear examples of what awaits us with the implementation of this agreement. ALCA is not only a commercial accord, but it also supports a series of parallel projects whose disastrous effects can be well illustrated by the questionable Plan Puebla Panama. This constitutes an enmeshment of projects that extends from highway projects to tourist services to industrial parks and factories. In sum, these are policies destined to permit the free exploitation of national resources by the transnationals.[203]

In South America FOBOMADE sees coming, through projects such as ALCA and PPP, the implementation of similar initiatives through a cautious strategy, detailed in a report on IIRSA titled "The Veins of ALCA: Regional Integration of IIRSA in South America: Bolivia, a country of transport and extraction of resources."

On its web site, FOBOMADE promotes this report, affirming that "In other countries, as in Central America and Mexico, these 'veins' have taken the form of the Plan Puebla Panama and have generated much resistance by organizations and movements within these countries. In South America, we have the equivalent of [the Plan Puebla Panama] in IIRSA."[204]

In February 2008, the Andean Coordinatorship of Indigenous Organizations (CAOI—Coordinadora Andina de Organizaciones Indígenas) advanced a position on IIRSA signed by 16 indigenous organizations, including CONVIVE (El Consejo Nacional Indígena de Venezuela—National Indigenous Council of Venezuela) and Maikiralasalli, a Wayuu organization from Venezuela's Zulia State. In the document titled "Resolution of Indigenous Peoples on IIRSA," CAOI said: "The facts demonstrate that IIRSA is provoking the accelerated destruction of the Amazon region, the ecosystem of the Plain, the Andes and the Basin, damaging indigenous territories, coastal communities, and river communities, displacing thousands of persons, with the loss of biodiversity, of ways of life, and is aggravating poverty while risking the survival of future generations."[205]

A paragraph later, the document states: "The governments of South America rub out with the elbow what they've drawn with the hand. The same [governments] that approved the Declaration of Rights of Indigenous Peoples (2007),violate all of those rights every day, applying projects such as IIRSA, affecting our lives, cultures, and dreams. All of these [countries] are also members of the Inter-American Development Bank that pushes IIRSA, and as a bank it's accountable to no one."

In this document CAOI also petitions the Venezuelan government to discontinue the programs framed by the philosophy of integration through grand energy infrastructure projects: "We ask President Hugo Chávez, in the case of the conflict in Zulia State, the Municipal Mara sector Socuy, with the indigenous Wayuu, Bari and Yukpa peoples, to cancel the coal mining concessions and to revise the IIRSA projects associated with this mining, in order to avoid the destruction of the Sierra de Perijá [mountain range], which would threaten the indigenous populations who inhabit the area, and which would make an undesirable contribution to global warming."

Coal Projects

On November 13, 2003, in El Menito, Municipality Lagunillas in the state of Zulia, President Chávez announced "We're returning coal [mining] to Zulia." Chávez proclaimed the decision to more than quadruple coal production in the region, from 8 million metric tons annually to 36 million metric tons. The chief of state revealed that the extracting company, Carbozulia de PD-VSA—whose administrative offices are in far-off Caracas—would be transferred to the administration of the Corporación de Desarrollo de la Región Zuliana. The official press release underlined the supposed re-territorialization of control of the industry, from which benefits would then flow to the surrounding communities.

While Zulia State is rich in both petroleum and coal, coal extraction is a more recent development than petroleum extraction. In 1976, the Ministry of Energy and Mines created Carbones del Zulia S.A. (Carbozulia). Geographically, the coal-mining industry occupies the foothills of the Sierra del Perijá—a formation that extends from the frontier with Colombia and the Guasare River to the Rio de Oro and the Casigua del Cubo. One of Carbozulia's affiliates, Carbones del Guasare, was formed in 1987 to operate from the Paso Diablo mine, extending through various small communities all the way to Santa Cruz de Mara, on the banks of Lake Maracaibo, where there was a shipping port to serve the world markets. All in all, Carbones del Guasare employs about 5,000 workers.[206] According to Carbozulia's web site, it has a concession for coal exploitation of 100,780 hectares (approx. 250,000 acres), of which barely 1,310 hectares are in production.[207]

The increase in coal production announced by President Chávez in 2003 was to come from the nearly 100,000 undeveloped hectares in the Zulia concession. But in order for this to happen, the Venezuelan state had to overcome the resistance of the indigenous peoples that live in the area as well as that of environmental organizations. And the increase had to come from Zulia, not from any other area in Venezuela There are coal deposits in the states of Táchira, Anzoátegui, Falcón, Mérida, Guárico, and Aragua; but according to estimates from the Ministry of Energy and Mines, Zulia State contains 87.5% of the reserves in the country.[208]

Environmental and anti-capitalist activists consider the coal-expansion projects to be in line with IIRSA. According to the People and Consciousness Studies Group of Maracay:

> This axis of integration–the Andean axis established in the IIRSA plan—where it enters Venezuelan territory in the State of Zulia, is called the "Axis of Western Development," and brings to final form the shipping-port model "Puerto Venezuela," which was baptized by the government of Rafael Caldera with the name of "Puerto America." One notices something significant in this: Puerto Venezuela or Puerto America was proposed in 1991, during the government of Carlos Andrés Pérez, by the engineer Luis Soto Luzardo . . . [At the time,] Hugo Chávez called this "Treason to the country." . . . [Now this same] engineer, Luís Soto Luzardo, is a member of the executive secretariat of Corpozulia, and was named to the post by Hugo Chávez.[209]

Lusbi Portillo (coordinator of the indigenous rights group Homoetnatura), says: "These works, as per the announcements by the engineer Soto Luzardo from Corpozulia regarding their construction in the basin of Lake Maracaibo, are the expression of the Axis of Western Development/Axis of Andean Integration (IIRSA/PPP), that has as a structural and motivating element the exploitation, transport and exportation of fossil energy."[210] Portillo, who has been working for decades in the Sierra del Perijá with the Wayuu, Barí and Yukpa, and is on the faculty of the University of Zulia, in Maracaibo, comments on the relationship between minerals and IIRSA.

> The general master plan—Puerto America—was elaborated by the Dutch company Alkyon Hydraulic Consultancy & Research in April 2002, and it was financed by that company, by the Dutch government, and by the government of the state of Zulia. The first module in its construction, Terminal Carbonero on Isla de San Bernardo, will serve to facilitate and increase the export of coal from 8 million tons to 36 million tons annually. The environmental impact statement for said module was conducted by the Dutch company Royal Has-

koning and financed by World Bank dollars, which paid the Aruban company Inter-American Coal. The Dutch Alkyon company, in the Plan for General Management, stated that the mega-port was not viable unless the national government or other entity subsidized it to the tune of $50 million (U.S.) annually.[211]

Biologist Carlos Portillo-Quintero has worked since 2001 to quantify the amount of deforestation occurring in different parts of Venezuela, including the northern part of the Sierra del Perijá. According to his studies, in a zone that extends from 80 to 250 meters above sea level, in the headwaters of the Guasare River and a few kilometers from the Manuelote Dam, mining has deforested between 2,000 and 3,000 hectares—to which one must add more than 10,000 additional hectares devastated by the collateral effects of mining. Portillo-Quintero also emphasizes the negative transformation of the way of life of communities affected by mining: "Today, the community of Carrasquero functions basically as a company town for this mine. Its inhabitants [have essentially abandoned] an agricultural or pastoral way of life; and many of them now seek employment on the mining staffs in the same manner as [those seeking work] in the petroleum industry in the city of Maracaibo."[212]

Portillo Quintero has delineated the consequences of new mines opening in the area. In the first place, the waters that feed the Socuy and Maché rivers will be affected, increasing the problem of scarcity [of clean, fresh water] that already exists in the municipalities of Mara, Maracaibo, San Francisco, and other towns located in the northwest part of Zulia State. In addition, they [the new mines] will drastically increase the rate of deforestation, negatively affecting climate stability and water flow in the lower basin of the Socuy River—zones inhabited by animals on the way to extinction, such as the Northern Spider Monkey (*Ateles hybridus*), the Jaguar (*Panthera onca*) and the Spectacled Bear (*Tremarctos ornatus*). Finally, Portillo-Quintero emphasizes the threat of loss of knowledge and of culture involved in changing the way of life of indigenous communities.

The author of this book has had the opportunity to converse with representatives of the indigenous communities opposed to the mining-expansion project. In March 2005, after several hours on a bus from Maracaibo, and then a journey of dozens of kilometers from La Orchila, we arrived at the house of Ángela González, spokeswoman of the Wayuu people. Two weeks before our arrival, representatives of the Ministry of the Environment and Natural Resources had visited the same area to deliver a report solicited by the office of President Chávez. After obtaining an early copy from a whistle blower, several environmental activists stated that the report was lacking in crucial areas. It did not detail the number of people who live in the affected area. It did not give data or evidence about the displacement of people by coal mining activities, nor did it list the damage that the mines located in the Guasare region would do. Neither did it say anything about the health effects on workers employed in the industry.

Ángela González, the Wayuu spokeswoman, received us amicably in her house, located a few minutes from the Maché River, whose rock formations are used as symbols by the coal companies that would dynamite them. She said: "They came—the technicians from Carbozulia—and they told us that they were going to build a project that would bring us good roads, that we wouldn't have to pay for them. They told us they would pay us, that we would be millionaires. They told my father that they would buy him out, that an international enterprise would buy everything and that he'd be left with a lot of money, that he could move to California or Houston."[213]

While we watched a sunset over the Perijás, Ángela described to us the future of the Wayuu if Carbozulia's intentions for the region were realized: "The consequences would be that we'd die of hunger. Where could we go, if this little piece of earth that we have, that God put aside for us, is the only thing we have? Where could we go?"

We asked Ángela about the Wayuu who held high government offices, and whose faces were reproduced on government publicity as a demonstration of its recognition of the rights of the indigenous peoples:

> Arcadio Montiel is Wayuu, our representative, our deputy in the National Assembly. The vice-president of Corpozulia is also Wayuu. But they never come to see their families; they don't come to any of the Wayuu communities. [Arcadio Montiel] is there because they give him money, they give him a bit to eat. And he doesn't talk to us. He's never come here. . . . Why didn't he come to give us the proposal? What he's doing now is an offense to the Wayuu.

Ángela bade us farewell with the stirring words: "ackaain wuaya juchirrua guaunmain jum wuinka": "We'll continue to struggle for our land and water."

An Encounter with the Zapatistas

The Wayuu are the largest indigenous ethnicity in Colombia and Venezuela, numbering more than 500,000 people and occupying a territory that crosses the frontiers between the two countries. On the Venezuelan side, they've formed their own organization to address the problems that affect them. This collective is called Maikiralasa 'lii ("the organization that won't sell out.") In July 2007, they attended the Intercontinental Meeting of Brother and Sister Peoples of the Zapatista Army held in the Selva Lacandona in Chiapas, Mexico. In their greeting to the assembly, they referred explicitly to the threat from coal mining that hung over their heads:

> Our struggle is against the mining development plans of the Venezuelan government and for the defense of our lands, rivers, and woods. That's why we're here. We're here to unite [with you], and [to ask] that you unite with us in our struggle. Therefore, we ask from the peoples of Chiapas and the Intergalactic Zapatista Commission* a statement in favor of our struggle, which is the struggle of the Wayuu, Bari, and Yukpa peoples in defense of the Sierra de Perijá-Socuy. We ask that the Zapatista people and comrades lend their voice to ours to demand that the Venezuelan government deliver the indigenous territories to their legitimate and true owners, and that it comply with the constitutional mandate and cancel all mining concessions granted by the state to transnational corporations to exploit coal in our ancestral and traditional territories.[214]

In an interview given to *El Libertario* (Caracas), Jorge Montiel, a member of Maikiralasa 'lii recalled how he had to dethrone the myth of a government in Caracas that proclaimed itself the defender of indigenous peoples:

> The Zapatista comrades told us, "Caramba! There in Venezuela they speak very well of this, the deputies and ministers . . ." No," we responded. "It's totally to the contrary. The deputies are with Corpozulia, they're with the transnationals. We also want to publicly declare that we are neither partisans nor opponents of Hugo Chávez: we're indigenous anti-imperialists and anti-capitalists. If we were with Chávez's opponents, we would be with the [conservative] opposition hurling charges. If we were Chávez partisans, we'd aspire to be deputies in the [national] assembly, the state legislature, or be councilmen. We . . . defend our own interest, which is the land."[215]

The Wayuu activists also had to respond to some individuals who, without ever having set foot Venezuela, vehemently attacked any questioning whatsoever of the Chávez government:

> At the beginning of a speech we gave in San Cristóbal, Chiapas, in the university, some Americans became very hot and bothered. They were very much partisans of Chávez. They said that we were right-wingers, because how could

---

* The Zapatistas have a sense of humor—tr.

we say such things when everything was well in Venezuela. But the comrades who spoke English—because we don't—asked them if they'd been to Socuy, if they'd seen the situation of the indigenous comrades. "No," they said. [Our comrades replied]: "Then why do you say that there's no problem? You have to go there first and then criticize [us]."

From the Arms of the Guerrilla to the Arms of Criticism

Pablo Hernández Parra defines himself as a "professional agitator." He carries around a flash drive with an archive of all of his Powerpoint presentations that he gives at workshops and conferences on matters related to the principal industry of Venezuela: energy production. In one of his presentations, "The Plans of the Empire in Latin America and the Strategic Plans of PDVSA," he contrasts official documents of the state petroleum company with those of IIRSA to demonstrate that both "coincidentally" outline the same routes to follow in the development of huge infrastructure projects, means of communication, and pipelines for the transport of oil and gas to world markets. Pablo is a communist veteran of the armed struggle and was a political prisoner under various democratic governments.

In 1963, he began his political life in the MIR and its military arm, Armed Forces of National Liberation, for which he was arrested and sent to prison for six years. His years in jail deepened his political convictions, and he affiliated himself with the Vantroi Cell, a nucleus of cadres who, before the pacification of the MIR, advocated armed struggle. In 1970, along with the Antonio Jose de Sucre Front's student and worker sectors, he founded a new organization called Red Flag (BR—Bandera Roja), which maintained guerrilla groups until 1977—groups in which he participated, forming part of a tendency called Red Flag-ML (marxist-leninist), after completing another prison term in 1971. In 1982, he spent another 23 months in prison on charges of subversion. After being released he was detained again, and was tortured by the Technical Judicial Police in Maracay. At the sentencing on the new charges, the judge substituted house arrest for imprisonment, sending Hernández Parra to the Isla de Margarita, where he lived until 1992.

Pablo formed part of the Grupo Soberanía (Sovereignty Group) in 2002 in defense of the state petroleum industry. It had been paralyzed for several weeks after the call of a general strike against the Chávez government by FEDECAMARAS (Federación de Cámaras y Asociaciones de Comercio y Producción de Venezuela—Venezuelan Federation of Chambers of Commerce and Manufacturers' Associations) and the principal union group of the moment, Confederation of Venezuelan Workers (CTV). The FEDECAMA-RAS/CTV general-strike strategy, that presumably sought to initiate another rightist coup d'etat, similar to the one months before, provoked a mobilization. Hernández Parra and other oil-industry experts traveled the country speaking to conferences and seminars about the strategic importance of the primary industry of the country. [PDVSA middle and upper management were deeply involved in the "petroleum strike," which turned out to be the most important part of the general-strike strategy.]

The old guerrilla recalls the beginnings of their efforts:

> Along with Victor Poleo, Francisco Mieres and Elie Habalián, I undertook to study the subject of petroleum. In the group, I was charged with the geopolitical part, which was the easiest part, and began to investigate, to disseminate little by little [knowledge of] the petroleum problem and to meet with the people of PDVSA. We did not defend the government, but lined ourselves up against the self-defined "meritocracy" in the petroleum industry through a forum we called "Inside PDVSA." Our fundamental analysis was that everything the "meritocracy" said was false. . . . Also, it was hiding the ties between PDVSA and foreign capital. We intended to demonstrate how the petroleum industry was in the hands of international capital through the "meritocracy" and how the petroleum strike was tied to Washington['s desire] to overthrow Chávez.[216]

But just as Hernández Parra affirmed that North American interests were conspiring against the Venezuelan president, he also maintained that they also provided support for him:

> Chávez arrived with neither a direction nor a program for government, and so he rapidly came to agreements with the international companies. Before the new Constitution was approved, Chávez approved the Gas Law in September 1999 that privatized the industry, just like [he approved] the Foreign Investment Law that assured foreign capital equal rights with respect to Venezuelan capital. Finally, when the Constitution of the Bolivarian Republic of Venezuela was approved, it included articles 299, 301 and 303 which permitted the privatization of PDVSA. To this moment, Chávez has performed the role assigned him by foreign capital, which is to privatize industry. Between the time in which Chávez signed these laws, in November 2001 and April 2002, when the [failed] coup d'etat took place . . . foreign and domestic capital pressured him to implement the privatization of the state enterprises.

According to Hernández Parra, one of the maneuvers that the leader of the Bolivarian Process made was to introduce nationalist functionaries such as

Gastón Parra Luzardo and Mendoza Potellá into the directorship of the PD-VSA, which provoked uneasiness in the PDVSA hierarchy: "In the end, there was a dispute over control of the spoils from petroleum income. This struggle triggered the petroleum companies, Bush, and the Venezuelan right to launch the [failed] coup in April 2002."

Given these statements from Hernández, the question arises: Were the international oil companies behind the attempted coup in 2002? Pablo's response leaves little doubt:

> The empire manipulates two actors; on the one hand it manipulates the government, and on the other the [PDVSA] meritocracy. Who would save the government from the petroleum strike by supplying petroleum? [Shipping and communications magnate] Wilmer Ruperti, who obtained the tankers and the gasoline. A peon of the empire, he resolved the government's problems. If they have to choose between Chávez and the meritocracy, the [oil] companies prefer the latter because they themselves created it.

Hernández Parra's hypothesis is not wild if one takes into account that in February 2003 the Venezuelan government gave ChevronTexaco and Statoil the go ahead for the Deltana Platform [drilling operation, in] one of the largest offshore gas fields.[217] The negotiations over this were announced via press releases and full-page ads in various Venezuelan periodicals that affirmed that the operation was "a victory of the revolutionary government against the conspiracy within PDVSA."

Hernández calculates that he's given around a thousand "Inside PDVSA" seminars over the entire country, an effort multiplied by dozens of volunteers; he also says that Grupo Soberanía joined with a sector of the state petroleum company:

> The people invited us to many places, to schools, a military base–Fort Tiuna, located in Caracas—neighborhoods, workers groups, universities; and we gave the forum [in all of them]. When we gave it for General Raúl Baduel, he took part in educating his troops. We ended up giving five or six forums within army barracks.

At the forums, Hernández et al. provided CDs full of documentation, which Grupo Soberanía made widely available and which were also sold by street vendors.

Despite its activities in defense of the state petroleum company, which during the petroleum strike was totally paralyzed, Grupo Soberanía began to have friction with the president of PDVSA, Alí Rodríguez Araque. According to Hernández Parra:

In December 2002, during the strike, we were being informed of all the negotiations being conducted by people like Alí Rodríguez, Bernardo Álvarez, and
Rafael Ramírez, and we began trying to deconstruct their dialogue. At that time
we obtained an internal [PDVSA] document in which Alí Rodríguez himself
outlined the future petroleum policies of PDVSA via mixed enterprises, via
privatization. We began issuing alerts about this proposed direction, and on
January 23, 2003, at a forum in Mérida, I denounced the fact that PDVSA was
being reorganized behind the backs of its workers.

In 2005, Pablo assessed the energy policies of the government following
the petroleum strike:

The Plan of Sowing Petroleum is nothing more nor less than Washington's
petroleum plan, a plan that Dick Cheney himself could have designed. Three
years after the attempted coup and the petroleum strike, the workers, especially
the petroleum workers, understand that their role during the sabotage was nothing other than recovering production that the capitalists had paralyzed; and the
role of the people was that of supporting the government so that it could carry
forward the empire's petroleum policy in the name of the "Revolution" . . . In
the face of the greatest delivery in the country's history of petroleum, gas, and
coal concessions [to transnationals], concessions that would cause irreversible
damage to the environment of the entire country, and would compromise the
well-being of future generations, why did the entire political flora and fauna
of the country, both of government and opposition, newspapers such as *Vea*
and *El Nacional*, television networks such as VTV and Globovision, fanatic
Chávez partisans and rabid opponents . . . with no exceptions, remain silent?
They didn't raise their voices, and in the end their complicit silence supported
and applauded that which in other epochs without doubt would have qualified
as "treason to the country" . . . That which happened in this new Macondo
[see *One Hundred Years of Solitude*] that is called Venezuela is nothing other
than that national and international capital led by the petroleum companies has
donned [the red vestments worn by Chávez's followers]; and they advance as
conquerors imposing their program of privatization disguised as "socialism of
the 21st century."(218)

Up to this point we've been arguing the first aspect of our hypothesis, that
the deepening role assigned to Venezuela by capitalist globalization has been
fostered by a government that, in a discourse repeatedly and loudly echoed
throughout the world, has argued that it's going down a different road. To
clarify our assertion to the contrary, we're adding here a few paragraphs
about what we understand to be capitalist economic globalization.

In order to sum up the socioeconomic changes that the planet has experi-
enced in recent years, we'll turn to one of the works of investigative sociology that has best documented and explained the type of capitalism that we live

under. At the beginning of the 1980s, renowned sociologist Manuel Castells dedicated himself to describing cultural, economic, and societal changes; he was convinced that we were at the dawn of a new era. (This was well before "globalization" studies became fashionable among academics and intellectuals.) After 12 years of research, and another four of writing/editing, in 1996 Castells' publisher released the first edition of his three-volume tome, *The Information Age*.[219]

In his book, Castells describes the appearance of a new socioeconomic structure, manifested in different forms in the various cultures and institutions of the entire planet, which is associated with the appearance of a new model of economic development, which Castells dubbed "informationalism" in *The Information Age*, but which he notes "in strict terms . . . should be called 'electronic informational-communicationalism.'"[220]

This new form of capitalism was made possible by development of micro-electronics-based, near-instantaneous worldwide communication, which allows formation of interactive networks that can adapt very quickly to new conditions. This is in contrast to older, largely one-way, vertical, hierarchical networks in which information flowed from the top down, due largely to their use of much slower, less efficient means of communication.

This new mode of economic development is defined as "informational" because productivity and competitiveness of the units or agents of this economy (be they companies, regions, or nations) depend fundamentally on their capacity to generate, process, and efficiently apply information. This is "global" because production, consumption, and circulation, just like the components (capital, labor, primary materials, management, information, technology, markets) are organized on a global scale in a direct form through a network of ties between the economic agents.

For Castells, the greatest transformations underlying the emergence of this economy are those of the management of production and distribution, and the process of production itself. The dominant economic sectors (in both goods and services) are organized on a worldwide scale in their operating procedures, forming a global network. The production process incorporates components produced in many places by many distinct businesses, and assembled for specific purposes and markets.

This web, or network, does not correspond solely to the model of a global enterprise that obtains its supplies from the entire world. This new system of production is based on a combination of strategic alliances and specific cooperative projects between large enterprises, their decentralized units, and networks of small and medium-sized businesses that connect among themselves or with larger businesses or business networks. What is fundamental about this networked industrial structure is that it covers the entire world, and its geometry changes continually in its whole and as it applies to each unit. In this structure, the most important element for the success of management strategy is to situate the enterprise (or industrial project) in the network in such a manner that it obtains a comparative advantage. In order for a business to operate in such a flexible geometry of production and distribution requires a very flexible form of management, which in turn depends on the malleability of the enterprise itself and to access to the communications and production technologies appropriate to it.

For the first time in history, the capitalist mode has no counterweight in determining social relations over the entire planet. And this type of capitalism is profoundly different from its predecessors. It possesses two distinctive traits: 1) it's global, as we just mentioned; and 2) its structure is in good measure determined by fluctuations in the financial network. At present, capital functions on a global scale in real time, and its primary functions are those of investment and accumulation, that is, to act as financing or investment capital.

The global economy has internal diversification in three principal regions and zones of influence: North America (USA, Canada, and Mexico—especially in the wake of NAFTA), the European Union, and the Asian/Pacific region. In contrast with this rich, powerful, and technological triangle, the rest of the world is organized in a hierarchical, asymmetrical web of interdependence, in which the different countries and regions compete to attract capital, human resources, and technology. Regional differentiation is a systemic attribute of the global economy.

At the same time, Castells does not regard the concept of a regionalized global economy as self-contradictory. In effect, even though regional differences exist, it's still a globalized economy because its agents operate through a global network that transcends national frontiers and geographic regions. In regard to politics, this economy is not indifferent to national governments, because they play an important role in the structure of economic processes. Nonetheless, the global economy is foremost, because that's the stage on which strategic production and commercial activities, such as the accumulation of capital, the production of information, and the management of information take place. The crucial thing in an information society is the complex interaction among the historical political institutions and the economic units that constantly grow more globalized.

The new international division of labor resulting from this process is constructed in turn of four different positions in the information economy:

1) the high-value producers, based upon labor in the information sector;

2) the high-volume producers, based upon low-cost labor;

3) the producers of primary materials, based upon natural resources;

4) the unnecessary producers, based upon devalued labor.

The essential thing to understand is that these different positions do not necessarily coincide with different nations. Rather, they are based upon networks and fluctuations that utilize the technological infrastructure of the information economy. The new international division of labor is not between countries, but between economic agents situated in the four positions indicated above. At the same time, it's obvious that some countries' economies are based almost entirely on one of these three "positions," the oil-producing countries (Saudi Arabia, Kuwait, Venezuela, etc.) being the most obvious examples.

From a sociological and economic point of view, there does not exist a global capitalist class, but rather a network of global, integrated capital whose movements and logic determine the economies of societies and influence them as a whole. This network of networks of capital unifies and governs the specific centers of capitalist accumulation, structuring the conduct of the capitalists who are in turn participating in the global network.

Castells does not agree with the prophecy that the state will end due to globalization. On the contrary, he points out that national competition will continue being a function of political states. At the same time, favorable local conditions as regards human and natural resources, and/or the availability of capital, are essential in attracting the multinationals. In this manner, the nation-states can utilize their regulatory powers to facilitate or block the movements of capital, labor, information, and goods within their borders. Nonetheless, in the 1990s nation-states were transformed from sovereign entities to strategic actors, occupying themselves with their own interests and the interests of those they supposedly represent, in an interactive global system of shared sovereignty. Therefore the nation-states are, and every day become more so, nodes in a network of ever-increasing power. In order to foment productivity and competitiveness in their economies, they have to closely ally themselves with global economic interests and follow global rules in line with the flow of capital, while at the same time asking their societies to wait patiently for the "trickle down" of benefits created by business initiatives.

Petroleum Socialism

In the international division of labor brought into being by global capitalism, roles are assigned to each region, owing in good part to what businessmen call "comparative advantages." Castells, as we saw, divides these into four "positions." Venezuela, like almost all of the other countries in Latin America, falls into the third "position"—producer of natural resources. In this sense, the Bolivarian government has continued the economic policies of its predecessors in basing its model of development on the intensive extraction of hydrocarbons. The current Venezuelan president has even designated the "black gold" project he wants to construct as "petroleum socialism." A press release from PDVSA sums it up:

> The President of the Bolivarian Republic of Venezuela, Hugo Chávez, referred to the construction of the socialist model based on the potential offered by petroleum resources, during his program, *Aló Presidente, Number 288*: "We are undertaking construction of a socialist model very different from that imagined by Karl Marx in the 19th century. This is our model: to rely on petroleum riches," said Chávez. The Venezuelan chief of state affirmed that "petroleum socialism cannot be conceived of without petroleum [extraction] activity," and that the resource "gives a peculiar configuration to our economic model."[221]

Venezuela sells petroleum in a "safe and reliable" manner to the international market, as high executives of PDVSA have said repeatedly.[222] Petroleum represents 70% of Venezuelan exports, of which the U.S. market absorbs 60% of that total. In that regard the leftist Venezuelan intellectual Domingo Alberto Rangel asks: "Is such a highly dependent country sovereign?" He immediately adds, "Petroleum destroyed some of the [country's] riches—the diversified agricultural economy dating to the 19th century—and synchronizes the most complete monoproduction ever seen in a Latin American country. . . . Liquid petroleum [has left] a brutal imprint on our process of creating an autonomous nation."[223]

It's seems reasonable to conclude that "petroleum socialism" fulfills the role assigned to Venezuela by economic globalization

In addition to this, another element must be considered in any evaluation of the first twelve years of the Bolivarian process: President Chávez has relied upon, in his exercise of power, the greatest revenues in the last 30 years in Venezuela. Economist Domingo Maza Zavala, director of the Banco Central de Venezuela until 2005, estimated that in the dozen years Chávez has been in power petroleum income amounted to $350 billion (US).[224] Between the commencement of the 1980s and 1999, Venezuela's gross domestic product remained nearly constant in a range of $95 billion to $120 billion. By 2005 it had risen to $133 billion; and it's kept rising. In 2006 it was $146 billion; in 2007 $159 billion; and in 2008 $166 billion.[225]

These statistics from CEPALSTAT are in fairly close accord with those supplied by the World Bank for the years through 2005, but diverge drastically from them for the years 2006–2008. The World Bank estimates Venezuela's GDP as $184 billion in 2006, $228 billion in 2007, and $314 billion in 2008. The World Bank figures seem more likely to be correct given the steep rise in oil prices between 2005 (roughly $50 per barrel) and 2008 (well over $100 per barrel throughout most of the year).[226] Whatever the case, petroleum income has been sky high in recent years.

This economic bonanza was duly publicized by the Venezuelan government. In 2005, for example, figures from the Economic Commission for Latin America indicated that Venezuela's GDP was the third highest in the region.[227] Nevertheless, despite the sudden increase in the country's revenues (as will be amply demonstrated in the following chapter), the transformations that occurred in Venezuela have neither significantly nor radically improved the quality of life of the majority of Venezuelans.

In counterpoint, it should be emphasized that during the Bolivarian Process—under a government that defines itself as being in transition to socialism—the most dynamic and voracious segments of the globalized economy appear to have amply benefitted. To cite one pertinent example, figures from 2007 establish that the telecommunications sector (mobile phones, Internet, cable television) garnered profits of more than $6 billion in Venezuela, continuing the trend of more than 15% annual growth.[228] According to data from CONATEL (Comisión Nacional de Telecomunicaciones—National Telecommunications Commission), the government regulatory agency, telecommunications companies invested $500 million more in 2007 than in 2006. In the cell phone market, the government company Movilnet remained in first place with a 39.9% market share.[229]

The financial industry has also prospered under the Bolivarian government. The banking sector in the first trimester of 2009 obtained profits of 1,065 billion Bolivars (approximately $5 billion U.S.), which was a 17% rise in comparison with the same period in 2008.[230]

A Benchmark for Globalization

Our hypothesis is that the installation of a charismatic, populist president with caudillo-like characteristics in Venezuela makes possible, with the least trauma possible, the adaptation of the country to the readjustments and transformations inherent in the globablized production process. One piece of evidence for this argument is the consensual imposition (behind nationalist rhetoric that masks the process) of a policy that reverses the (incomplete) nationalization process in the energy industry; and that nationalization process was a particular obstacle to the free flow of capital that characterizes the present phase of capitalism. This reversal was characterized by the return of foreign investments in the industry, accompanied, on the legislative side, by legal instruments that offered guarantees to foreign investors. To put it in Manuel Castells' terms, this is an example of the nation-state utilizing its regulatory capacity to facilitate the flow of capital within its territory.

As well, in 1999 the U.S. and Venezuelan governments signed the "Convention between the Government of the United States of America and the Government of the Republic of Venezuela for the Avoidance of Double Taxation and the Prevention of Fiscal Evasion with Respect to Taxes on Income and Capital." That's a long and bloated name for a legal mechanism under which U.S. citizens and businesses pay only minimal Venezuelan withholding taxes on their dividends and interest.

As regards Venezuela's role of safe provider of energy to world markets, and the legal accommodation of its principal industry to international economic tendencies, we'll make but one comment: The Bolivarian government has pushed its population as never before to internalize its role as dependents, and as dependents on income from hydrocarbons. Each and every one of the questions posed in the past by the traditional Venezuelan left about the social and environmental consequences of petroleum monoproduction has been abandoned by that same left since Chávez assumed power. And that's why a film such as *Nuestro petróleo y otros cuentos* (see Chapter 1) is considered politically incorrect and rarely seen throughout the world.

As an example of this censorious attitude, the author of this book recalls one particular incident involving a young member of the PCE (Partido Comunista de España—Spanish Communist Party), who had been assigned by the PCE to do political work in the San Agustín district of Caracas. Upon seeing *Nuestro petróleo* at one of its first public presentations, this young militant grabbed his head with both hands and exclaimed, "This film cannot be seen in Spain!"

Michael Hardt and Antonio Negri state in their book *Empire*[231] that governments discipline [their people] in accord with the contemporary form of global "sovereignty." To paraphrase Hardt and Negri: A disciplinary society is a factory-society. The application of discipline is at the same time a form of production and a form of government, so that disciplined production and a disciplinary society tend to coincide almost completely. . . . The character, the structures, and the hierarchies of the division of social labor expand and become every time more defined according to the measure that civil society is gradually absorbed by the state; the new norms of subordination and the disciplinary (authoritarian) capitalist regimes spread throughout the entire social terrain. Precisely when the disciplinary regime reaches its highest level and most complete application, it manifests itself as the extreme limit of the social accord.

And, leaving behind Hardt and Negri, this new social accord, in the words of the leader of the Bolivarian Process, is "petroleum socialism."

From "Fascist" to "Bolivarian"

As the Bolivarian government showed more evidence of the influence of globalization, the type of economic actors that emerged and prospered under its mandate also changed. Wilmer Ruperti, following his meteoric enrichment that began with the petroleum strike in 2002, has dedicated himself to the communications media, inaugurating a 24-hour news and entertainment channel, Canal i. He also bought the radio station chain Radio Rumbos and a small Caracas tabloid, *Diario de Caracas* ("Caracas Daily"). And he tried unsuccessfully to acquire one of the traditional Venezuelan national newspapers, *El Universal*.[232] Juan Carlos Escotet the owner of the fifth largest bank in the country, Banesco, is an apologist for the government's economic policies on the state television outlets. He has said that "now the Venezuelan entrepreneurs have a better and better market thanks to the improvement of the buying power of the public and the social climate."[233]

However, the best illustration of the compatibility of the local sectors representative of the global economy and the Bolivarian process is the Venezuelan businessman who's a model of prosperity in the age of informational capitalism: Gustavo Cisneros.

Gustavo Cisneros was born in Caracas in 1945, and according to *Forbes* magazine possesses a fortune of $6 billion, placing him in 149th place on the list of richest people in the world. in 2009. His riches come, principally, from his telecommunications and related businesses, the most important being Venevisión International, Venevisión Productions Movida (in the U.S.), and Venevisión y Cervecería Regional, all grouped together under the banner of the Cisneros Group. The businesses that form the Cisneros Group operate in more than 50 countries in America, Asia, and Europe. Cisneros, a prominent opponent of Hugo Chávez during Chávez's first years as president, was named by *Newsweek* as the "vertex" of the plot to overthrow Chávez via the failed coup d'etat in April 2002.[234]

In a speech he delivered on January 10, 2003, Chávez referred to the entrepreneur in terms that clearly defined him as one his greatest adversaries, saying, "[T]here goes a fascist, there goes a coup d'etat plotter who is the owner of a television channel here in Venezuela, a man called Gustavo Cisneros. He's one of the people most responsible for what is going on in Venezuela and I accuse him before the people and before the world of being a coup d'etat plotter and a fascist."

A year and a half later, surprisingly, Chávez met with Cisneros on June 18, 2004 with Jimmy Carter as an intermediary. Two days after the encounter, in explaining his meeting with Cisneros, Chávez substituted "mister" for "coup d'etat plotter" and "fascist": "I told Mister Cisneros 'welcome' and gave him my hand, saying what pleasure it gave me that we could sit and converse because he's a Venezuelan, and we were going to have a coffee and talk, and I would do it with any Venezuelan who truly wanted to come to talk about serious things."[235] In the following days, in an interview with Eleazar Díaz Rangel, the editor of the daily *Últimas Noticias* ("Latest News"), a paper with pro-government leanings, President Chávez said: "[Cisneros] knows that he, his media, his business, and his family can coexist with this [Bolivarian] Project when he respects the Constitution and the laws, and recognizes the authorities as he has been doing."[236]

Cisneros also spoke of the meeting:

We spoke extensively about the problem of poverty in Venezuela. President Chávez and I share the same opinion: the matter of poverty has to unite the country, above all in view of the large growth in the number of homes that fall below the poverty line. For my part, I insisted that once the referendum process is finalized, the national dialogue must focus on the search for solutions to this [poverty] problem. I maintained that Venezuelans should channel their forces to improve education and to stimulate national entrepreneurial capacities, in order to compete successfully in world markets.[237]

Both men have repeated that on the day they met they did not make a pact and, aside from their statements, no one knows the contents of their conversation. Nonetheless, it's a verifiable fact that the editorial line of the Venezuelan TV station owned by Cisneros, Venevisión, changed after the conclave, going from one extreme to the other. An indication of the sudden ideological shift can be seen in the "Final Presidential Election Report, 2006," produced by the European Union, following its role as international observer of the presidential election in 2006, in which Chavez won re-election: "The tone of Televén [another station] and Venevisión was in general little critical of the two principal coalitions, but, from a quantitative point of view, the two stations openly favored the official position. Venevisión dedicated 84% of its political coverage to the official coalition and only 16% to the 'Unity' [opposition] coalition, while Televén gave 68% of its coverage to the Chávez coalition and 32% to [the Unity coalition]."[238]

What would a television channel owned by business tycoon Gustavo Cisneros have to gain by so generously promoting the political interests of a president who affirms that he's "constructing socialism"? The answer is obvious: to be, without competition, the broadcast channel with the biggest audience in a country of 28 million. Effectively, after the government decision not to renew the license of Radio Caracas Televisión (RCTV), Venevisión's traditional competitor, Venevisión could count on the highest viewership levels in the history of the small screen in Venezuela.

RCTV, the oldest private station in the country, transmitted for 54 years on channel 2. On May 27, 2007 at 11:59 pm it terminated its broadcasting. The fundamental reason for the government's decision not to renew its license was the participation of the station in the failed coup d'etat in 2002, its refusal to transmit a series of programs by followers of Chávez [at the time of the coup], and to incite military and civilian rebellion against a democratically elected government. However, Venevisión had the same type of coverage with the same type of slant, and its license was renewed on May 27, 2007, three years after the Chávez-Cisneros-Carter meeting.

RCTV was the channel with the highest viewership in Venezuela (approximately 36% of the audience), followed closely by Venevisión (approximately 34%). These two channels came close to monopolizing both television audience and advertising income. Over the decades they developed a ferocious competition for viewers. This contradicts the government's line that it was "democratizing broadcasting space" [by denying RCTV's license renewal]. The exit of RCTV obviously and greatly benefitted Venevisión. Five months after RCTV went off the air, Cisneros' Venevisión was drawing 51% of the audience.[239] By September 2008 that figure had risen to 67%, Televén being a distant second with 28% of viewers.[240]

Venevisión's advertising revenues are not insignificant. Broadcast (over-the-airways, in contrast to cable) television receives 60% to 65% of advertising revenues in Venezuela. Mari Pili Hernández, a journalist and ex-Venezuelan Vice-Minister of Exterior Relations for North America, and also manager of television Channel 1, gives us an idea of the magnitude of small-screen marketing in Bolivarian times. In regard to the refusal to renew RCTV's broadcasting license in 2007, she said: "Last year, 2006, the reported advertising profits of RCTV was approximately 360 billion Bolivars [at 2010 exchange rates, $180 million U.S.]. As in every year, the advertising pie grows. The estimate for this year is above 420 billion Bolivars." The social communicator and defender of President Chávez assertively asked: "This money, now, given that RCTV is no longer on the air, where did this money go?"[241]

The answer isn't surprising. John da Silva, a Venezuelan blogger specializing in marketing, says: "[L]et's do an exercise, using as a benchmark the [advertising budget of the type used by] Movilnet–the state cell phone company If we go strictly by the numbers, we'd be investing about 60% of the advertising monies in over-the-airwaves television, of which Venevisión would get 67% [of the revenues formerly received by RCTV], Televen 28%, and Globovisión 5%."[242]

The Chamber of Telecommunications Services estimates that in 2006 advertising expenditures for Venezuelan cell phone companies were $150 million.[243] Assuming that these expenditures remained static through 2008, this would mean that Gustavo Cisneros' TV advertising revenues rose from roughly $30 million in 2006 to $60 million in 2008 (given that on-the-air TV gets 60% of advertising monies, and that Venevisión's share of the market rose from 34% in 2006 to 67% in 2008).

The evident coexistence pact between one of the richest businessmen in the world and the leader of the Bolivarian Process marks a refinement in the complex interactions between the institutions promoted by the Chávez movement and the globalized economy. Appreciating this is key to understanding the unfolding of the conflict over the airwaves in Venezuela. If Venevisión represents in its area the local node best tied to the global capital network, RCTV personified the historical business model whose traditional modes of generating income have been progressively displaced by the information flows characteristic of our time [and the global economy]. (This also explains the tensions over control of petroleum income in Venezuela. For example, the confrontation between the historical Venezuelan business grouping, FEDE-

CAMARAS, whose members are concentrated in economic sectors in decline [agriculture, cattle, manufacturing, etc.] and the emerging "socialist" business group, EMPREVEN [Empresarios for Venezuela], whose members have ties to state activities in banking, financing, construction, and tourism.)

Regarding RCTV, as *El libro blanco sobre RCTV* ("White Book on RCTV") reveals, the company is the property of Peter Bottome, Marcel Granier, Alicia Phelps, Alberto Tovar Phelps, and Guillermo Tucker Arismendi. Its founding, by the entrepreneur William H. Phelps, was the product of the familiar process of the accumulation of wealth which began with the exportation of coffee and which crystallized in 1920 with the importation and distribution of products characteristic of the industrial revolution: Singer sewing machines, Underwood typewriters, and Ford automobiles.

The information technologies that arrived late in the 20th century were not an exact analog to the industrial-revolution technologies that arrived in Venezuela in the 1920s. The owners of RCTV didn't appreciate this. The one who correctly calculated the direction of change was Gustavo Cisneros.

In his biography, he writes:

> In the middle of the 1990s, Grupo [Cisneros] paused to evaluate the situation. This introspective effort produced two important decisions: one of them was that we concentrate on rapidly growing businesses that we were familiar with and understood—or that we thought we could learn quickly—including television transmission and programming, telecommunications, and the Internet; the second was the decision to reduce our presence in Venezuela to the absolute minimum, leaving in the country only Venevisión and the companies closely tied to it.[244]

In 1992, Grupo Cisneros created the cell-phone network Telcel, and in May 2006, two years after the meeting between Chávez, Cisneros, and Carter, and with the approval of the National Telecommunications Commission, Grupo Cisneros bought the third-largest cell-phone company in Venezuela, Digitel, which had at the time of purchase two million customers.[245]

The Myth of Multipolarity

Another piece of evidence indicating the Bolivarian accommodation to present economic tendencies is the development of a discourse that justifies and mystifies the insertion of the Venezuelan economy into the planetary circulation of capital. From the presidential palace of Miraflores, the symbolic center of power in Venezuela, we have heard repeatedly that Hugo Chávez is the vanguard of a movement dedicated to combating the political and economic power of the United States. This has resurrected the anti-imperialist Latin American rhetoric from the Cold War period. This political line insistently asserts that, in the face of the unilateral power of the U.S., the Venezuelan president is laying the building blocks of a new order on the foundation of Venezuela's hydrocarbon potential. Even though this self-serving myth is vulnerable to even the most minimal critical analysis, it has become the basis of the government's program, promoted from Caracas and hailed by Chávez's followers both inside and outside of the country.

An official notice from the Venezuelan Ministry of Foreign Relations opens with the statement: "Every day we're nearer to obtaining a multipolar world, propelled and impelled by the President of the Republic, Hugo Chávez Frias."[246] Another note states: "The rapprochement with Russia implies also the backing of a friend that, because of its power, is capable of dissuading any destabilizing attempts emanating from the United States. Without doubt, at the heart of the accords is the shared desire to build on a world level multipolarity that limits the initiatives from Washington."[247] Another: "Venezuela said goodbye to 2006 with a strengthened international image that allowed it to defeat foreign campaigns whose purpose was to weaken the advance of Venezuela's foreign policy. With a vertex whose sides are composed of regional integration and support for the consolidation of a multipolar world, Venezuelan foreign policy received important backing from more than seven million voters in the presidential elections of December 3rd."[248] One more: "Chancellor Nicolás Maduro Moros assured us that the goal of the Bolivarian government in the matter of foreign policy is to advance the construction of a multipolar world and a new alliance of poles of power to break the imperialist hegemony and to build a world based on economic development, social justice, true peace, respect for international law, and the building of dialogue between civilizations."[249]

The claimed construction of multipolarity, as state policy, is defined in various official documents. The "General Outlines of the Social and Economic Development Plan of the Nation 2007–2013" stated in its "New International Geopolitics" section that "The construction of a multipolar world implies the creation of new poles of power that represent the breaking of North American imperialism, in the pursuit of social justice, solidarity, and guarantees of peace through the deepening of fraternal dialogue between peoples, respect for the liberties of thought and religion, and self-determination of peoples."[250]

One of the strategies outlined to achieve this multipolarity is "energy internationalization." The definition of this strategy outlined in this press release plunges to new depths of double think: "[This strategy has] the objective of increasing the capacity for exploration, production, and commercialization integral to energy, through initiatives for regional energy integration with foreign investments not controlled by the hegemonic axes, under the aegis of mixed enterprises."

This goal of constructing multipolarity is, in turn, echoed by various government ministries. For example, the "Report and Account of the Ministry of Popular Power for Housing and Habitat" for the year 2007 states that the reordering of the country has a third strategic objective: "the impulse to the new multipolar system." What does international geopolitics have to do with housing projects in Venezuela? The complexity of the answer transcends the limits of this humble book.

What concerns us is that the dream of constructing a multipolar planet confronting the unilateralism of the United States is nothing new. On the one hand, to explain that the imbalances of the planet are the exclusive fault of the U.S. is to grossly simplify the complex realities. In this sense we agree with the outline of Michael Hardt and Antonio Negri. To paraphrase what they say in their book *Multitude*: The contemporary global order can no longer be understood in terms of the imperialism practiced by modern powers, an imperialism based principally on the extension of the sovereignty of the nation state onto foreign territories. That which is emerging today, in contrast, is "networked power," a new form of sovereignty, that includes as principal nodes the nation states, along with the supra-national institutions, that is, the principal capitalist corporations and other powers.[251]

The authors call this new form of global, interconnected sovereignty "Empire," which does not imply that the influence of the U.S. on a global scale is the same as that of Haiti. To paraphrase them again: In the network of the Empire not all powers are equals. Much to the contrary, some nation-states have enormous power, and others almost none, and the same occurs with the rest of the components of the network, the corporations and other institutions. But despite the inequalities, they see themselves obligated to cooperate to create and maintain the present world order with all its divisions and internal hierarchies.

Completing this concept, and complementing the above, is the fact that already by 1997, two years before the arrival of Hugo Chávez as the President of Venezuela, multilateralism had become the predominant tendency in the functioning of the world. Let's follow the reasoning of the Spanish sociologist Manuel Castells in *The Information Age*. The period following the Cold War was characterized by growing multilateral interdependence among the nation-states. One factor in this growing multilateralism was the loosening of the military blocs constructed by the superpowers, NATO and the Warsaw Pact. NATO's functions were redefined in the latter half of the 1990s. Its purpose became that of performing security tasks in the name of a wide consortium of nations, and wherever possible, in conjunction with the UN. This novel approach was taken in the name of "global security."

This was first seen in the 1991 Gulf War, whose purpose was to confront a threat to the petroleum supplies from the Middle East, implying a symbiotic relationship among the most capable military powers (the US and the UK) and those who in part financed the operation (starting with Japan, Germany, and the Arab emirates); this symbiotic relationship was masked by rhetoric about "aggression" and the "civilized world."

This new security system had been constructed, fundamentally, as a shield against [what the powers that be project as] permanently reconfiguring "barbarous" forces [replacing the Eastern Bloc as the frightening enemy du jour]. Aiding in this construction was the view that the world's nation-states–including the most powerful—were enveloped in a constantly changing web of interests and negotiations. Castells notes two exceptions to the tendency of integration of nation-states in this system of collective security: the Russian Federation, even though it's a military superpower, and China, which is on the way to becoming a superpower. However, even there he points out the great difficulty either of these entities would have in organizing a coalition of permanent allies to support its interests; and, even if they achieved it, that still wouldn't contradict the multilateralism of the new security system, but only add complexity to it.

By the time of Hugo Chávez's ascendency, global geopolitics had been ruled by multilateralism for some time. This multipolarity was most evident in the economic field. The club of economic superpowers called the G-8, along with a few others, was in the center of the economic web. The web's executive arms were the International Monetary Fund and the World Bank, charged with regulation and intervention in the name of the basic rules of global capitalism. The G-8's informal meetings, such as those at Davos, Switzerland, aided in creating personal/cultural cohesion in this economic elite.

As well, as we mentioned earlier, there is still regional variation in the global economy, with the three regions being comprised of North America, the European Union, and the Asian-Pacific-Rim region. To these, Castells adds, due to their booming economies, India and Brazil. All of the other areas of the world organize their economies around these epicenters in relationships of multiple dependency.

There's no doubt that the global economy is profoundly asymmetric, but not in the simplistic sense of having a center and surrounding peripheral zones, or a simple North-South divide, as preached by the Venezuelan government. To paraphrase Castells in *The Information Age*: Because the North and the South are so diverse internally, it makes little sense to analyze them using North-South categories. The new international division of labor does not take place among countries, but among economic agents situated in the four positions (see page 117) of a global structure of networks and capital and information flows.

Words versus Facts

McDonald's commenced operations in Venezuela in 1985, with the opening of its first fast-food joint in Caracas. Seven years later, with the creation of the company Alimentos Arcos Dorados de Venezuela, it began offering franchises across the nation, allowing vertiginous expansion. At present, McDonald's has 60% of the fast food market in Venezuela, half again as much as the rest of its competitors combined. In March 2009, it had 135 locations in the country and, according to Woods Staton, coordinator of the brand name in Latin America, the Venezuelan outlets had the highest monthly invoicing by restaurant in the region: 45,000 sales per month, which is the equivalent of feeding 90,000 persons per month.[252]

After ten years of Bolivarian rhetoric, the habits of consumers have not reverted [to pre-McDonald's habits], nor have they improved, as one would expect under a revolutionary process. (It's worth noting that the very upscale Louis Vuitton store in Caracas, which sells $1,000 handbags, generates more profits than any other Vuitton store in South America.) In contrast, consumers' wants are the same as those that predominate in any other part of the capitalist global village. A local publication specializing in publicity and marketing observed in July 2006: "When the Venezuelan needs to eat without losing time, when he doesn't have anywhere to leave the kids, or when he doesn't want to cook, one of the most frequent options is McDonald's."[253]

Paradoxically, McDonald's has been one of the biggest advertisers on Televisora Venezolana Social (TVES), the channel created by the government to replace RCTV after the recission of its license. "On TVES, be it Che McDonald's or McGuevara's, the capitalist sponsorship doesn't stop the socialist rhetoric," a government supporter bitterly complains on the pro-government web site APORREA.[254]

This data about McDonald's is significant because it illustrates the superficiality of the changes that have occurred over the last decade in Venezuela. As we've detailed, at the same time that the government affirms that its petroleum policy is sovereign and anti-imperialist, it deepens its relationships with the transnationals. Thus all of the supposed progressive economic policies that it announces, with a huge splash in the communications media, do not correspond to reality. An example of this is the state's alignment with the postulates of third worldists, that Venezuela is in the vanguard of an imaginary agricultural revolution: "Venezuela not only guarantees petroleum sovereignty, but also fortifies nutritional sovereignty."[255] These are the words of national assembly deputy Henry Tachinamo, a member of the Economic Development Commission. And, parallel to this declaration, a coordinator of the state program that distributes foodstuffs at low cost, Mercal, Fabiola Díaz, stated that 75% of food is imported.[256]

How can a government maintain such contradictions? A partial explanation is given by Guy Debord, the French revolutionary and writer. In 1967, in *Society of the Spectacle*,[257] he wrote that in the evolution of capitalism, spectacle would come to dominate society:

> The spectacle is the ruling order's nonstop discourse about itself, its never-ending monologue of self-praise, its self-portrait at the stage of totalitarian domination of all aspects of life. The fetishistic appearance of pure objectivity in spectacular relations conceals their true character as relations between people and between classes: a second Nature, with its own inescapable laws, seems to dominate our environment. But the spectacle is not the inevitable consequence of some supposedly natural technological development. On the contrary, the society of the spectacle is a form that chooses its own technological content.

Debord, the most well known exponent of situationism, would find confirmation of his thesis through the observation of a president threatening not to sell petroleum to the U.S. [at the time of this translation in July 2010]—a threat orgiastically celebrated by his followers around the world–a president who at the same time negotiates with his supposed enemies. The same happened in reverse at the time of the "petroleum strike" in 2002, when the petroleum transnationals and the U.S. government orchestrated the withholding of gas and oil from the Venezuelan government–and still the government negotiated with its enemies. With what seems like eerie foresight, Debord put it like this in 1967: "When the real world is changed into simple images, the simple images change into real things, and into the efficient motivators of hypnotic behavior."

One piece of evidence favoring this interpretation of the so-called Bolivarian Revolution comes from an unsuspected place, which on its face should be considered a serious threat to the interests of the Revolution: the U.S. embassy in Venezuela. Between the years 1998 and 2003, during a period of great tension between the two governments, Ambassador John Maisto frequently repeated a phrase that became doctrine: "Don't watch what Chávez says, watch what he does."[258]

American intellectuals, rebels against all that emanates from the U.S. establishment, opt exclusively to watch what Chávez says.

The Real Economic Role of the Chávez Government

Victor Álvarez, during the first eight years of the Bolivarian government, held high posts in various state institutions, including being the head of the Ministry of Basic Industries and Mining. Later, he dedicated himself to economic research, and his results contradict the assertions made by President Chávez. Nonetheless, he has reaffirmed his fidelity to the belief system of 21st century socialism. In a polemic interview, he provided an evaluation that summarizes, better than we could, the real economic role of the Chávez government:

> The dependent culture generate vicious cycles very difficult to break. One of the most pathetic is the absolute fact that we import because we don't produce, and we don't produce because we import . . . The financing of social costs, particularly those dedicated to social missions, does not have as a source taxes paid, but rather the abundant income that the country receives from petroleum. Therefore, we're not dealing with a mechanism of progressive redistribution of income through which the state treasury takes the resources of those who have the most and directs them to those who have the least . . .

Notwithstanding the growing criticism of the Bolivarian government against capitalism, after ten years of revolution the official data reveal that— far from diminishing—the weight of the mercantile economy in the gross domestic product has actually increased. Its participation continues to be majoritarian, and therefore defines the capitalist nature of the present Venezuelan productive model. The size of the private sector of the economy went from 64.7% in 1998 to 70.9% at the close of 2008. The size of the social economy went from 0.5% in 1998 to 1.6% at the close of 2008.

The monetary illusion that wage earners have bettered their situation hides the reality that the situation of the owners of capital has improved much more than that of the workers. The sectors that have seen the greatest rate of growth from year to year, and in absolute terms as regards the gross domestic product, are telecommunications, sale of goods, service industries, and financial [services] and insurance . . . Sectors such as agriculture and manufacturing have lost weight relative to the gross domestic product, or have shown lower growth rates. Despite the [growth of the] agricultural sector in Venezuela, during the years 1998–2008, . . . with the vegetable segment growing by 35% and the animal segment by 23%, [the agricultural sector's] share of the gross national product, its relationship to the total size of the economy, only reached 4.39%. This is inferior to the 12.1% of the economy it comprises in Colombia and 6.22% in Latin America as a whole.[259]

129. PDVSA "Informe de gestión anual 2008" (July 2009) http://www.pdvsa.com/interface.sp/database/fichero/free/4878/582.PDF

130. Guillermo Rodríguez Eraso. "Evolución de la industria petrolera en Venezuela," in *Sembrando el petróleo: 100 años de historia.* Fundación Venezuela Positiva: Caracas, 2001.

131. Domingo F. Maza Zavala, "Lo bueno y lo malo del petróleo en el siglo XX," in *Sembrando el petróleo: 100 años de historia.* Fundación Venezuela Positiva: Caracas, 2001.

132. Simón Alberto Consalvi, "Las mil y una noches del petróleo en Venezuela," in *Sembrando el petróleo: 100 años de historia.* Fundación Venezuela Positiva: Caracas, 2001.

133. Rodríguez Eraso, op. cit.

134. Maza Zavala, op. cit.

135. Ibid.

136. Raúl Sosa Rodríguez, "Los hechos demuestran las dificultades de la sociedad venezolana de regresar a la austeridad y comprender que la bonanza en los últimos decenios depende de factores extremos incidentales," in *Sembrando el petróleo: 100 años de historia.* Fundación Venezuela Positiva: Caracas, 2001.

137. Ramón J. Velásquez, Prologue to the book *Pobreza, reto del siglo XXI*, by Heraclio Atencio. Alafadil Editores: Caracas, 1996.

138. Miguel Otero Silva, *Casas Muertas*. Los Libros de El Nacional: Caracas, 2008.

139. Heraclio Atencio Bello, "Introito," in *Sembrando el petróleo: 100 años de historia.* Fundación Venezuela Positiva: Caracas, 2001.

140. Ibid.

141. Miguel Angel Burelli Rivas, "Uslar Pietri y la siembra del petróleo," in *Sembrando el petróleo: 100 años de historia.* Fundación Venezuela Positiva: Caracas, 2001.

142. There are numerous examples. For example: Prensa Presidencial, "Pueblo y soldado: Fórmula perfecta para hacer una verdadera Rvolución" http://www.aporrea.org/actualidad/n137165.html; Prensa Presidencial, "Debemos sembrar el petróleo y utilizar la riqueza racionalmente para el desarrollo" http://www.minci.gob.ve-noticias-prensa-presidencial/28/7547; Prensa Presidencial, "Presidente: la siembra del petróleo esta en march" http://www.mv.gov.ve/noticias/index.php?act=ST&f=2&t=31668

143. Granma Internacional, "Venezuela lanza estrategia petrolera hasta 2030" (August 2005) http://granmai.co.cu/espanol/2005/agost/vier19/venezuela.html

144. To see the Venezuelan Constitution in full, see http://www.constitucion.ve/constitucion.pdf

145. To compare the original articles and reform proposals see http://www.aporrea.org/actualidad/n99947.html

146.Victor Poleo, http://www.soberania.org/Archivos/informe_pcv.pdf

147. Luis Manuel de Limas, "Victor Poleo: la nacionalización es un disfraz" *El Tiempo*, June 2007.

148. Victor Poleo, op. cit.

149. http://www.iconoclasistas.com.ar

150. Rodríguez Eraso, op. cit.

151.Mazhar Al-Shereidah, "La dimensión imaginaria en la nacionalización petrolera." *Revista Venezolana de Economía y Ciencias Sociales*, Vol. 1, No. 12, April 2006, pp. 125–146.

152. Petroguia, "Mapa Energético de Venezuela 2005–2006"

153. After the approval of the new Constitution in 1999, the Congress was officially renamed the National Assembly, and became a one-chamber body.

154. Cited by Pablo Hernández Parra in "Empresas Mixtas, privatización final de PDVSA" (August 2005) http://www.sobernia.org

155. Ibid.

156. Radio Nacional de Venezuela, "Ingreso petrolero venezolano ha mejorado significativamente" http://www.rnv.gov.ve/noticias/?act=ST&f=&t=63786

157. Rafael Uzcátegui, "Introducen demanda contra las empresas mixtas en el TSJ" (January 2008) http://www.aporrea.org/energia/n107881.html

158. PRV-Tercer Camino, "A la nación venezolana, Defendamos nuestra soberanía." Caracas, June 2008.

159. PRV-Tercer Camino, "Crítica parcial a la Constitución Nacional del año 2007." Caracas, August 2007.

160. Rafael Uzcátegui, *Reforma constitucional: globalización, disciplina y estatización.* Caracas, October 2007.

161. Coordinadora Democrática, "Proyecto País." Caracas, October 2002, pp. 26-27.

162. Pablo Hernández, *El verdadero golpe de PDVSA: las empresas mixtas I.* Caracas, 2006.

VENEZUELA ◆ 133

163. Arthur Lepic, "Chevron-Texaco, primer mecenas de la vida política estadounidense" (April 2005) http://www.voltairnet.org/article124459.html

164. http://www.chevron.com/chevron/speeches/article/02122002_latinamericanupstreamprogressandpitfalls.news

165. Agencia France Press, "Construirán gasoducto" (July 2002) (Link no longer available)

166. Servicio de Noticias del Estado, "Manos a la obra con el Gasoducto Colombia-Venezuela-Panamá: Uribe. (Bogotá, December 2003) (Link no longer available

167. Ministerio de Comunicación e Información, e-mailed press release, July 15, 2004: "Poliducto colombo-venezolana dará apertura al mercado asiático"

168. Prensa Presidencial, "Formalizarán ingreso de Venezuela y Colombia al Plan Panamá Puebla" (2005) (Link no longer available)

169. PDVSA, "Presidentes de Colombia, Panamá y Venezuela inician construcción del Gasoducto Transcaribeño" (2006) (Link no longer available)

170. BBC Mundo, "Cronología de un desencuentro" (November 2007) (Link no longer available)

171. YVKE Mundial, "Presidente Chávez responde a acusaciones de Uribe de tener 'proyecto expansionista'" (November 2007) http://www.radiomundial.com.ve/yvke/noticia.php?1442

172. Aporrea, "Chávez anuncia que no tendrá ninguna relación con Colombia mientras Uribe sea presidente" (November 2007) http://www.aporrea.org/actualidad/n105478.html

173. Luigi Bracci Roa, "Uribe es un 'mafioso' al organizar ataques de funcionarios de EEUU contra Venezuela" (January 2008) http://www.radiomundial.com.ve/yvke/noticia.php

174. BBC Mundo, "Venezuela: tanques a la frontera" (March 2008) (Link no longer available)

175. Agencia Bolivariana de Noticias, "Chávez destacó la necesidad de reactivas las relaciones con Colombia (July 2008) (Link no longer available; agency has been renamed Agencia Venezolana de Noticias: http://www.avn.info.ve/)

176. YVKE Mundial, "Venezuela y Colombia relanzan sus relaciones comerciales y lucharán contra el narcotráfico" (July 2008) http://www.radiomundial.com.ve/yvke/noticia.php?7768

177. YVKE Mundial, "Presidente Chávez en desacuerdo con PCV y PPT por candidaturas y marcha del viernes" (July 2008) http://www.radiomundial.com.ve/yvke/noticia.php?7674

178. Interview in *El Libertario*, No. 39, 2004.

179. Prensa Presidencial, "Presidente panameño llegó al país para desarrollar jornada de trabajao" (March 2009) (Link no longer available)

180. Prensa Presidencial, "Venezuela y Colombia debatirán basados en la amistad y la confianza" (April 2009) (Link no longer available)

181. Chevron. "Venezuela: Highlights of Operations" http://www.chevron.com/countries/venezuela

182. Prensa Presidencial, "Chevron-Texaco invierte 400 millones de dólares en Venezueal" (March 2004) http://www.aporrea.org/actualidad/n14722.html

183. *El Universal*. Interview with Ali Moshiri, November 8, 2007.

184. De Limas, op. cit.

185. Radio Nacional de Venezuela, "Entrevista con el Viceministro" (March 2004) (Link no longer available)

186. Maria Pila García-Guadilla, "Ecosocialismo del siglo XXI y modelo de desarrollo bolivariano: los mitos de la sustentabilidad ambiental y de la democracia participativa en Venezuela." *Revista Venezolana de Economí y Ciencias Sociales*, Vol. 15, No. 1, January–April 2009.

187. Asociación de Amigos de la Gran Sabana, "El modelo bolivariano de desarrollo en Venezuela: Impactos ambientales y sociales."Alerforo: Caracas, 2006.

188. Martin Murphy, BBC Mundo. "El gran gasoducto del Sur" (January 2006) (Link no longer available)

189. Ibid.

190. Agencia Bolivariana de Noticias, "Jefe de estado alertó sobre intereses que buscan impedir proyecto del gasoducto" (April 2008) http://aporrea.blogspot.com/2006_04_26_archive.html

191. Amigransa, Orinoco Oilwatch, "Sociedad civil exige detener proyecto del gasoducto suramericano" (May 2006) http://www.biodiversidadla.org/content/view/ffull/23555

192. José Baig, BBC Mundo, "Gasoducto del Sur: Proyecto chiflado" (April 2006) (Link no longer available)

193. Ivon Rincón Moreno, "Ambientalistas exigen suspensión del proyecto del Gran Gasoducto del Sur." *(March 2006) (Link no longer available)

194. Ivon Rincón Moreno, "Lideres indígenas rechazan gasoducto." *Correo del Caroní*, March 2006.

195. Ibid.

196. Carlos Chirinos, BBC Mundo, "Sin gasoducto al sur" (October 2008) (Link no longer available)

197. Pilar García-Guadilla, op. cit.

198. See http://www.iirsa.org/acercadeiirsa.asp?codIdioma=ESP

199. IIRSA, "Comunicado de Brasilia" (September 2000) http://www.iirsa.org/BancoMedios/Documentos%20PDF/comunicado_brasilia_esp.pdf

200. Lusbi Portillo, "ALCA/IIRSA, Plan Colombia y el Eje de Desarrollo Occidental" (March 2004) http://www.aporrea.org/actualidad/a7588.html

201. Sandro Cruz, "Chávez: El ALCA no es una solución para nuestros pueblos" (November 2003) http://www.voltaire.net.org/article120536.html

202. See "Chávez propone el ALBA como alternativa al ALCA." http://www.nuestraamerica.info/ler.hlvs/3790

203. "Integración (silenciosa) de la Infraestructura Regional Sudamericana (IIRSA)." http://www.rebelion.org/hemeroteca/economia/030917iirsa.htm

204. "Las venas de ALCA" (September 2003) (Link no longer available)

205. CAOI, "Resolución de Pueblos Indígenas sobre la IIRSA" (February 2008) http://www.aporrea.org/tiburon/a51387.html

206. "La revolución neoliberal del carbón." Alterforo: Caracas, January 2006.

207. http://www.carbozulia.com.ve

208. Ministerio de Energía y Minas, "Recursos carboniferos en Venezuela" (2006) http://www.carbozulia.com.ve

209. Grupo de Estudio y Trabajo Pueblo y Conciencia, "Carbón, la muerte negra." *El Libertario*, March 2007.

210. Lusbi Portillo, "Chávez actúa como procónsul del Imperio" (August 2006)

211. Lusbi Portillo, "ALCA/IIRSA, Plan Colombia y el Eje de Desarrollo Occidental" (August 2006) http://www.aporrea.org/tecno/a8043. htm
212. Juan Pablo Nuñez, "Entrevista con Carlos Portillo. El Libertario, No. 45, November 2004–January 2005.
213. Rafael Uzcátegui, "Interview a Angela, Wayuu en luch contra el carbón." El Libertario, No. 43, June–July 2005.
214. Wayuu Maikiralasa'lii, "Mensaje de los pueblos indígenas de Venezuela a todos los pueblos reunidos en Chiapas" (July 2007) http://colombia.indymedia.org/mail.php?id=69618
215. Pepe el Toro, "Entrevista con Jorge Montiel. El Libertario, No. 51, November-December 2007. See GOTOBUTTON BM_|_ http://www.nodo50.org/ellibertario/PDF/lib51.pdf
216. Rafael Uzcátegui, interview with Pablo Hernández Parra, Caracas July 2009.
217. Venpres, "Gobierno entrega operaciones de Plataforma Deltana a transnacionales Chevron-Texaco y Statoil" (February 2003) http://www.aporrea.org/actualidad/n4987.html
218. Pablo Hernández Parra, "Los planes del imperio y el papel de PDVSA" http://www.soberania.org/Articulos/articulo_1611.htm
219. Manuel Castells, The Information Age. Wiley-Blackwell, 1999.
220. Manuel Castells, "Informationalism, Networks, and the Network Society: A Theoretical Blueprint", p. 10. (2004) http://citeseerx.ist.psu.edu/viewdoc/download?doi=10.1.1.114.1795.pdf
221. Prensa PDVSA, "Chávez: Estamos construiyendo un socialismo petrolero múy diferente de que imaginó Marx" (July 2007) http://www.aporrea.org/ideologia/n98719.html
222. See http://www.soberania.org/Articulos/articulo_061.htm
223. Domingo Alberto Rangel, "Venezuela ¿Nación or emirato petrolero?" Sembrando el petróleo: 100 años de historia. Fundación Venezuela Positiva: Caracas, 2001.
224. La Jornada, February 2, 2009, p. 21. "La revolución se hizo gobierno."
225. CEPAL, "Producto interno bruto total a precios constantes de mercado (dólares de 2009)" http://www.website.eclac.cl/sisgen/ConsultaIntegrada.asp?id
226. http://www.google.com/publicdata?ds=wb-wdi&met=ny_gdp_mktp_cd&idim=country:VEN&dl=en&hl=en&q=gross+domestic+product+venezuela
227. Miguel Angel Santos, "Programas sociales y tasas de participación laboral" (July 2007) (Link no longer available)
228. Dinero, No. 230, 2008. "Telecomunicaciones: competencia con limtes." (Link no longer available)
229. Vanessa, Pérez Díaz, El Nacional, March 24, 2007, p. E6.
230. Laclase.info, "La banca obtuvo ganancias por BsF. 1.065, 5 millones en el primer trimestre del año" (Link no longer available)
231. Michael Hardt and Antonio Negri, Empire. Cambridge, MA: Harvard University Press, 2001.
232. María Angélica Correa, Zeta, No. 1667, July 19, 2008. "Un toque del Rey Midas de la marina venezolana."
233. Radio Nacional de Venezuela, "Empresarios privados tienen ahora mayor mejor mercade en Venezuela" (June 2008) http://www.rnv.gov.ve/noticias/index.php?act=ST&f=4&t=70839
234. See
235. Aló Presidente #194 (June 2004) http://alopresidente.gob.ve
236. Prensa Presidencial "Presidente: Gobierno no ha hecho pacto con Cisneros" (June 2007) http://www.aporrea.org/medios/n97140.html
237. Gustavo Cisneros, "¿Que ocurrió en la reunión Chávez, Carter y Cisneros? El propio Gustavo Cisneros cuenta la historia." Noticiero Venevision, July 2007. http://www.noticierovenevision.net/pop_up/que_ocurrio/index.htm
238. Misión de Observación Electoral de la Unión Europea, "Informe Final Elección Presidencial Venezuela 2006" (Link no longer available, but see http://ec.europa.eu/external_relations/human_rights/election_observation/index_en.htm)
239. Ultimas Noticias, October 5, 2007, p. 58.
240. Campo Magnético, "Se viene la preventa 2009." TvAbierta, September 2008. (Link no longer available)
241. Agencia Bolivariana de Noticias, "Maripili Hernández: Caso RCTV tiene un trasfondo económico" (June 2007) http://www.aporrea.org/medios/n95863.html
242. Camp Magnético, op. cit.
243. Producto, No. 282, May 2007. "Inversión Celular."
244. Robert Bottome, "Grupo Cisneros: Un caso (íngrimo) de éxito venezolano" (Link no longer available)
245. "Conatel autoriza venta de Digitel al grupo empresarial Cisneros" http://www.aporrea.org/actualidad/n77816.html
246. Prensa MRE, "Propuesta de multipolaridad impulsada por gobierno venezolana cobra mayor fuerza" (April 2005) http://www.aporrea.org/tiburon/n59199.html
247. Diego Ghersi, "Mundo multipolar" (Link no longer available)
248. Manuel Lozano, "Integración y multi-polaridad, ejes de política exterior" http://www3.rebelion.org/noticia.php?id=42969
249. Prensa Ministerio de Relaciones Exteriores, "Canciller Maduro explicó restrucración de Cancillería" (September 2006) (Link no longer available)
250. República Bolivariana de Venezuela, "Lineas generales del plan de desarrollo económico y social de la nación 2007-2013"http://www.portaleducativo.edu.ve/Politicas_edu/planes/documentos/Lineas_Generales_2007_2013.pdf
251. Michael Hardt and Antonio Negri, Multitude: War and Democracy in the Age of Empire. Penguin, 2005.
252. El Universal, March 26, 2009. "McDonald's elevó en 26% sus ventas en América Latina."
253. Producto, No. 272, July 2006. "Hasta en el llano."
254. Simón Rodríguez Porras, "McDonald's en la Televisora Venezolana Social" http://www.aporrea.org/medios/a62563.html
255. Agencia Bolivariana de Noticias, "Diputado Tachinamo sostuvo que Venezuela garantiza soberanía alimentaria" (July 2009) (Link no longer available; agency has been renamed Agencia Venezolana de Noticias: http://www.avn.info.ve/)
256. Jorge Guzmán, "Justa distribución de alimentos por parte de Mercal consolida el poder popular" (May 2008) http://www.abn.info.ve/reportaje_detalle.php?articulo=763
257. Guy Debord, Society of the Spectacle. Rebel Press: London, 2004.
258. Juan Agulló, "La estrategia de la tensión" (September 2008) http://www.rebelion.org/noticia.php?id=72661
259. Omar Lugo, Yolanda Ojeda, and Gerardo Prieto, "El capitalismo es un mal necesario para el Socilismo del Siglo XXI." El Mundo, August 31, 2009.

CHAPTER 4
Populism and Militarism

Before addressing the matter of autonomous social movements in Venezuela over the last decade, we should consider several matters that are essential to understanding the Bolivarian government in all its complexity. Owing to the region in which Venezuela is located, we'll begin by talking about the political changes that have occurred in Latin America in recent years, and the place of the Venezuelan government in the context of those changes.

In a summary of the political changes that have occurred to the south of the Rio Grande in the last two decades, Uruguayan writer Daniel Barret considers the reactions to neoliberal "structural adjustments."[260] In the 1990s, multitudes reacted against these "reforms," a testimony to these reforms' failure to cement, without fissures, a place [for the states which adopted them] in the worldwide market. Parallel to this, a worldwide avalanche of social initiatives demanded the right of peoples to determine their own destinies. These initiatives were known as the "anti-globalization movement."

In Latin America, movement-type responses to the failure of neoliberalism caused the fall of several governments: De la Rúa in Argentina (2001); Sanchez de Lozada in Bolivia (2003); Lucio Gutiérrez in Ecuador (2005); and Carlos Mesa in Bolivia (2005). All of the social movements that brought down these governments sprang from the grassroots of society, had little formal organization—in contrast with vanguardist fronts and other organizations in the 1970s in Latin America—and functioned through contagious effect in rebelling against and refusing to put up with situations that had become intolerable. In Argentina they [social initiative participants] raised the cry that transcended borders: "¡Que se vayan todos!" [This translates roughly to "Out with all of them!" or "They all must go!"] Every one of these social initiatives, although they shared common traits, had characteristics peculiar to the societies in which they arose. Unfortunately, these dynamic initiatives did not represent a real, sustainable alternative, nor did they signify structural advances for Latin America's social movements.

At the same time, there was another response to neoliberalism, an institutional-electoral response, whose immediate consequence was what some have called the "turn to the left" of the Latin American electorate. Thus, we have two primary types of response: the spontaneous in-the-streets type, which led to the fall of governments; and the political-party type, which led to the installation of new governments. Daniel Barret recognizes that, effectively, in electoral terms, there has been a turn to the left; but at the same time he mentions that this obscures what he terms "the renewal of hope":

> To a certain extent, there exists the renewal of a sentiment much like that of the 1970s, considering things in evolutionary and progressive terms, [a sense] that history is advancing now, and that it didn't [previously]. People tend to think that it's an unstoppable wave, when all one has to do is review the history of Latin America to understand that these types of things have occurred in other moments and that they were perfectly reversible, as reversible as "existing socialism" [i.e., the Soviet Union and Eastern Bloc] when many imagined its base and pillars were infinitely stronger [than the current progressive "wave" in Latin America]."

The Uruguayan anarchist provides a specific year as an example:

> If you take the year 1953, there were more populist, nationalist governments than there are today. Those that had populist/nationalist characteristics were the government of Federico Cháves in Paraguay; that of Carlos Ibáñez del Campo in Chile; that of Gustavo Rojas Pinilla in Colombia; that of Getúlio Vargas in Brazil; that of Juan Domingo Perón in Argentina; and that of Jacobo Arbenz Guzmán in Guatemala.

Social Democratic Governments and Populist Governments

In regard to this electoral "turn to the left," Barret makes an important distinction: that between populist governments and social-democratic governments, [in part] because the social and political dynamics that produce each type are different. Social-democratic governments are typically the product of long-standing political parties that rose out of the labor movement; this is not the case with populist governments. Another characteristic distinguishing social-democratic from populist governments is that the social democrats place more emphasis on the functioning of parliamentary democracy than the populists. Two current examples of social-democratic governments are those of Luís Inácio Lula da Silva, who is a product of the Labor Party in Brazil, and who is currently in power, and Tabard Ramon Vasquez Rojas of the Broad Front in Uruguay, who left office in March 2010.

In the social democracies there exists neither the desire nor the intention of founding a new world, while in the populist states that is the case. Therefore, populist governments generate greater hopes and expectations—and thus sow more confusion—than social-democratic governments. The rhetoric of the populist governments is much more markedly revolutionary than that of the social-democratic governments. The social democrats accept the logic of the government-opposition game, and also conduct their affairs in the framework of alternating parties leading the government. In contrast, the populist rationale is that of the unfolding of a historic project, that is to say, a project of infinite length, and therefore it's difficult for the populists to even think of relinquishing power.

The political dynamics that characterize these different approaches to government have an intimate relationship with the social movements. In broad strokes, social-democratic reformism, once installed in power, slowly loses its ability [to inspire and] to call [upon its supporters and the social movements] to act. Populism, in contrast, generates much more enthusiasm, and therefore has a much greater capacity for state cooptation of social movements.

Against the background of this Latin American reality, Daniel Barret draws his conclusions. The two trajectories—the spontaneous movements that overthrow governments and the social-democratic/populist movements that install governments—present a basic dilemma to Latin American social movements: either the statist road or the autonomous road. Barret puts it like this:

> In this moment, in this pivotal swing of the pendulum in Latin American history, it appears that the statist road is that being chosen. Not only [is this important] because of election results, not only because of what this [course] represents in terms of demobilization and in some cases dismemberment of the social movements, but also because of what it represents in terms of hopes and expectations: it means the displacement to others of the task of realizing historic goals and commitments.

Populism as a Manner of Exercising Power

If the electoral "turn to the left" in Latin America has produced on the one hand social-democratic governments and on the other populist governments, that of Hugo Chávez is definitely of the latter type. And since the situation in Venezuela is the topic of this book, we should describe populism more fully.

In recent Latin America history, "populism" refers to a series of political approaches/short-term movements led by charismatic personalities during the 20th century. The leading example is that of Juan Domingo Perón in Argentina in 1946–1955 and again in 1973–1974. Other examples include Getúlio Vargas in Brazil (1946–1954), Alberto Fujimori in Peru (1990–2000), and Carlos Menem in Argentina (1989–1999).

Latin American social science possesses a vast bibliography on the width and breadth of the conditions and contexts in which populist governments have arisen in the region. There has been much argument about the reduction to a single category of the multidimensional phenomena that accompany every concrete example of populism. Nonetheless, Kenneth Roberts has created an outline that allows us to draw a first approximation of the concept, starting with five traits [261]:

1) Personal, paternalistic, increasingly charismatic leadership;

2) A coalition that crosses class lines, concentrated in the most subordinate social sectors;

3) A top-down process of political mobilization that transcends the institutionalized mediation mechanisms, or that subordinates them to direct ties between the leader and the people;

4) An amorphous or eclectic ideology, expressed in a discourse that elevates the subordinated sectors, in other words, a discourse that is anti-elitist;

5) Economic projects that utilize redistributive methods in a dependent-client context, and whose benefits are massively distributed with the purpose of constructing a material base to obtain the backing of the popular sector.

Populism in Venezuela

After the death of the dictator Juan Vicente Gómez in 1936, a process began that researcher Juan Carlos Rey calls "mobilization populism." It developed through the remainder of the 1930s and 1940s, culminating in the failed attempt in 1948 to install a democracy based in the masses. Three dynamics converged in this populist variant: 1) An intensive and extensive social mobilization process, which had generated a mass without political roots that could join new organizations and shift loyalties; 2) An exclusionary situation, presided over by an oligarchic regime, in which political, social and economic participation was restricted to certain sectors of society; and 3) The emergence of a new elite consisting of middle-class urban groups that felt alienated from the existing sociopolitical order, which blocked their participation [in the running of society] and gave them no recognition.[262]

The governments which followed the Gómez dictatorship initiated restricted liberalization, but didn't deliver true democratization. Societal access to the political process continued to be blocked by institutions such as the indirect election of the congress and president, and the continuance of oligarchies in which political recruitment took place via cliques and family ties. In these oligarchies, what mattered in political selection was wealth, personal ties, prestige, and the influence that all these provided. It was in this post-Gómez period that the development of the first political parties in the country began.

Following the overthrow of the government of Rómulo Gallegos in 1948, and ten more years of military dictatorship headed by Marcos Pérez Jiménez, the democratic experiment inaugurated in 1958 took a new form: conciliatory populism, with a wide consensus about the "rules of the game" among the principal political and social actors in the country. These rules were agreed upon in the Pact of Punto Fijo between the Democratic Action, COPEI, and Republican Democratic Union parties, which was signed on October 31, 1958. This pact meant that elected governments could count on the moral and material support necessary to avoid overthrow, and that they could successfully mobilize the combination of social and collective resources required to realize their decisions. And in the making of political decisions, [the political parties and the various governments] adopted a series of informal rules and institutional regulations.

This conciliatory populist system, instituted at the beginning of 1958, was based in the recognition of the plurality of interests, as much among those in the majority as those in the minority, and in the creation of a complex system of negotiation and accommodation among the various actors. Through this system the various social-democratic governments derived the necessary social consensus regarding the basic rules of the political order, reconciling two necessities upon which governability rests in a democratic regime: first, the guarantee that the powerful minority's interests would not be threatened by the government's decisions; and second, the maintenance of the confidence of a majority of the population in the machinery of representative democracy as a means of satisfying their aspirations.

Between 1958 and 1984 there were two fundamental factors upon which conciliatory populism was based: first, the central role played by the state as the principal actor and promoter of the development process, as well as in the sharing of its benefits; and second, the roles played by the political parties and various subordinate groups as mediators between the state and the rest of society.

During the first years of this period, the primary government objective was to guarantee that the elected presidents weren't overthrown by military coups or by armed civil insurrections. However, the governmental elite was conscious that the regime would endure only if the masses maintained their confidence in the ability of representative democracy and in the political parties and their leaders. This required the immediate placation of the most urgent and pressing needs of the people, as well as the assumption through programmatic means of the promise to progressively extend democracy. This meant that the social-democratic regimes became ever more involved in the political, social, and economic spheres, in the continual diminishment of inequalities.[263]

Bolivarian Populism as a Continuation of the Old Populism

Nelly Arenas and Luís Gómez Calcanó have clearly established the similarities between the Bolivarian Process and the country's first government with populist tendencies: the so-called Democratic Action triennial [period] when it ruled between 1945 and 1948. In 1941, General Isaías Medina Angarita was designated President of Venezuela. On October 18, 1945, a military coup in which Democratic Action participated overthrew Medina Angarita, under the excuse that his government had impeded the democratic demands of the people and represented the continuation of [the rule of former dictator] Juan Vicente Gómez. After the coup, the military ceded power to civilians, with which Rómulo Betancourt—leader of Democratic Action–assumed the presidency and called elections in 1947, which his candidate, the writer Rómulo Gallegos, won. The following year, Gallegos was the victim of another coup d'etat.

During the three years in which Democratic Action was in power, its leaders were carriers of a new social "contagion," advocates of a new order that conflicted with the old. This new social order demanded a radical rupture with the "excluding, anti-national, anti-democratic, and corrupt" past.[264]

It didn't matter that after the death of dictator Gómez in 1936 the governments of López Contreras and Medina Angarita had instituted some reforms:

everything in the period prior to 1945 was an expression of the "opprobrious Gómez regime," in the words of Betancourt. The overthrow of the old order became the base of the new government's prestige.

Another element at the time was nationalism which, in the economic sphere, manifested itself as questioning of the relations between the nation and the world market, with petroleum being the most important component. Democratic Action, in the 1945–1948 period, denounced the "surrender" of the Gómez regime, which AD characterized as subordinate to petroleum imperialism; therefore AD advocated, at least rhetorically, a different model of development. This AD nationalism was supported by a foundational myth: that of Simón Bolivar. This supplied the ideological and moral instruments for a supposed refounding of the republic. In the words of Rómulo Betancourt, the epic change initiated in 1945 represented a "second independence," which was utilized as an element of the intense social mobilization in support of the new government.

Just as would happen decades later with the Bolivarian Process, the AD government of 1945–1948 convened a constituent assembly to "refound" the institutions that would rule the country, and it obtained a large majority [in support of its reforms]. The political minorities were criminalized as inheritors of the Gómez legacy, and because of this one could characterize the AD style of government as sectarian. This led to the assimilation of the state by a political party (AD), which erased the border between the hegemony of a new state and the hegemony of a political party.

Between 1945 and 1948 the Venezuelan state received, in comparison with previous years, a considerable income from the sale of petroleum, which allowed it to promote populist social policies. "It operated in practice as if there existed no material restrictions on its actions."[265] For example, on December 14, 1945 President Betancourt eliminated the tax on the consumption of gasoline and wheat flour, reduced the price of kerosene, lowered the price of passenger transport, and decreed a reduction in rent and electric rates.

The AD government of 1945–1948 was supported, as well, by a civilian-military alliance with the National Armed Forces, in which these Forces became "an instrument of the people." Betancourt distinguished himself from the traditional political class through his nationalist rhetoric, his anti-imperialism, and his symbolic identification with the people, marking in this manner the beginnings of Venezuelan populism.[266]

Militarism as Part of Venezuelan Culture

The cult of Simón Bolivar provides the foundational myth upon which the political culture of Venezuela has been erected, beginning with the Democratic Action government of 1945 and continuing through the Bolivarian Process of the present day. The cult of Bolivar, the axis of the supposed "national identity," has been built upon a long and efficient collective elaboration which has mystified—by including falsification of and omission of certain historical conditions—the civilian relationship with the military. The most well known of these mystifications is founded on Bolivar's letter of August 5, 1829 to the British official in charge of negotiations with Bolivar. There's a single sentence in it that supposedly demonstrates Bolivar's anti-imperialist tendencies. Its most salient feature is that it asks how it's possible not to oppose "the United States, that appears destined by Providence to plague the Americas with misery in the name of liberty." However, this is taken out of context. In the same letter, Bolivar pledges his submission to the British crown:

> In sum, I'm far from opposing the reorganization of Colombia in accord with the tested institutions of learned Europe. On the contrary, it would make me infinitely happy and would reanimate my forces to aid in such a work that one could call salvation and that could not be achieved without difficulty without the support of England and France. With this powerful assistance we'll be capable of everything, without it, no.

The great importance of the military as guarantor of public efficiency, obedience, and order is an expression of the ideological web woven in the Venezuelan collective unconsciousness. This military worship began to develop during the war of independence against Spain in the 19th century, beginning with Bolivar—as the insurgent commander when Venezuela won independence in 1821—and continuing with successive leaders who have characterized themselves as "strong men" have capitalized on it.

However, Bolivar was not the first popular Venezuelan strong man, but rather José Tomás Boves (1782–1814) who, as the head of a nominally pro-Spanish army of 10,000—of whom fewer than 200 were Spaniards—during the war of independence, managed to gain the sympathy of the people, owing to his charisma and knowledge of campesino culture, taking advantage of the campesinos' resentment of the ruling white creole class, to which Simón Bolivar belonged. The Venezuelan historian Laureano Vallenilla Lanz states that Boves "freed the slaves from their servitude. He was the first to began to equalize the castes, elevating mulattos and zambos [persons of mixed black and Indian ancestry] in his army to high places in the military hierarchy. His popularity came to be immense."[(267)]

After Boves' death, another resident of the Venezuelan savannah, José Antonio Páez (1790–1873), of humble background and strong character, and who rose through the ranks and fought on the side of the independence forces, put himself at the front of Boves' troops in order to incorporate them into Bolivar's army: "To pass from one file to the other," notes Lanz, "they did nothing more than change commanders; in the dark recesses of his mentality and his inclinations . . . Páez was the legitimate heir of Taita Boves."

A general who won several battles against the Spanish during the war of independence, Páez was elected first president of the republic in 1830, and soon became the principal holder of public debt and the possessor of huge agricultural plantations; he controlled the meat monopoly, gaming houses, and taxes. "Liberty had arrived for those who managed to become owners; the society continued to be classist. The [former] usurping class was the only one that suffered losses, with the incorporation of the high officials [of the revolutionaries] as latifundistas (huge land owners)."[(268)]

At the end of the 19th century, Venezuela survived on the export of coffee, which was cultivated in its Andean zone [in the northwestern part of the country]. The so-called "Andean hegemony" arose in this region, where the rural plantation constituted the principal economic unit; and that unit was based upon individual power and personal loyalty, two preconditions of the cult of the strong man (caudillismo). As well, during the first half of the twentieth century, all of the Venezuelan presidents were from this region, comprised of Mérida, Táchira, and Trujillo states.

Juan Vicente Gómez is the father of the modern Venezuelan state, for, among other reasons, organizing a professional army with national reach; in the first years of his rule he established the Military Academy of Venezuela, which was largely responsible for the professionalization of the army. Gómez altered the constitution on seven occasions in order to legitimize his retention of power, surrounding himself with a series of intellectuals who attempted to give ideological coherence to his mandate. The most well known of these was the historian Vallenilla Lanz, who with his book *El Cesarismo democrático* argued for the necessity of a tropical caesarism: "the necessary gendarme," "the only one who is suitable to our normal evolution." And it was precisely the dictator Juan Vicente Gómez who elevated Simón Bolivar to a guiding star and erected a statue of him in every village and city center.

During 51 years of the 20th century, Venezuela was governed by civilian and military strong men, who were defined by possession of a charismatic personalty, a wide network of relations, and a considerable and permanent source of economic resources; they embodied the concept of order and national progress. In this manner, the military man and the military—understanding the first as both the individual figure and social symbol, and the second as the institutional apparatus and means of action—have been essential and decisive components in Venezuelan politics, especially, in a very singular manner, through the entire length of the 20th century.

The characteristics of this militarism are as follows:

1) The cult of the male military hero;

2) The perpetual recurrence of the cult of the strong man (caudillismo) and the macho values associated with him;

3) The predominance of insight and clear-sightedness of the leader as regards his playing the collective leading role;

4) The conception of politics as a matter of urgency or emergency, and not as a process of collective construction and historical continuity; that everything starts anew with new individuals in power;

5) The valuing of military force as the corporeal apparatus bearing the ideals of purity, redemption, and efficiency, and existing above the institutions created by civil society, which are perceived as antagonistic and subordinate.

Bolivarian Populist Militarism

If in the course of this text we've questioned the existence of a socialist revolution in Venezuela, we're not arguing–as some do–that we live in the presence of a military government with dictatorial traits. Rather, as we'll show, since the year 1999 government power has become increasingly militarized; and under the cover of leftist rhetoric the Chávez government has continued Venezuela's militarist tradition.

In its actions, the Bolivarian movement has promoted a renewed militarism in the following ways:

1) Discourse influenced by Fidel Castro. President Chávez promotes himself as the "comandante-presidente," an appellation used by a good number of his followers. Chávez, in his discourse, has continually described the conflict within the country in military terms and with allegories about bellicose confrontations, mixing events of the struggle for Venezuelan independence with references to traditional warfare. For example, he called the electoral campaign in 2004, a recall election called by the opposition, the "Battle of Santa Inés (after an actual battle that took place on December 10, 1859).

This type of speech inspires antagonism on both sides, among both friends and enemies. It's based on the "external enemy" strategy, in which the enemy is represented by the president of the United States, whose "army of occupation" [in Venezuela] is composed of those who dissent from official policies, the "enemy within," who are complicit with imperialism and conspire without respite. An example of this polarizing, us-versus-them narrative is provided by an official press release: "[T]he chief executive of Venezuela ordered that the National Armed Forces press the Venezuelan people to accelerate defensive preparations of all kinds because the internal enemy is becoming emboldened."[269]

Implicit in this discourse is the idea that the highest honor is to die for "the national interest." Since 2004, the primary slogan of the Venezuelan army has been "Country, Socialism, or Death"; at the same time followers of Chávez consider themselves "citizen soldiers." The continual presentation of exaggerated caricatures of enemies and imaginary threats creates fear and immunizes society and [the government's] policies against change.[270]

2) The symbolic. Despite civilian clothing being appropriate to his office, President Chávez attends official ceremonies in military dress. The red beret, worn by the military coup plotters (including Chávez) during the 1992 coup attempt, is an important part of the Bolivarian outfit. El Paseo de Próceres ("the parade ground of the exalted") in Caracas is a military site opened by the dictator Marcos Pérez Jiménez, and is used as much for military parades as for civilian demonstrations in support of the government. The symbolism of starting and ending the inaugural march of the Fourth World Social Forum at this site, in January 2006, is obvious.[271] As well, the Paseo is used on independence days for political acts. For example, the first swearing of allegiance of the Bolivarian Revolutionary Movement (MBR–200, the military movement founded by Chávez that was responsible for the 1992 coup attempt) was held there on December 17, 1982, the anniversary of the death of Simón Bolivar. In 1997, MBR–200 chose April 19, the date of Venezuela's declaration of independence from Spain, to hold a meeting there in which it decided, contrary to its original (electoral) abstentionist and insurrectionist principles, to participate in the elections the next year and to support Chávez.[272]

3) The Exercise of Power. Since the arrival in power of the Bolivarian movement, a great number of medium-level and high-level public offices have been held by military men. Already in 2003, the researcher Inés Rolando Garrido revealed that there were 310 military men in managerial posts in state enterprises, autonomous institutes, government financial funds, ministries, state government posts, and mayoralties.[273] The leadership of Chávez is incontestable, as is, through the Bolivarian movement, the development of a cult of personality. As well, the government uses the "leader-people" relationship in any collective context, wherever and whenever it wants.

4) The relationship with society. The Bolivarian movement has continually organized itself in emulation of military structures. Units of Electoral Battle (UBEs—Unidades de Batalla Electoral), battalions, militias, fronts, patrols, civilian-military reserves, etc. At the same time, it has demanded that the popular-participation organizations, created by the state, have military-type training and be incorporated in the so-called National Bolivarian Militia, which since 2008 has been a new element in the structure of the National Armed Forces. President Chávez even asked, on March 8, 2009 (International Women's Day!), for the creation of a military corps comprised entirely of women.[274] Diligently, four months later, on July 26, the Minister of Popular Power for Women, María León, stated that 1,200 women would be sworn in as members of the Combat Corps of Women.[275] As well, some of the slogans emanating from above, and adopted by the base of the Bolivarian Movement, clearly imply subordination to authority. The speeches and orders of President Chávez are replete with military references, such as "knee on earth"(the posture assumed by soldiers in battle) and "Commander Chávez orders [you] on this front." In April 2009, the government declared that a law to regulate social property should include as beneficiaries communities that have "organization, political formation, technical capacity and military instruction."[276]

5) The preponderant role assigned to the National Armed Forces. The army has, in fact, a more important organizing-administrative role than the political parties that support President Chávez, from the PSUV to its satellites such as Fatherland for All (Patria para Todos) and the Communist Party of Venezuela. The National Armed Forces, in 2000, developed the first social policies of the Bolivarian government, under the name Plan Bolivar 2000. Presently, the armed forces preside over the Mercal Mission [the nutrition mission] and other important policies and projects, in addition to providing logistics and infrastructure for most public acts of the Bolivarian Process.

6) The armed forces' budget. The national budget for 2009 provides the Ministry of Defense with the seventh largest appropriation of those given the 27 ministries. This means that the military receives three times the amount of money destined for nutrition and housing, four times more than is allotted for protection of the environment, nine times more than the budget for culture, and twelve times as much as is allotted to sports. The greatest gap is between the allotment for the military and that for indigenous communities; there the amount given the Ministry of Defense is 58 times the amount given to the Ministry of Popular Power for Indigenous Peoples.[277] As well, according to the Stockholm International Peace Research Institute, Venezuela ascended from 55th place to 18th place on the list of military arms importers during the years 2004–2008, acquiring $2.038 billion dollars worth of arms during that period, of which $1.944 billion were bought from Russia. Venezuela is only surpassed as an arms importer in Latin America by Chile, which came in at eleventh place among world arms importers.[278]

A good part of the above-mentioned dynamics were put into practice based on the ideas of Argentine sociologist Norberto Ceresole, one of the intellectuals who was influential during the first years of Chávez's mandate.[279] Ceserole advanced the concept of strong man-army-people as the fundamental axis upon which the Bolivarian Process rotated:

All of these elements—"order," or "popular mandate," a military leader becoming a strong man or national head, the absence of effective, intermediary civilian institutions, the presence of an important group of "apostles" (nucleus of a future civilian-military party) that intervene with generosity and magnanimity between the strong man and the masses, the absence of preexisting ideologically driven parasitic [entities], comprise a model of change—in truth, a revolutionary model—that is absolutely new, although in line with clear historical traditions.(280)

Domingo Alberto Rangel, a Venezuelan marxist intellectual, points out the military substrate of the Bolivarian project:

We insist that "Bolivarian" and "socialist" is a contradiction as grating as that of "socialist" and "patriotic"; [this contradiction] is tolerated and continues because the regime is both military and militaristic. In what sense is the regime military? In the only sense that determines the nature of a political regime. . . . Those who monopolize the decisions in this regime are military men.(281)

Rangel goes on to insist that making socialism compatible with the armed forces is impossible:

To be a socialist and a patriot is already a grating contradiction. Socialism is internationalist, a struggle to abolish frontiers and to transcend, as always in history, the nation-state stage that humanity entered four or more centuries ago. A socialist patriot is like a boiling ice floe or a solid liquid, a contradiction in itself. Why then, has a similar grotesque contradiction prospered in Venezuela over the last eight years [since Chávez assumed power]? Because in a world of farce, anything is possible.

Humberto Decarli, a Venezuelan anarchist and labor activist, has refuted the supposed progressive character of the Venezuelan army:

The myth of the democratic and institutional armed forces is overturned because such a thing has never existed in the country. One is dealing with a petrified form at the service of the powers of the day, and above all else the reigning political, socioeconomic, and cultural powers in these times of globalization. Is not an army with a specific role in Betancourt's project of collaboration between powers, and which now occupies a space as one of the fundamental powers in a country where democracy does not exist, anything but a caricature of government by the people?(282)

The Bolivarian Process lost its revolutionary pole star long before it assumed power in February 1999. Its degeneration commenced when it permitted the values of militarism to seep into the core of its struggle, when it consciously incorporated the logic of power as its form of social thought. John Holloway notes:

[I]f we rebel against capitalism it's not because we want a different system of power, rather it's because we want a society in which power relations have vanished. You can't construct a society without power relations through conquest of power. Once you adopt the logic of power, the struggle against power is already lost.[283]

260. Daniel Barret, "El dilema es estatismo o autonomía." Talk delivered at Alternative Social Forum, Caracas, 2006.

261. Nelly Arenas and Luis Gómez Calcaño, *Populismo Autoritario: Venezuela 1999-2005.* Cendes, UCV: Caracas, 2006.

262. Juan Carlos Rey, "La democracia venezolana y la crisis del sistema populista de reconciliación." *Revista de Estudios Políticos*, No. 74, 1991.

263. Ibid.

264. Neritza Alvarado Chacín, "Populismo, Democracía y Política Social en Venezuela" (Link no longer available)

265. Arenas and Gómez Calcaño, op. cit.

266. Susanne Gratius, "La 'tercera ola populista' de América Latina." Fundación para las Relaciones Internacionales y el Diálogo Exterior, October 2007. (Link no longer available)

267. Laureano Vallenilla Lanz, *El Cesarismo democrático.* Libros de El Nacional, Colección Ares: Venezuela, 1999.

268. Ibid.

269. VTV, "Presidente Chávez: Mandatario regional que pretenda desestabilizar el país será reducido por la ley" (August 2009) http://vtv. gob.ve/noticias-nacionales/22018

270. Heiner Busch and Wolfgang Kaleck, "La Fabricaión de la imagen del enemigo: El viejo truco del militarismo" (May 2005) http://www.grupotortuga.com

271. Rebelion.org, "VI Foro Social Mundial comienza con una marcha inaugural" (January 2006) http://www3.rebelion.org/noticias/2006/1/25956.pdf

272. Margarita López Maya, *Del Viernes Negro al Referendo Revocatorio.* Editorial Alfadil: Caracas, 2005.

273. Cited by Arenas and Calcaño, op. cit.

274. Mariela Acuña, "Ministerio de la Mujer tendrá cartera y nuevo nombre." *Ultimas Noticias*, March 9, 2009, p. 2.

275. VTV, "Ministra León anunció juramentación de 1200 mujeres combatientes para el mes de agosto" (July 2009) http://vtv.gob.ve/noticias-nacionales/21345

276. Marco Ruíz Gerenciar, "Empresas socialistas requirirá formación politica." *Ultimas Noticias*, April 17, 2009, p. 19.

277.*Gaceta Oficial de la República Bolivariana* de Venezuela, No. 39.147, March 29, 2009.

278. International Institute of Peace Studies (SIPRI), *SIPRI Yearbook 2008.* SIPRI: Stockholm, 2008. http://books.sipri.org

279. Ceserole was an enigmatic man. He was a left supporter of Peronism in Argentina and a member of the Montoneros guerrilla group in the 1970s. In 1987, he was an adviser to the military men who attempted to overthrow then-President Raúl Alfonsin. He was also known for his nationalist posturing and his Holocaust denial, most notably around the time of the bombing of the Israeli embassy in Buenos Aires in 1992, in which 29 were killed and 242 wounded. He died in 2003, while an adviser to Hugo Chávez.

280. Norberto Ceserole, *Caudillo, ejército, pueblo. La Venezuela del presidente Chávez* (January 1999)

281. Domingo Alberto Rangel, "Un Régimen militar." *El Mundo*, July 19, 2007, p. 4.

282. Humberto Decarli, *El Mito democrático de las Fuerzas Armadas Venezolanas.* Ediciones Comité de Relaciones Anarquistas: Caracas, 2006.

283. John Holloway, *Change the World Without Taking Power: The Meaning of Revolution Today.* Pluto Press: London, 2005.

Photo by Rafael Uzcáteguie.

Photo by Mafias Verdes

Two images from the national demonstration in Caracas on March 31, 2005 against coal mining in the Sierra de Perijás

CHAPTER 5
Social Movements

The two fundamental characteristics of the Bolivarian Movement, militarism and populism, are incontestible, so we'll go on to describe the resistance initiatives of the last decade. However, before continuing, we should consider something that clarifies our analysis: the capabilities of the social movements to establish themselves and to develop their autonomy. Given the complexity of the contemporary world, and the obvious limitations of the workers' movement in it, there are many actors capable of bringing down the ruling hegemonies. As Castells notes in *The Information Age*, these actors are of a collectively conscious type, whose impact, as much in defeat as in victory, transforms the values and institutions of society, and which we label "social movements."

The principal social movements that immediately preceded President Chávez's rise to power were concentrated in the principal cities. In order of importance: Caracas, Maracaibo, Valencia, Barquisimeto, and Maracay. Only the indigenous and environmental movements were well developed in the less populated parts of the country. The environmental movement included the Federation of Environmental Organizations and Groups (Federación de Organizaciones y Juntas Ambientalistas), the Ecological Front of Aragua (Frente Ecológico de Aragua), and the Ecological Front of Carabobo (Frente Ecológico de Carabobo). The indigenous groups and organizations were members of the National Indigenous Council of Venezuela (Consejo Nacional Indígena de Venezuela).

The cooperative movement was concentrated in the central and western parts of Venezuela, in the Aragua, Carabobo and Lara areas, with CECOSESOLA (Central Cooperativa de Servicios Sociales de Lara—Cooperative Federation of Lara Social Services) being the most important of the cooperative associations, and one which lasts to this day. The Neighbors Associations (Asociaciones de Vecinos) were very important in Caracas in the 1980s and early 1990s.

The student movement impelled important mobilizations, and its nuclei were in the major public universities, such as the Central University of Venezuela, the University of the Andes, the University of the Plains, and the University of the East. Some of the most important groups were the Union of Revolutionary Youths (UJR—Unión de Jovenes Revolucionarios), the Movement of Renewal 80 (Movimiento de Renovación 80), and the Disobedience Group (Grupo Disobediencia).

The women's movement was divided between, on the one hand, academic-oriented groups tied to the country's principal public universities, such as the Network of Venezuelan University Studies on Women (Red de Estudios Universitarios Venezolanos de La Mujer), Woman and Environment (Mujer y Ambiente), and Against Violence (toward women) (Contra la Violencia), and on the other hand to groups with ties to the social organizations of the left, such as the Popular Feminine Circles (Círculos Femeninos Populares) and Women's Houses (Casas de la Mujer).

Why are social movements and not others—for example, the working class, in contrast to earlier times when it was believed that the proletariat constituted the primary historical force that would make the revolution--the primary actors? And why are the social movements the actors that lead to revolution? How do we view these movements?

Our viewpoint is not statist-centric, something which has predominated in a good part of the Venezuelan and Latin American left, and which has as its object state power, and through it the creation of change. The state, which exists as node in the network of social and global power relationships in which we're immersed, is neither a physical destination nor a tool which can be mechanically bent and folded to one's purposes. Its supreme purpose is its own perpetuation; it demands individual sacrifice in the name of the chimeric "general well-being," which in reality consists of safeguarding the privileges of the dominant sectors at the expense of those who sacrifice themselves (and others). "The state, as such, is the inevitable negation and annihilation of liberty in its entirety, of all individual and societal freedom."[(284)]

What about the social movements' relationship to the leftist political parties? The political party is an organizational form whose struggle is directed toward the taking of power, subordinating everything to that objective, including supposed principles. One example is the critique of machismo within leftist parties, where that critique is considered a "distraction." This, of course, implies an impoverishment of the struggle against real oppression. The very form of the political party, be it vangaurdist or parliamentary, presupposes an orientation toward the taking of state power, and political parties make no sense outside of that context. The party is the means of controlling class struggle; it's the means of subordinating innumerable movements to the goal of controlling the state. Resistance becomes marginalized; it becomes very much secondary to that goal. Therefore, the hierarchical transformation of the struggle becomes the hierarchical transformation of our lives, our struggles, the hierarchical transformation our very being.[285]

Returning to social movements, what accounts for their combativeness? Their autonomy. And autonomy is the capacity to rule oneself and to question what one has inherited from the past. The term is a compound of two Greek words: "auto" and "nomos," which in combination literally mean to make your own laws for yourself. Autonomy in politics is the practice of human beings defining, in a free manner, their own trajectories in life. In a collective context, it means that people decide, in the most democratic manner possible, every aspect of daily life that affects them, from work, to the use of free time, to nutrition, etc.

The opposite of autonomy is heteronomy, that is living under rules made by others. This is drummed into us from birth: the "naturalness" of living under rules made by others, of being subservient, of always following the dictates of others. These things, as well as the institutions that impose them, are considered sacred and not subject to discussion.

An individual starts to become autonomous when he or she begins to ask if this or that must always be so, or if things would work better if done differently. Because of this we can say that autonomy is a discussion without end, one that should never stop, and which therefore is arriving at ever-changing (and improving) conclusions. If the state, the government, armies, and jails are unjust, shouldn't they be replaced with something better? An autonomous individual never forgets that it's individuals who make the laws that govern society. And therefore they should be replaced whenever they act against the common good. Individual autonomy is created by free reflection and deliberation. It becomes concrete when one becomes sovereign over oneself and one's acts.[286]

Autonomy has several consequences: it democratizes society; it dissipates centralized power; it tends toward equality; and it makes possible individuals becoming social "subjects" (actors, not objects) who participate actively in the autonomous project. Who has the right to autonomy? Everyone who demands it.

In what sense does autonomy revolutionize the theory of revolution? It breaks the tradition that sees a centralized state as necessary to bringing about change; and, likewise, it breaks the tradition that sees hierarchical and centralized organizations, such as political parties, as necessary to the conquest of power.

Social autonomy cannot be separated from individual autonomy. A revolution commences when the people form their own autonomous organizations, when they make their own rules and their own forms of organization. And therefore the revolution ends when these autonomous organizations are domesticated, subjected, or reduced to a decorative role.[287]

Having considered autonomy, let's now consider whether the Bolivarian government has reinforced or diminished the autonomous capacity of Venezuela's social movements.

Autonomy in Social Movements

When one struggles for emancipation, one of the preconditions is the construction of an autonomous culture that fosters in oppressed individuals a new, empowered identity. But how does one construct autonomy from below?

The Uruguayan author Raul Zibechi, in his book, *La mirada horizontal* ("The Horizontal View"), has identified five dynamics that impel "counter-hegemony" in grassroots social movements:

1) Construction of one's own narrative [both individual and social] and a vision of the world that is antagonistic [to domination/submission and hierarchy]. The organization should foster intellectual independence in its members. Only autonomous individuals can create communications organs that are independent of conventionality, of bosses, of set-in-concrete ideas. To be autonomous is to be critical and self-critical, which is equivalent to going against the current of dominant practices and ideas; and this is achieved through a process of study, self-education, and debate.

2) The opening of autonomous spaces outside of the reach and logic of the market, where it's possible to build local, democratic, and autonomous entities. A long practice in spaces that aren't contaminated, or scarcely contaminated, by the dominant logic (including that of political marketing) can give rise to new forms of life [and organization], new ways of conduct, that will lead to a different, counter-hegemonic, autonomous political culture. One could call these "cultural laboratories" in which people can weave ties face to face, directly, in a self-directed manner and without intermediaries—spaces that are sufficiently free and open to allow experiment without fear of errors or failures, and the only way to create conditions that invert, or subvert, the dominant values.

3) The counter-hegemonic spaces should function in accord with the values held in common by the social movements. They should be "horizontal" spaces, not hierarchical, a web that avoids concentration of power. At the same time, they should value diversity as a strength. One's identity can only unfold and maintain itself if one cares for and supports the differing identities of others. Difference enriches.

4) Daily practice constructs a collective identity in search of a new civilizing model. From common practice born [in individual] differences comes a new form of democracy that consists of brotherhood, which leads directly to the realization of community. The goal is neither to take power nor final victory; the goal is the people themselves.

5) Construction of integrated spaces and narratives which unite all aspects, complexities, and concerns of the human being.

Zibechi adds that the forces of change have to look out horizontally, toward the interior of their own files, searching within the people themselves for the means of resolving problems, and in this way creating–and recreating–the new world of the oppressed.

Social Movements and Leftist Political Parties

Reviewing the situation of the social movements in Venezuela at the end of the 1990s, we can show that the election of Hugo Chávez was a response to the qualitative and quantitative growth of the social movements–and, in general, to the forces that opposed the existing politico-economic system. To appreciate this, we should outline in broad strokes the history of these movements prior to 1998.

The historian Margarita López Maya, who supported the Bolivarian Process during its first years, has for decades monitored and analyzed what she calls "the politics of the street": the genealogy, demands, and types of mobilization by popular, non-hegemonic groups and organizations.

From 1958 through the first years of the 1970s, her studies showed that the number of protests in Venezuela aimed at social rights (wage demands, public services, etc.) was almost the same as the number aimed at civic and political ends. The high number of protests with political motivations coincided with the period of armed guerrilla struggle, conducted especially by cells of the PCV and MIR, both of which had engaged in armed agitation on several fronts in the countryside and had also carried out sabotage and "propaganda

of the deed" in the principal cities. The highest percentage of violent protests (as a percentage of all protests) in the entire democratic period (1958 to
present) occurred in 1963, an election year in which the armed left called for
abstention; in that year, violent protests accounted for 47.7% of the total, and
64.3% of protests were motivated by political and ideological demands.[288] (This
is in stark contrast to the years 1973–1999, when social protests amounted to
75% of the total.)

The armed struggle reached its apogee in the years 1960–1969, with some
organizations continuing it until 1982. However, its impetus was never comparable to that of the insurgencies in other Latin American countries. In an
interview conducted for this book, Pablo Hernández Parra, who participated
in the Antonio José de Sucre Front, told us that, in total, the Venezuelan
guerrillas did not conduct more than ten offensive actions against military
objectives, but rather concentrated the majority of their efforts against civilian objectives, especially against persons they thought were informers, and
on defense against the army.

In 1968, the MEP (People's Electoral Movement), which split from Democratic Action, became the first far left political party to participate in a presidential election. It won the highest number of votes ever garnered by a leftist
political party in Venezuela until the 1990s: 719,461, which corresponded to
19.34% of the total.[289] The highest total came in 1993 when the La Causa
R presidential candidate, Andrés Velásquez, received more than 1.2 million
votes, which corresponded to 21.95% of the vote, although voter participation dropped sharply from that in the previous presidential election, from
81.92% in 1988 to 60.16% in 1993. [This seems to indicate a drastic overall
decrease in public confidence in the Venezuelan political system in the wake
of the Caracazo, and at the same time a distinct turn to the left among those
who retained faith in it.—tr.]

After the PCV renounced armed struggle, an important segment of the
party split off after questioning the PCV's support for the Soviet Union. So in
1971 the Movement Toward Socialism (MAS—Movimiento Al Socialismo)
was formed, and took part in elections from 1973 on. Its high point (in terms
of percentage of the vote) came in 1993 when it supported the Social Christian candidate, Rafael Caldera, who received approximately 600,000 votes,
10.59% of the total, and La Causa R received more than 1.2 million votes,
which corresponded to 21.95% of the vote .[290] Other leftist organizations,
such as the PCV and MIR, also participated in Venezuelan elections prior to
the ascension of Chávez in 1998, but none ever received more than 1% of
the vote.

López Maya offers an explanation of why all the efforts of the insurgent and electoral left didn't result in concrete organizational gains. The Venezuelan state, financed by petroleum income, was able to contain the protests of the 1970s through the mid 1980s. Its efficacy in minimizing conflicts in good part disarticulated attempts at independent organization of the popular sectors. Frequently, protests were simply the forerunners of negotiations between the union bosses and the political parties and institutions of the state, in a tripartite process (unions, businesses, government). This explains why, even when there were a lot of them, protests did not lead to social movements or organizations. With the sustained deterioration of the economy and the delegitimization of the political system at the end of the 1980s, the situation changed irreversibly. Protests took on a more pugnacious role in the political struggle, and redistributive demands could no longer be satisfied by the client-oriented and conciliationist mechanisms of the past.

The recession inaugurated by the economic crisis after the abrupt devaluation of Venezuelan currency in 1983 catalyzed the fragmentation of the conciliationist populism inaugurated in 1958. The conflict expressed in the sharpening of the politics of the street was not a result of agitation by the leftist political parties. This was demonstrated in 12 massive and spontaneous community demonstrations in 1988, all demanding rights. These prefigured like nothing else the crisis of governability brought to a head on February 27 and 28, 1989: the Caracazo.

The Caracazo

The Caracazo ["the Caracas blow" or "the Caracas explosion"] has been described as the first revolt in the world against neoliberalism. It took place on February 27, 1989 under Carlos Andrés Pérez, who in December 1988 won the presidency for the second time. During his first term, 1973–1978, he nationalized the petroleum industry and followed a full-employment policy, governing in the midst of a bonanza of income caused by the high price of oil, which was the product of crisis in the Middle East and OPEC. In 1988, he symbolically represented an epoch of prosperity, and the electorate returned him to office. (At that time, the prohibition against re-election of presidents was not absolute; the Constitution allowed it 10 or more years after a president left office.)

The then-president's excessive confidence in his popularity was one of the reasons why, after asking for financing from the International Monetary Fund, he applied an IMF-inspired austerity program. One of its measures, a steep hike in transportation prices, provoked a massive and violent popular protest, which was essentially a nationwide riot. In the various uprisings, those participating in them broke into warehouses and supermarkets and found in their storerooms the products that the merchants had been hoarding for weeks, in the expectation that the government would remove price controls.[291]

On February 28, the government suspended constitutional rights, while the army simultaneously put down the popular uprising with considerable violence. The official figures listed 276 dead, which didn't agree with the figures given by the deputies of the La Causa R party, who put the number at 379 dead. Student organizations, human rights groups, and foreign journalists estimated that there were more than a thousand victims of the military repression that followed the rioting.[292]

Angel Cappelletti, an intellectual Argentine academic who at the time resided in Venezuela, writes:

[The events of] February 27 signify a plebiscite, a profound, unusual affirmation of democracy. The people (from the margins to the middle class, from unemployed workers to students without a dime and university graduates without jobs) took to the streets demonstrating their faith in democratic principles, moved by the conviction that, all people being equal, everyone had the right to all the wealth society has to offer. . . . It's certain that neither the politicians nor the oligarchs were the direct objects of the people's anger, without doubt because they weren't on hand, or the "mob" didn't manage to reach them. The army rapidly and efficiently performed its essential task and made sure [the politicians/oligarchs] were not affected by the revenge of the people without a rag on their backs.[293]

The events of the Caracazo demonstrate that the democratic consensus imposed in 1958 was insufficient to meet the needs of the majority. So, the history of Venezuela can be divided into events before and after the Caracazo: the "before" characterized by the agreements reached behind closed doors by the principal political parties—Democratic Action and the Social Christians—and the "after" characterized by the appearance of a constellation of diverse, heterogenous social initiatives which did not have an organic, direct relationship with either the left parliamentary parties or insurgent organizations.

Some of these grassroots social groups and initiatives that began to appear in 1989 revived images of the national liberation struggles in Latin America. And these struggles did—with the exception of the student movement—have correlates in Venezuela. But the relation between the new social movements and the doctrinaire left organizations was cloudy, when it wasn't nonexistent.

Going back to the pacification of the leftist armed struggles in 1969, many expressions of resistance were concentrated in two sectors: the public universities and state cultural activities/management. It's reasonable to speculate that these two areas became "zones of tolerance" that were permitted because they served to alleviate the pressure of insurgent groups such as MAS and MIR that didn't want to participate in institutional or electoral struggles.

Researcher and activist Maria Pilar García-Guadilla believes that the new social movements had begun to gestate in the decade that effectively ended the armed-struggle period:

> At the end of the 1960s, new organizations and social movements sprang up in Venezuela that were different from the existing social organizations, not solely in their identities and strategies, but also in their objectives. We're not dealing here with corporate-like organizations such as the unions nor with formal social organizations that did not mix in the political sphere, such as the nonprofit foundations and civic associations, of which more than 300 existed in Venezuela in the 1960s. One is dealing with, on the contrary, social organizations that at times were structured, but at other times little structured, and which had, informally, a base in the principles of participation, equality, and social solidarity, and wanted to see the inclusion of these principles in the political environment; also, these groups were reclaiming their right to participate in decision making on matters that affected them, be it on a local, regional, or national scale."[294]

Demands from Below after the Caracazo

Reviewing the statistics on the number of and motivations for protests between 1990 and 1999 allows us to describe the tendencies of the most relevant social actors. In 1991, more than 70% of demonstrations were tied to failures in public services, especially lack of water and the poor physical condition of the schools.[295] This is in contrast, as we mentioned earlier, with the motivations for protests in the first years of Venezuelan democracy. Effectively, demands for economic and social rights widely surpassed political demands during the entire decade of the 1990s. In 1998, 78% of protests concerned economic and social rights, while only 18% concerned political demands.[296]

Secondary school and university students were notable actors in this epoch. The influence of the left—especially Red Flag (BR–Bandera Roja),

MAS, and in lesser measure the PCV—was clearest in this sector. BR was a marxist-leninist organization that had been one of the last to abandon the armed-struggle strategy, which accounts for its acceptance among student rebels.

Many students at the time were members of the Union of Revolutionary Youths (UJR), which at the beginning of the 1990s constituted the major "school of cadres." The UJR controlled an important number of student unions, which were called student centers. It fought many battles, which on several occasions resulted in students being killed by the police or military. These battles were fought over demands regarding the education sector (reduction of the education budget, rejection of privatization proposals, the poor condition of schools, and refusal of obligatory military service) or the nation as a whole (resignation of President Carlos Andrés Pérez, the high cost of living, or rejection of the abolition of certain labor rights). It's necessary to underline the existence of a clear class identity within these unions of students: after the murder of students by the police or military there were—with a certain degree of spontaneity—days of national protest.

The union organizations were a second factor in the conflict, especially in 1996 when the National coordinatorship for the Defense of the Present System of Social Services (Coordinadora Nacional por la Defensa del Actual Régimen de Prestaciones Sociales) was formed. More than 100 workers organizations—along with other civil groups—belonged to it.

The popular communities were also protagonists in the protests, which were of a spontaneous and reactive nature, demanding increased efficiency in the carrying out of the government's social policies. Community participation characterized many actions: the blockade of streets, rioting, the looting of supermarkets, etc., and the so-called civic strikes. These strikes resulted in paralysis of commerce, transport, and education, but were only of local scope. According to the records of the human rights group PROVEA, in 1992 there were 225 street blockades, 222 marches, 22 civic strikes, 17 lootings, and 11 riots. In 1994 there were 293 street blockades, 176 marches, 10 civic strikes, 32 lootings, and 11 riots. Four years later in 1998, some of these figures had diminished: 113 street blockades, 77 marches; 19 civic strikes, three lootings, and no riots.[297]

One communitarian experience from those years stands out, The Assembly of Caracas Barrios (Asamblea de Barrios de Caracas):

A space of interchange of debate and coordination, which was born from the roundtable of attendees at the First International Meeting on the Rehabilitation of Barrios. . . . The Assembly of Barrios, which lasted until 1993, came to unite representatives from more than 200 Caracas barrios around very diverse debates and proposals. . . . It had a key ingredient: the emphasis on discussions, proposals and struggles specific to barrios.[298]

One salient point here is that the demands of the barrio organizations and those of the leftist political parties and collectives had little in common. The leftist parties and collectives considered demands for public services or for the ending of evictions as reformist. Another point worth mentioning is that the persistence and strength of the Assembly of Barrios motivated a number of leftist organizations, including anarchist organizations, to attempt to take over the Assembly, and in doing so they brought their internal disputes with them.

The Caracazo events coincided with the founding of the first generation of Venezuelan human rights organizations. Between 1985 and 1989, three NGO began to raise human rights issues in the press: the Network of Support for Justice and Peace (Red de Apoyo para la Justicia y la Paz) in 1985; the Venezuelan Program of Education-Action on Human Rights (PROVEA— Programa Venezolano de Educación-Acción en Derechos Humanos) in 1988; and the Committee of the Families of the Victims of the Events in February and March 1989. These three organizations, along with other initiatives on human rights, diversified and enriched Venezuela's human rights terrain.

Venezuelan environmental groups during the 1990s developed growing levels of cooperation among themselves, with a basis in two events. The first was the approval of the Criminal Environmental Law in 1992, a piece of legislation which defined crimes against the environment and provided punishments for them. The second was the wide mobilization in 1997 to impede the Management and Regulation Plan for the Use of the Forest Reserve of Imataca. The Imataca Forest is one of the largest in Venezuela, consisting of nearly nine million acres along Venezuela's coast and the frontier with Guyana, and the Plan would have allowed large-scale exploitation of its mineral deposits and timber reserves. Both the Environmental Law and the Imitaca Plan stimulated widespread responses, via an informal, decentralized web of organizations. The responses were as diverse as street demonstrations, the issuing of reports, appearances in the communications media, and lobbying at high government levels. A few of the groups involved were the Venezuelan Federation of Environmental Organizations and Councils (Federación Venezolana de Organizaciones y Juntas Ambientales), Association of Friends of the Gran Sabana (Asociación de Amigos de la Gran Sabana), and the National Ecological and Social Union (Unión Nacional Ecológica y Social); there were many others.

A similar network, although smaller in scale, was constructed by the indigenous movement. In August 1990, 21 indigenous peoples formed the National Indigenous Council of Venezuela. In July 1993, two massacres of Yanomami people revealed the government's failure to defend indigenous communities, and that unleashed protests by a number of groups, including the Organization of Indigenous Peoples of Amazonas State (Organización de Pueblos Indígenas del Estado Amazonas) and the Regional Organization of the Indigenous Peoples of Zulia State (Organización de Pueblos Indígenas del Estado Zulia). The first of the massacres occurred in the Venezuela/ Brazil frontier region Parima-Surucucus in Amazona state, in which at least four indigenous people were murdered. The second occurred in the Wayumi community, and 16 to 20 indigenous people were slaughtered there. Both massacres were conducted by small-scale miners.

At the same time, a slow but perceptible expansion of counter-cultural initiatives increased the complexity of the dissident universe; and these initiatives/expressions were resistant to the mediation of political parties. The decade began with rock bands influenced by punk, new wave, and ska; and the music expressed the unrest of a generation. It was so popular that it was issued on a mass basis by the country's largest music companies. Sentimiento Muerto (Dead Sentiment), the band most representative of Venezuelan rock in the 1990s, reflects the climate of the decade with its song "Educacion anterior" (Previous Education) on its CD "El amor no existe" (Love Doesn't Exist):

> Politicians talk about youth
> They want us to work
> With the example they've given us
> Now I understand why we're unemployed
> How can they want me to do anything?

On a more underground level, there was a radically politicized punk current that, in the case of Caracas bands, developed two streams: one tied to the leftist political parties that were the inheritors of the armed-struggle tradition, and the other more universal and anarchist. The leftist bands included groups such as Holocausto, 27-F, Devastación, Víctimas de la Democracia, and Primero Venezuela; their logo was the same as that of the Socialist League

(Liga Socialista), with the addition of a mohawk. The anarchist bands included Allanamiento Moral, Autogestión, and Octavo Pasajero.

Leftist Local Governments and the Collapse
of the Traditional Parties

The events of 1989 prepared the ground for a number of lines of attack on the "democratic" regime that represented the interests of the existing powers. The Caracazo inaugurated a period characterized by a growing sense of ungovernability. Two political party organizations partially capitalized on the unrest: they took power locally in some areas, something no nontraditional party had done previously.

The first group was La Causa R, the most recent example of something new and organic on the Venezuelan left. It was founded by Alfredo Maneiro as a "movement of movements," including "alternative" unions, community groups, and, to a lesser extent, elements in the Central University of Venezuela. La Causa R created a space called The House of Calm Waters (La Casa del Agua Mansa) as a debating space, and it also issued various publications. In 1983 and 1988, it participated in the presidential elections, to little effect. However, it rose meteorically in the regional elections in 1989, vaulting to national prominence. In those elections, Andrés Velásquez, a worker and the leader of the union branch of La Causa R, won the governorship of the State of Bolivar; La Causa R candidates also won two mayoral races in the state, which is an important industrial region. In December 1992, days after the second attempted coup d'etat of the year, Velásquez won re-election by a wide margin, and the La Causa R candidate, Aristóbulo Istúriz, won the mayor's race in Caracas. In the presidential elections of 1993, the La Causa R candidate came in fourth place, but La Causa R did better in the congressional elections: it elected nine senators and 40 deputies, which made it the third largest party in the Congress, and which also made it the most successful Venezuelan leftist political party; those nine senators and 40 deputies far surpassed the number of leftist legislators ever elected in Venezuela by any other political party.

The second party organization that capitalized on the social convulsions of the 1990s was the Convergence party which, along with a multitude of small political organizations, created an electoral movement popularly known as El Chiripero ["the cockroach movement," so called because of the large number of small organizations that comprised it], which in 1993 supported the presidential candidacy of Rafael Caldera, who ended up with just over 30% of the popular vote, according to the figures from the government's National Electoral Council. However, only in the widest sense can one consider Caldera's candidacy as a break with the hegemony of the traditional parties. Caldera was the founder of the Social Christian COPEI party in the 1940s, and as a young deputy he defended the prohibition against the spread of Communist and anarchist ideas in Venezuela, stating on July 4, 1944 that he believed "in the most firm and sincere manner that there would be no benefit to the collectivity in lifting the very just, very legitimate, and very democratic suppression of anarchist and communist propaganda."[299]

During his first administration (1968–1973), Caldera was accused of violating human rights toward the end of the armed-struggle period in the country, and of infringing on the autonomy of universities by ordering the army to occupy them. Paradoxically—and paradox is something liberally strewn throughout Venezuelan history—two decades later he was supported by some of the same leftist organizations he had helped suppress 45 years earlier, including the MAS, the PCV, and the MEP.

After having been cast aside by the new generations of COPEI, the party he founded, Rafael Caldera returned to the battle in his capacity as senator for life [a post granted to ex-presidents] in an extraordinary session of the National Congress held hours after the attempted coup d'etat of February 4, 1992. He made a speech, taking advantage of the fact that it was being televised to the entire nation. The upshot of the speech was that the cure for the military attempt was total condemnation for the military men involved in the attempted coup. The former Social Christian president then broke with the country's elites:

> The country awaits another message . . . It's difficult to ask the people to immolate themselves for liberty and democracy, when one thinks that liberty and democracy are incapable of giving them something to eat and of impeding the exorbitant rise in the cost of living, when it hasn't been able to put an end to the sickness of corruption, which every day before the eyes of the world is consuming our institutions. This situation cannot be ignored.[300]

In harmony with the unease of the country, and in contrast to the majority of the ruling class, Rafael Caldera washed away in ten minutes his old political image and cast himself as the candidate of youth, as an aspirant in the presidential contest the coming year. His calculations didn't fail him.

The 1990s: A Turbulent and Tension-Filled Decade

The social dynamics of mobilization in Venezuela in the 1990s were complex, not aligned with the political parties, and with dissimilar levels of connection among their parts. Things were neither mechanical nor linear. The [various social movements and upheavals] during the 1960s and 1970s were intermittent in their intensity; ithey ebbed and flowed. The 1990s were similar in that respect. In December 1995, the human rights group PROVEA stated, in its annual report:

In the last three reports, which cover October 1991 through September 1994, the average number of peaceful demonstrations was more than a thousand per year, contrasting with 581 over the period we're analyzing [October 1994 through September 1995]. In sum, there's a decrease of around 40%, which seems to have a relation to the demobilized, apathetic social situation; to this we can add confirmation of a tendency noted in 1994, in which political-globalization demands and proposals from, in particular, the popular movements and civil society in general, were almost absent from the local, regional, and national panoramas.

In its annual report published three years later in December 1998, the month in which Hugo Chávez won the presidency for the first time, PROVEA stated:

Beginning with 1994, popular expectations of the government of Dr. Caldera, who offered to reverse the neoliberal economic policies; the participation in the government of progressive and leftist forces that had previously participated in the popular protest but who now opposed or contained it; the absence of leadership and political proposals that unify the popular movement and civil society; and the effects of the economic crisis have influenced a large part of the population to invest their time in satisfying their own needs and ensuring their own economic survival to the impairment of their participation in matters of public interest, be they social or political . . ."

In the 1990s, the visions of a different world were fragmented and isolated, without pretensions of totality. Mobilizations were, mostly, defensive reactions against governmental policies. With the exception of La Causa R taking local power between 1989 and 1995 in Bolivar State, there were no other concrete examples of development of a counter-hegemonic political culture.

The forces of the left focused on access to local budgets to develop social-welfare policies, when not ensuring mere personal survival; likewise, the left sought places of power within university administrations, without taking initiatives that would have resounded in the halls of academia, or flown in the face of the dominant values and practices. There were few community means of communication, and few radical or alternative publications to bring to national or regional attention the proposals, debates, and accusations of the social sectors in conflict. But there were several anarchist and leftist periodicals at the time, including *La Voz de los Trabajadores*, *Correo A*, *El Libertario*, and *Tribuna Popular*. Theoretical elaboration was scarce, and independent, radical book publishing houses were even scarcer. Except for Editorial Ruptura, which belonged to the PRV, and Centauro Ediciones the only leftist and social movement publishing was done via the universities. Public debates were limited to the universities—with all the academic overtones that implies—as were commemorations of historical events, such as the Cuban revolution, the deaths of students massacred by police, and the armed struggle in Venezuela. The social collectives, including organizations of the left such as BR and the PCV, didn't have public sites where they could hold cultural or political activities, or even remembrances of their own historical events. In the decade of the 1990s there was no library or center of documentation beyond those supported by the state where one could research, for example, the history of armed struggle in Venezuela. This says much about the left's priorities and weaknesses in the decade.

But not everything was wrong with grassroots social dynamics in the 1990s. One must contrast the above limitations with the relative youth of Venezuelan non-political-party-oriented civil society, which was developing in the context of a worsening local economic crisis; as well, it was developing while projects aimed at transforming the world were at a low ebb, following the dissolution of the Eastern Bloc. The internal dynamics of social struggles in Venezuela involved the development of relationships among the oppressed, which among other things allowed them to help ensure their [mutual] survival. As well, one should realize that the potential and capabilities of social movements are not static but dynamic, and such movements appear and disappear in complex situations. If the will for change in Venezuelan society displayed different [and often depressing] symptoms during the 1990s, at the end of the decade the initiatives from those on the bottom were in the full process of self-configuration, recomposition, and development.

284. Mikhail Bakunin, "The Paris Commune and the Idea of the State" http://flag.blackened.net/daver/anarchism/bakunin/paris.html

285. Holloway, op. cit.

286. "Recuperar la autonomía: propuesta libertaria par el momento actual," *El Libertario*, No. 52, March 2008.

287. Raúl Zibechi, *La mirada horizontal. Movimientos sociales y emancipación*. Editorial Nordan: Montevideo, 1999.

288. Margarita López Maya, *Del viernes negro al referendo revocatorio*. Alfadil Ediciones: Caracas, 2005.

289. Consejo Nacional Electoral, "Elecciones Presidenciales: Cuadro Comparativo 1958–2000."

290. Ibid.

291. PROVEA, *Informe anual octubre 1989-septiembre 1990 sobre la situación de los derechos humanos en Venezuela*. PROVEA: Caracas, 1990.

292. Ibid.

293. Angel Cappelletti, "La epifanía de los cerros o la sinceración democrática." *Revista Orto*, No. 21, May-August 2001.

294. Maria Pila García-Guadilla, "El movimiento ambientalista y la constitucionalización de nuevas racionalidades: dilemas y desafios." Revista Venezolana de Economía y Ciencias Sociales, Vol. 7, No. 1, January–April 2001, pp. 113–132.

295. PROVEA, *Informe anual octubre 1990–septiembre 1991 sobre la situación de los derechos humanos en Venezuela*. PROVEA: Caracas, 1991.

296. López Maya, op. cit.

297. PROVEA, *Informe anual octubre 1993–septiembre 1994 sobre la situación de los derechos humanos en Venezuela*. PROVEA: Caracas, 1994; and PROVEA, *Informe anual octubre 1998–septiembre 1999 sobre la situación de los derechos humanos en Venezuela*. PROVEA: Caracas, 1999

298. Andrés Antillano, "La lucha por el reconocimiento y la inclusión en los barrios populares: la experiencia de los comités de Tierras urbanas." *Revista Venezolana de Economía y Ciencias Sociales*, Vol. 11, No. 3, September 2005.

299. Corina Yoris-Villasana, *18 octubre de 1945: legitimidad y ruptura del hilo constitutional*. Universidad Católica Andrés Bello: Caracas, 2004.

300. Rafael Caldera, speech to a joint session of congress, February 4, 1994. (Link no longer available)

March of "informal sector" workers in Caracas in December 2007

Public sector healthcare workers march in Caracas
in August 2009 demanding labor rights

CHAPTER 6
The Bolivarian Political Process

In March 1994, after two years in prison for his involvement in the attempted coup d'etat in February 1992, Hugo Chávez was pardoned by President Rafael Caldera. In 1995 and 1996, Chávez crisscrossed the country expounding the strategy of insurrection and electoral abstention of his organization, MBR-200. Despite propounding this position, in 1997 Chávez created the Movimiento V Repúblicano (MVR); and the following year he was its candidate for president.

The MVR, in the wake of the wave of discontent that followed the Caracazo, correctly analyzed the situation and gathered the diverse social currents to its diffuse ideology, giving the impression that its "electoral Bolivarianism" was the legitimate expression of the social initiatives and the left in Venezuela. On December 6, 1998, Hugo Chávez won power with 56.2% of the votes, a total of 3,673,685.

Many of Chávez's protagonists have loudly proclaimed throughout the world that he radicalized Venezuelan democracy and that because of this, massive, enthusiastic majorities have taken part [supported Chávez's candidates and policies] in subsequent elections. If so, this is coherent with a revolutionary process. If a radical change in political direction favored the people, they would show their support for it via, among other methods, the vote. But the official figures give lie to this contention.

Participation in all three of the years in which Chávez was up for election—1998, 2000 (after a constitutional change requiring an election), and 2006—was significantly lower than at the high point of Venezuelan electoral participation, 1968. And, overall, participation has been declining ever since then. One need only look at historical participation rates (supplied by the National Electoral Council) to confirm this: 1958, 93.42 %; 1963, 92.21%; 1968, 96.73%; 1973, 96.52%; 1978, 87.55%; 1983, 87.75%; 1988, 81.92%; 1993, 60.16%; 1998, 63.45%; 2000, 56.31%; 2006, 74.7%. It's worth noting that four years after the Caracazo (which took place in 1989) there was a huge decrease in participation, and that, overall, this decrease has persisted under Hugo Chávez.

A critical reader could object that the rate of participation increased between 2000 and 2006, and that one could interpret that as reflecting the taking hold of the Bolivarian Process and a subsequent increase in voter enthusiasm. But let's look at regional elections. One expects a decrease in participation in off-year elections (as compared with presidential elections), which is normal in a politics-as-usual situation. But what about a revolutionary situation, where the effects of revolutionary change are most strongly felt in day-to-day life? In such a situation, one would expect high participation in local elections. In November 2008, mayoral and state governmental elections took place. According to the CNE, only 65.6% of voters took part in those elections. These results lead to the conclusion that Hugo Chávez has injected enthusiasm into the presidential election process, but not into the local races where one would expect increased enthusiasm and participation as a reflection of a truly revolutionary process—if such a process existed.

Neutralizing the Powers of the Multitude

When the Chiripero (see pages 163–164) succeeded in putting Rafael Caldera in power in 1993, it represented a break with the practice of Democratic Action and the Social Christians taking turns in the presidential palace (something which commenced in 1958 with the signing of the Pact of Punto Fijo).(See page 123) Caldera's election generated a level of expectations only comparable, in a Latin American context, to that which existed with the fall of the PRI in Mexico in 2000.* Needless to say, Caldera blew the opportunity. (See pages 164–165)

After the landslide that carried Hugo Chávez to power, who in a few months had overcome the lead of Irene Sáez—a former beauty queen who at one point held a huge lead in the polls—as well as the ancient rivals Democratic Action and the Social Christians, who felt obligated to close ranks around a single candidate, the Bolivarian Movement began to dissolve the social web that carried it to power. The dispersion, diversity, and fragmentation of the wide movement of the discontented, which had translated to votes for Chávez, obligated Chávez to crowd it out in order to neutralize the seismic potential [of such movements of the discontented] revealed nearly a decade earlier during the Caracazo. The first step in this direction was the

* The Partido Revolucionario Institucional (originally the Partido Nacional Revolucionario) is the utterly corrupt, brutal, and authoritarian political party which ruled Mexico from 1929 to 2000. It currently holds power in most Mexican states and has a plurality in the Mexican congress.

convening of a Constituent Assembly, which would *relegitimize* the powers of the state and to draft a new Constitution that would *refound* the republic.[301] This was an early and important manifestation of one of the most important characteristics of the Bolivarian Movement: the electoralization of the citizen-participation movements.

On April 25, 1999, an advisory referendum approved the calling of the Constituent Assembly; on July 27 the members were elected; and on November 17 a referendum approved the new Constitution. Researchers Nelly Arenas and Luís Gómez Calcaño, in *Populismo Autoritario: Venezuela 1999–2005*, describe the moment: "Given that the so-called revolution sprang from an initially conspiratorial—and therefore vanguardist—project, that transformed itself almost overnight into a heterogenous electoral movement, it had neither the time nor opportunity to build an organized, social base." The leaders of the left, now inside the Bolivarian Process, argued for the necessity of organizing [the popular movements] as *bases of support* for President Chávez. Veteran Venezuelan journalist Guillermo García Ponce declared in an interview:

> I would say the fundamental failing is the lack of organization of the people, of their organized participation in the management of the government and the consequential weaknesses in the political and ideological formation of those who participate in the process . . . Until now the process has developed with the support of the armed forces, the charismatic character of the President and his great oratorical powers, and the national demand for change, but it lacks the organized, united, and conscious people.[302]

The events of 1999 were key in initiating the path of institutionalization of the forces that operated outside of the state, and of incorporating them into its ambit. In the first place, it's necessary to emphasize the fact that the calling of the Constituent Assembly was not a result of the social movements. In 1994, a number of organizations had called for such an assembly, but their appeal "didn't find an echo in the people, being perceived as far from popular sentiment."[303] Until 1998 it didn't appear on the list of demands of the social movements. In that year, it became one of the promises of the Patriotic Pole, the coalition that supported Chávez.

The new regime rapidly managed to institutionalize the social movements, first through the selection of the delegates to the Constituent Assembly, and later in the new state bureaucracy. In these processes, a group of leaders [of the social movements] was isolated from the body of the movements. This separation congealed into the separation of those who issue orders and those who take them. In the language of the Zapatistas, the leaders didn't command obedience, but began their training in demanding command.

The triumph of Hugo Chávez and the Constituent Assembly process snatched from the social movements their zeal for social renewal; they took on an agenda and an identity far from their origins, and that agenda and identity were within the new power structure. In this sense, the scenario for the local ecological movement, visualized by the researcher and activist María Pilar García-Guadilla, was fulfilled:

> If the inclusion of the demands and values of the environmental movement in the new Constitution opened a space for the creation of new and more democratic relations with the state, it could also have had negative effects on the autonomy and survival of the environmental movement. There are two outstanding challenges: Once the visions and values promoted by the [environmental] movement have been institutionalized, there might emerge differences in interpretation of conflicts that would destroy the previous unity and that would reduce the effective power of the movement . . . Another consequence of institutionalization could be political demobilization . . . the politicization of the leaders of the environmental movement and their transformation into political actors . . . that would create a vacuum in leadership of the movement, and would foster the cooptation of [its] elected representatives.[304]

Let's make it clear that we're not evaluating the Constitution of 1999 as a product, but rather as a process whose unspoken motivation was to transform anti-systemic dynamics into state powers, as well as to instill the belief in the efficacy of public officialdom. The elections and the subsequent adoption of the new Constitution in 1999, including what was destined to become the content of a new social pact, were imposed from above, with more emphasis on the results than on the process. In this manner, the Bolivarian Movement was rapidly molded by those in power into an organic unity very different from the cohesion of its different grassroots currents. As a consequence, it manifested itself in a vertical manner, responding to the mobilizations called by elites in a manner typical of the electoral process. It adopted as its own a statist discourse, and became systematized in a series of hierarchies.[305]

The Constitution of 1999 was an advance over the Constitution of 1961 as regards human rights. Given the characteristic "progress" in the field of human rights over the years, it could hardly have been otherwise. Nonetheless, as we've discussed previously, the new Constitution tied Venezuela to economic globalization.

The state did not have the power to contain the multiplicity of social movements and dynamics prior to 1999, but after Chávez's election it homogenized them and swallowed them whole. As a natural consequence, centralization was followed by cooptation. Time and again the elites have defined the reasons for mobilizations, their form, and even the manner in which participants should organize themselves.

To confirm this, we'll evaluate the principal forms of "popular participation" that are promoted in the Bolivarian government's propaganda: the Bolivarian Circles, the Cooperatives, the Seized Factories, and the Community Communications Media.

The Bolivarian Circles: A Laboratory of State Cooptation

The idea of organizing nuclei composed of a few persons and distributed around the country sprang from the head of Hugo Chávez when he was a presidential candidate. In a book of interviews, published before his first electoral victory, the leader of the Bolivarian Process stated:

> We're going about forming electoral circles, with a base in what Simón Bolivar outlined during the process of forming Bolivia, of the electoral power of the people, including placing them as an additional power . . . We, taking a little of that, revising it of course, are taking this to the grassroots, trying to install it in every hall, every site, wherever is possible, to organize an electoral circle of five, ten persons, and [we intend] that this will go on multiplying like a huge network.[306]

On June 10, 2001, on his radio program *Aló Presidente*, Hugo Chávez called upon his followers to organize themselves into Bolivarian circles:

> We're going to organize everyone into Bolivarian Circles of fishermen, Bolivarian Circles of women, Bolivarian Circles of farm workers, Bolivarian Circles of young people . . . [B]efore ending the program, we're going to offer this: you can fax or telephone to give us the lists of the Bolivarian Circles; remember, between seven and eleven [participants], because it's always good to have uneven numbers in this type of thing, and that's also a recommendation for the hours of decision and discussion. It's good between seven and eleven, in order to be the most efficient, correct, and remember that I'm going to start giving instructions as the leader . . . and I thank you for recognizing this and that you'll continue to recognize it.[307]

Even if this organizational form was popular among Chávez's followers, there was never a verifiable number of participants. In October 2001, Diosdado Cabello, Minister of the Office of the Presidency, stated that there were 10,000 participants,[308] while other officials stated that there were three million participants.[309]

Even though the Bolivarian Circles defined themselves as a nongovernmental organization, this was not credible given their ties to the government.[310] Their organizational manuals made this clear: "The maximum leader of the Bolivarian Circles will be the President of the Bolivarian Republic of Venezuela. The national and international site in which registrations of Bolivarian Circles will be compiled is the Miraflores Palace [Venezuela's presidential palace]."[311] The only requirement for Bolivarian Circles was to be Bolivarian. The objective was to give impetus to the construction, consolidation, and development of the objectives of the 1999 Constitution, under the ideological orientation of the independence heroes Simón Bolivar, Ezequiel Zamora, and Simón Rodríguez.

In March 2002, President Chávez announced that 140 billion Bolivars—about $62.5 million US—would be delivered to the Bolivarian Circles for community initiatives.[312] Later that year—and the next—the Bolivarian Circles undertook important mobilization work on behalf of the government, especially during the failed coup d'etat of April 2002. They were also active at the end of that year, when the general strike [which included the petroleum strike] was called by FEDECAMARAS and by the primary opposition-controlled union federation, the CTV.

On December 15–17, 2003, the Bolivarian Circles held their first and only ideological congress, with about 700 delegates attending. One account of the congress states that the majority of the concerns raised at the congress had to do with how the Circles could effectively participate in matters of state. The first of these concerns had to do with the coming (October 2004) mayoral and state elections, and the possibility of choosing candidates via grassroots elections; but in the end, Hugo Chávez chose the candidates. The second concern was maintaining direct contact with comandante Chávez, without intermediaries. The third concern was to ask the government for more resources for Circle projects. The fourth was to dislodge infiltrators and corruption from public organisms. The fifth was to participate in the planning and execution of government programs, such as the Local Public Planning Councils. And, finally, the sixth was the desire to hold periodic regional and municipal congresses.[313]

The true work of the Bolivarian Circles was to aid in the implementation of the social policies, the "missions," in the people's zones. However, there were also accusations about the training of these cells as combative civil forces to confront oppositional protests, and to control turf in the people's zones. The first National Coordinator of the Bolivarian Circles was army general Miguel Rodríguez Torres, who left the political police (DISIP) to organize the Bolivarian Circles and then, in 2002, returned to DISIP as its head.[314]

In 2004, the Bolivarian Circles model of organization was in crisis. First, because the calling of a recall referendum against the president imposed, from above, new political priorities. In order to undertake an electoral campaign and to mobilize voters on election day, the government created the Units of Electoral Battle (UBEs). The goal was the creation of 8,500 UBEs, as well as 130,000 Electoral Patrols (Patrullas Electorales), each composed, in theory, of 10 members, which would add up to a total of 1,300,000 patrollers.[315] This siphoned off energy from the Bolivarian Circles.

The second problem was the internal conflicts within the Bolivarian Circles about who would exercise control, after Chávez. Two coalitions disputed hegemony within the movement: the National Front of Bolivarian Circles (Frente Nacional de Círculos Bolivarianos) and the National Network of Bolivarian Circles (Red Nacional de Círculos Bolivarianos). These two groups traded accusations of corruption, influence peddling, and authoritarianism.

After his victory in the recall referendum, Hugo Chávez organized his support into new, hierarchical types of organization, such as the Units of Endogenous Social Battle (Unidades de Batalla Endógenas Sociales), which were created by decree from the former Units of Electoral Battle. The members of the Bolivarian Circles, without debate, joined the new organization. The former national coordinator of the Circles, Rodrigo Cháves, declared in 2005 that "[T]he Bolivarian Circles are being minimized, because even though they are a symbolic element of the Bolivarian movement and play a protagonistic role, the process has changed and with it the structure."[316] Without consulting the Circles, which according to some government officials had three million members, the leftist intellectuals in the government justified the effective death of the Bolivarian Circles and the adoption of new forms of social organization.

The journalist and director Aram Aharonian of the Telesur TV network notes:

There was an added value at the end of the [2004] referendum campaign: the political machine which mobilized 900,000 volunteers was now converted . . . into a social and economic machine to defend the national process of change. Now it discharged its energies into the "social battle." With the same impetus and commitment, the [electoral] patrollers set about taking [control] over the social and social-assistance challenges of the dispossessed masses, applying the same logistics. It's an attempt at social oversight of the work of the communities . . . It's a defense structure of the Bolivarian Revolution . . .[317]

As can easily be seen, the social dynamics of the Bolivarian Circles did not surge from the heart of the popular social movements, which had mortgaged their autonomy when they assumed an electoral agenda; rather, the Circles were a concerted effort to support the objectives and priorities of the power elite. If the constituent process had been the first test grounds in the institutionalization of the social movements, the Bolivarian Circles demonstrated the capacity of the government to create, direct, and dissolve–according to the needs of the moment–channels for the cooptation of its base of support

The Community Councils, or the Discreet Charm
of Third World Revolution

In September 2005, we [Caracas' anarchists] received an e-mail from Sao Paolo notifying us of an upcoming visit to Venezuela by Michael Albert and Lydia Sargent, the editors of *Z Magazine*. The e-mail invited us to contact Ezequiel Adamovsky, the Argentinian who would act as their translator during a possible meeting with us in Caracas. Since 1999, we've met with dozens of people who have traveled to Venezuela from all corners of the Earth to observe directly what is called the Bolivarian Revolution and to hear the views of the local anarchists on it. On this occasion we would be hosting well known writers whose opinions we had read on the Internet, and so instead of a private meeting we planned an open forum which we called "The Global Resistance Movement: A View from Argentina and the United States." Our Argentine friend, Ezequiel Adamovsky, who works for the *El Rodaballo* ("The Flounder") magazine and who is a participant in the public assemblies in his country, accepted the proposal. We produced a flyer which we photocopied and distributed in the usual places, and also made an announcement on the Internet. A few days later, Ezequiel decided that he preferred a private meeting rather than a public forum. We didn't understand why, but we agreed.

On the date we met, October 21, the night in Caracas was cool and clear. One of us had gone to pick up Michael Albert, Lydia Sargent, and Ezequiel at the place they were staying, the Embassy Suites Hotel in the eastern part of Caracas. Traffic was heavy enough that it delayed the start of the meeting, but it was a nice evening and we waited. I don't know if Albert had an exhausting day or was bothered by the long ride through the crowded streets of Caracas, but upon arriving the first thing that he said was that anyone who speaks against George Bush was an ally. There were no cordial greetings, no outstretched hands, no "good to meet you" pleasantries—only silence.

Normally in these types of meetings visitors attentively listen to what we have to say, to our version of affairs, our version of history, and then they contrast it with other versions they've heard during their visit. This time things were different. Michael Albert took it upon himself to explain the political situation in Venezuelan to the dozen Venezuelans who had patiently awaited his arrival. According to Albert, he had been meeting the prior week with government officials at various levels in order to familiarize himself with the intentions of the government. One meeting after another. When we asked him if he'd had any contact with the community or with any social organizations in their habitats, their spheres of action, he said no. His first experiences of the Bolivarian Process occurred in one air-conditioned office after another, save for the night on which we met. The following day, Albert left the country.

Michael Albert's anarchist perspective [on Venezuela] seemed strange to us, and it seems even stranger given that he appears to have accepted as true each and every statement made by officials whose salary depends on speaking well of the government they serve. The night Albert met with us, thanks to Adamovsky's translation, we learned of a Venezuela in which for the first time in their lives the poor had access to education and health care, where the functioning of the ministries was based in assemblies, and where flowers spontaneously broke through the pavement. During Albert's presentation, which we followed attentively, there was a moment in which Albert lowered his voice and told us that the officials of the state petroleum company, PDVSA—which Chávez had supposedly nationalized—had told him of a plan they'd devised to expropriate the multinational oil companies whose talons were sunk into the country. (Months later we learned that the plan of expropriation consisted of "mixed enterprises.")

And he ceded no credibility to our arguments. According to Albert, our allegations "had to be corroborated." (One presumes he'd corroborated all of the allegations from the government officials he'd visited.) The only smile during that visit with Albert came when we suggested that he watch *Nuestro petróleo y otros cuentos*, which had just appeared with English subtitles thanks to an Indymedia collective affiliated with the radical U.S. environmental group Earth First! This suggestion was met with a grimace.

When Michael Albert told us about the imminent creation of a network of popular organizations, which would turn subcomandante Marcos and the Zapatistas green with envy, we told him about the history of the Bolivarian Circles—something which, of course, had to be corroborated. Albert insisted that he had seen with his own eyes convincing and impressive diagrams of popular networks in the offices of (army) General Jorge Luís García Carneiro's Ministry of Popular Participation and Social Development. From there on the conversation became intolerable for him, for us, and, especially, for the translator. Michael Albert, in that no man's land that divides a heated conversation from a shouting match, told us that he wanted his book on participatory economics to be printed by the millions and distributed free on the streets of Caracas. One of our compañeras then told the Harvard-graduate economist that he was an ignoramus. To date, Albert's books have not been freely distributed in Caracas.[318]

All this is pertinent owing to the fact that the Powerpoint diagrams that so impressed Albert in the Ministry of Popular Participation and Social Development's offices correspond to the Community Councils (CCs—Consejos Comunales), the organizing form that supplanted the Bolivarian Circles and the Units of Endogenous Social Battle. Their origis dates to June 12, 2002, when the Law of the Local Public Planning Councils (CLPP—Ley de los Consejos Locales de Planificación Pública) was enacted. Its purpose was defined as the incorporation of the citizenry in the planning process for municipal-level public policies and programs. In this law, the Community Councils were mentioned for the first time: "[T]he members of CLPP will be obligated to fulfill their functions to the benefit of the collective interests; they will maintain a permanent tie with the networks of parochial and community councils."[319]

The functioning of the CLPP in practice was limited by the municipal governments themselves, which rejected the permanent comptroller role the law assigned to them. The researcher María Pilar García-Guadilla stated in a report: "[S]ome mayors, as much members of the opposition as officialists [Chávez supporters], have felt threatened as regards their functioning and have put impediments in the path of conforming to the law. . ."[320] However, the jealousy of the authorities was not the only obstacle. Other factors were the legal vacuum regarding Community Council election proceedings; fraud in those proceedings; the naming, in many instances, of officials of mayoralties and municipal councils as representatives of the communities; and the absence of financial resources for community projects."[321]

This situation makes clear that the need to generate social mobilization with electoral ends was the impulse behind the Community Councils. In January 2007, after being elected to a second presidential term, Hugo Chávez announced his next governing program called Five Constituent Motors. One of these "motors" was the enabling faculty, through which the president, in the Council of Ministers, could proclaim laws without consulting the legislature or the people. A second "motor" was reform of the Constitution, for which it was necessary to hold a referendum, which took place at the end of 2007. The third was an educational crusade. The fourth was the implementation of a "new geometry of power." The final "motor" was called "explosion of Community Power." Hugo Chávez describes it:

> This motor of the Bolivarian Socialist Project is that with the most power. But this explosion . . . of the Community Power is going to depend for its development on the success of the other four motors. It's going to depend on the laws [created through the] enabling [motor] to a good extent, on the reform of the Constitution, on the National Moral and Illuminating Journey,[322] on the new geometry of power, and on other factors. That's why it's urgent that we take up the task immediately.[323]

Barely three months after this announcement, the Law of the Community Councils was approved without input from the grassroots. Once again, a form of organization was imposed from above, from outside of the social movements, and was formulated on paper prior to being put into practice.

This is how the Community Councils were tied directly to Chávez's executive power: They were separated from the CLPP; the Organic Law of Municipal Public Power was reformed to suppress their relationships with the mayoralties and parochial councils; and presidential commissions were formed with the specific goal of tying the Community Councils to the regime. [324] The crowning touch was that the official in charge of organizing the Community Councils from above was an army man, General Jorge Luís García Carneiro, the Minister of Popular Participation and Social Development. In February 2006, García Carneiro announced his goal of creating 50,000 Community Councils nationwide. Eight months later there were 16,720.

One of the purposes of the CCs was that they receive financial resources to help develop community projects. The Law of the Community Councils provided for direct transfer of resources from the government. García Carneiro, before evaluating a single project, announced that each proposal would be funded to the tune of 30 million Bolivars (around $13,000), paid through the fund established for that purpose: 2.2 billion Bolivars, equivalent to about $982 million US.

At the same time, García Carneiro told the CCs that in addition to receiving money for their projects they would be responsible for selecting mothers in the barrios who would receive a state subsidy: "[T]he Community Councils will have as a responsibility the conducting of a census of housewives, who will receive economic aid of 388,000 Bolivars [about $173 US] monthly."[325] At the time, that constituted about 95% of what a minimum-wage worker earned—405,000 Bolivars in the urban zones. All of this government largesse was, of course, made possible because of income from the petroleum industry.

The Community Councils as a Subordinate Social Movement

The Law of Community Councils impeded from the start the possibility of Community Council autonomy. Its Article 2 states that they have to register with the Local Presidential Commission of Popular Power, the final link in the hierarchic chain. That is to say, the ultimate coordinating organism is the National Presidential Commission of Popular Power, which is appointed by the president (Article 30), which in turn appoints the Regional Presidential Commission of Popular Power "subject to approval by the President of the Republic" (Article 31), which in turn appoints the Local Presidential Commission of Popular Power for each municipality, "subject [of course] to approval by the President of the Republic" (Article 32). In the world of the Community Councils, all roads lead to Caracas (and the Miraflores Palace).

The environmental activist and researcher María Pilar García-Guadilla has investigated the experiences of the CCs. Here are some of her conclusions:

In a manner similar to the other community organizations that sprang forth under the shelter of the Constitution of 1999, the Community Councils give the appearance of being a communitarian actor with the capacity to self-diagnose the problems in their ambit, of stimulating the strengthening of communities and their roots in the geographic spaces they inhabit, and of raising the potential of the community groups that have sprung forth as a consequence of the policies of President Chávez. [But] the objectives and the rhetoric from most of the political, social, and governmental actors about Community Councils do not correspond to practice. While the president's objectives and rhetoric concern empowerment, transformation, and democratization, the observed practices point toward dependent clients, cooptation, centralization, and exclusion for political reasons. To deliver resources to the communities when there exist neither the expertise nor the mechanisms that ensure transparency, makes the Community Councils vulnerable to [unfounded] demands, dependent-client practices, and cooptation . . . Up till now, the majority of the Community Councils lack the capacity to go beyond small changes and improvements in the areas they occupy. They lack, also, the capacity to enrich social and cultural identities, and so contribute to the pluralism of urban ways of life because they do not impel movement toward an autonomous, alternative, and pluralistic society, one separate from the state that permits hegemony [top-down control] in the matter of social transformation.[326]

The Community Councils as basic organizing cells created by the government have always been pressured to undertake functions far from those relating to their communitarian ambit: in the first place, functions of the PSUV (which was created in 2006 to supplant the MVR). The CCs have been pressured to integrate themselves into the PSUV's proselytizing activities, and into the creation and training of cadres. In the second place, [they've been pressured] to take on security and defense functions, following the social-intelligence policing theory developed by Bolivarian government officials.

On July 9, 2009, the Bolivarian News Agency revealed that 450 members of the Community Councils in Caracas had participated in "Forum II," an organizing meeting called by DISIP, the political police. The stated purpose of the Forum, which was held in the Military Academy Theater in Fort Tiuna, was to create a network of social intelligence among the Community Councils, DISIP, and the army.[327]

Another facet of this government use of the Community Councils is the integration of the CCs into the National Bolivarian Militia, a force of civilians with military training that forms part of the Venezuelan army. On September 29, 2008, the commander of the National Bolivarian Militia stated: "Our goal is to organize and register 15 million Venezuelans in the militia. How do we plan to do this? Well, we calculate that in the future, in the medium term, we'll have 50,000 Community Councils in the country. If we manage to register persons in each of them, then we'll have it."[328]

A third facet of the police/military functions delegated to the Community Councils is their participation in citizen security work in the barrios in cooperation with the so-called Community Police. As can be seen in the *Manual de normas y procedimientos del servicio de policía comunal* ("Manual of Rules and Procedures of the Community Police Service"), this involves coordination with the CCs on local security and crime-prevention activities (Article 4.1). Three of the functions played by the Community Police are 1) To identify the principal causes that produce criminal behavior in every community; 2) To foment the creation of Integral Safety and Prevention Committees in Community Councils throughout the nation; and 3) To create plans of action to prevent and control crime, in coordination with the communities.

One of the primary activities of the Community Police is the construction of a "network of primary information" along with conducting a "diagnostic" to "have an optimal familiarity in their area of responsibility." This "diagnostic," as the manual clearly states, should detail socioeconomic and demographic information, along with expectations and worries of the populace, and should also include information on territorial extent, native and foreign population, organizations in which community members participate, the transit and public order situations, and "all of the problematic things that affect the order and tranquility of the community."[329] Is this a policy designed to combat lack of personal safety or to give the government eyes and ears in every community?

Of course it's possible to find Community Councils all across the country that have established cooperatives, constructed sports fields, or planted trees in the local plaza.[330] This is in line with their being executors of small-scale good works while being directly accountable to the central government.[331] Having said that, the CCs have restricted autonomy, are instruments of the central government's power, and have not generated a political culture different from the forms of citizen participation developed in the country since the coming of democracy in 1958.

The Committee of Victims Against Impunity, a popular organization formed by family members of victims of police abuse, puts it like this:

> [W]e maintain that [the CCs] constitute a para-governmental organizing apparatus and have been promoted by the state itself. There exists sufficient evidence to demonstrate that this community organization has come to respond to partisan interests . . . [T]he good will of the individuals who provide organizational life to the Community Councils does not negate the clear fact that the Community Councils are organisms of the Venezuelan state, which has promoted and financed them, and provided them with legal status, with a purpose that is nothing but the control of the popular movement.[332]

There have been a growing number of accusations against CCs regarding irregularities in the handling of resources delivered to the Councils [by the central government] for development in their areas. In 2007, for example, the human rights group PROVEA revealed that 70.4% of the accusations it was aware of regarding the construction of housing tied the CCs to "presumed acts of corruption, use of poor quality materials, shoddy construction, structural failures, as well as failure to complete projects."[333] Lamentably, the Community Councils have become executors of state policies, and have therefore rapidly been beset by the vices common to the government apparatus.

Bolivarian Cooperatives

In 1998, the year Hugo Chávez was first elected, the number of cooperatives registered in the country was 762. The Special Cooperative Associations Law was passed in 2001. In 2006, authors Betsy Bowman and Bob Stone estimated that there were 108,000 co-ops in the country.[334] Later that year some government officials estimated that there were 250,000.

In the years 2004–2006, many leftist media outlets on the international level reported on the "cooperative boom" taking place in Venezuela. The promotion of cooperatives constituted one of the pillars of "endogenous" economic development in the country. Nelson Freitez, a researcher of the cooperative movement, explains the ascendancy of cooperatives in Venezuela: The official promotion gave the impression that credit from the state was a subsidy rather than a loan that had to be repaid. Also, the knowledge and skills were in place for the creation and legal registration of cooperatives, and abundant financial credit resources were available. And the official promotion of cooperatives stressed the ease of creation rather than how demanding [running cooperatives] often is. An additional factor was that the attempt to create a cooperative economy was maintained through the intentions of the people and the transference of government economic resources [to the nascent cooperatives], with no understanding of the cooperative process.[335]

So, the state prioritized the contracting and delivery of economic resources to legal entities in cooperative form to such an extent that between the years 2002 and 2004 one often heard that the best way to get credit from the state was to solicit it as a cooperative. And many cooperatives were formed with that sole purpose.

However, that's not the most outstanding irregularity. Several organizations that defended labor rights lodged complaints about the use of cooperatives as a means of circumventing labor laws. Cooperatives that were not complying with the labor regulations received contracts from public institutions—a means of politically correct outsourcing. Freites describes this as follows:

One shouldn't ignore the effect of the promotion of a "social economy" that certain sectors of the public administration have facilitated: the emergence of precarious and unprotected forms of labor via contacts with cooperatives that take on the work formerly realized by salaried workers. In search of cost reductions, various government entities have taken advantage of the provision of services by the cooperatives which, according to the Special Law of Cooperative Associations, don't pay [minimum] wages and are not subject to labor laws . . . These undesirable practices constitute a true negation of the objectives of the "social [cooperative] economy," by which we mean the exploitation of labor and the denial of the rights of those who perform it.[336]

An example of this situation is provided by the cooperatives that collected garbage in Caracas during the years 2003–2008. During that time the government garbage collection service was replaced by private cooperative firms. The workers in those firms were paid weekly and had no social security or benefits, and worked in dangerous conditions.[337]

Recent figures seem to indicate the true dimensions of the cooperative movement in Venezuela. In April 2006, the National Superintendency of Cooperatives (SUNACOOP—Superintendencia Nacional de Cooperativas (National Superintendency of Cooperatives), along with the National Institute of Statistics (INE) undertook a census to determine the quantity and type of cooperatives in the country, although the results were never officially divulged. Elias Ejuri, president of the INE, stated in September 2007 that the census had been concluded and that its results were known in short form.[338] However, in August 2009 they still hadn't released the data. But, in a nonofficial capacity, the INE released the conclusions: The census revealed that there were 47,000 collective associations, of which only 33.5% were active—some 15,745 cooperatives. And 75% of those were in the service sector.[339]

Another study conducted by the researcher Luís Alfredo Delgado and released in 2008 estimated that there were 20,000 active cooperatives, which was the highest number in Latin America, twice the amount in the runner up, Argentina. But a majority of these cooperatives were those that already existed in 2001.[340] Another indicator was provided by Juan Carlos Alemán, head of SUNACOOP, who stated that the cooperative sector comprised 18% of the country's labor force, 2,214,965 workers. This was in contrast with the INE's estimate of 2% of active workers, corresponding to 222,770 workers.[341]

In reality, the most successful cooperative experience took place in the central part of the country prior to the Chávez government. In 1967, a group of ten cooperatives in Barquisimeto decided to found a cooperative organization with the purpose of providing funeral services to its associates; thus was born the Lara Cooperative Federation of Social Services (CECOSESOLA). After 40 years of work the organization is now comprised of 60 community organizations with 15,000 members. The activities of the member groups include agricultural production, funeral services, healthcare, transport, savings and loans, mutual aid funds, and distribution of food and household items.

CECOSESOLA operates the largest funeral service in the region, and its consumers' bazaars—huge markets of vegetables, fruits, and other food and manufactured products—supply 25% of the inhabitants of Barquisimeto, a city of one million. Following the successful management of six community health centers, CECOSESOLA, with its own resources, founded the Integral Cooperative Center of Health in 2009, which would benefit the inhabitants of the western parts of the city—the most disadvantaged districts—and which includes the largest hospital in the region.

In an interview with the Venezuelan anarchist periodical *El Libertario*, Teofilo Ugalde, a member of CECOSESOLA via the Kennedy Cooperative and the School Cooperative, outlined the differences between the experiences of the CECOSESOLA cooperatives and those sponsored by the government:

> One sees the [government-sponsored] cooperatives today. What is the first thing they do? Take a course to learn how to do a project or how to present it [for funding]. Who do they have to speak to in order to get a government contract? There are also cooperatives whose problem is "to what organization? to what European NGO can we write to send us money?" They have failed, and we've seen it. . . . This is the result of the process. . . . When we speak of not asking for money from the government, it's not because we're anti-Chávez, but rather that what we want . . . is to do things for ourselves. This question of being autonomous means not being dependent on the state or whatever, to work with our own capabilities, with which we build little by little. In other regions they say, "Ask the government." And they see it as the most natural thing in the world. It's not like that here. At times, when we've been asked to approach the government, the reply has been, "No. We're going to come up with something."[(342)]

The Co-Managed Factories

In the middle of 2007, two Germans were in Venezuela familiarizing themselves with the takeover of factories in the country. Their curiosity had been stimulated by attending a meeting in Berlin where they saw the documentary *Five Factories: Workers' Control in Venezuela*, by Dario Azzellini.[(343)] The images in the documentary so excited the pair that they flew to Caracas and visited every one of these productive centers that prefigured the revolution– the ones that appeared in the film. Before going to Venezuela, they contacted the Venezuelan anarchists in order to get their perspective on the Bolivarian Process.

The visit prompted them to write a report on their experiences with the "occupied factories" in Venezuela. They detailed the experiences of the two instances of "workers control" most emphasized by the Bolivarians at the international level: Alcasa and INVEPAL (Industria Venezolana Endógena del Papel). They explained the situations in these factories as follows:

Alcasa [an aluminum factory in Ciudad Guyana] was one of the two great pilot projects of co-management, in which an old radical leftist guerrilla, Carlos Lanz, was named the manager by the government in order to "change the relations of production." . . . Alcasa employs 3,000 workers. Frankly, the factory should be closed immediately because of the health damage it causes. After 20 years of service, the workers are highly contaminated shells of human beings, because the aluminum shavings destroy their lungs. All of them know this and yet they remain. They argue that they've endured it for 20 years and they have to feed their families, and they have to endure it for some years more. This brings them to reject the proposals made by the extreme left management that they reduce the work week. They fear that doing this will lead to an extra shift, which in turn will lead to their losing the possibility of working overtime. This leads the factory management to conclude that the workers are too egotistical and "obsessed with money," and therefore it's necessary that they receive more political education by means of a course.

Some of the machines that Alcasa bought when it was founded 40 years ago are still in service, and the most modern are 20 years old. The technology is obsolete and some of the machines no longer work. Production capacity is barely at 60%. [The factory] is in economic equilibrium, but if the price of aluminum doesn't go up in the coming years the damage will be immense. As well, in the capitalist sense, it appears that neither the state nor the management [of the factory] have efficiency and yield as goals. In private, management complains that the government bureaucracy blocks the financial measures necessary to updating the factory's technology.

Inside the factory there are locales in which politico-ideological education is imparted. Management has hired the personnel that conduct these courses. In them, for example, there is discussion of the difference between "normal" (bourgeois) and "strategic" (revolutionary) planning, with citations from Marx, Gramsci, Adorno, etc., with no mention of the actual situation in the factory.

Wages vary according to qualification and seniority, and there are differences between white collar and blue collar employees. Nonetheless, the workers have a relatively high wage. With wages previously equivalent to 500 Euros per month, which was three times the minimum wage, today the monthly wage is [only] double that of the minimum wage.

Of the co-management that was announced at the start, there remains almost no trace. In 2005, three workers were elected to the [board of] Production Management, and later a worker was elected representative to the Management Council, which met with the workers from time to time. Roundtables with debates about work didn't take place, and the [workers'] assemblies seem to solely occupy themselves with matters such as cleaning the restrooms and the distribution of work clothes. If you asked any worker if he supported co-management, you wouldn't get a real response. Only "well, production has been going up," or "I like to work as always." If you persisted with more concrete questions, you'd hear things like: "It's better if I don't say anything, I don't want problems." No worker [we talked with] spoke about participation in the strategic planning regarding work precesses or the administration [of the factory].

In fact, the situation had worsened for some workers. The workers in the old service businesses that had sprung up during the outsourcing process had organized themselves into cooperatives in order to maintain employment. Now, the members of these cooperatives participated in the production process, side by side with those who belonged to the factory's staff, but were not included in the "co-management." They weren't permitted to take the company's buses to and from the workplace, nor to use the canteen. They didn't get bonuses–among them the year-end bonus, which corresponded to three or four months' wages–and they didn't have health insurance. This happened because their wages didn't depend on the collective bargaining agreement, but on the cooperative which had a service contract with the factory. Therefore they received a specified amount for specified activities and nothing more. The worst thing was that the members of the different cooperatives didn't communicate among themselves and neither did they collectively denounce the situation. Each worker remained alone with his anger and frustration. Action in solidarity with the workers of the plant appeared as a mere abstraction . . . and when some members of the cooperatives denounced this situation, some of the "politicos" suggested that they participate in the political "education" courses previously mentioned.

The Endogenous Venezuelan Paper Industry (INVEPAL) is a paper factory located in the center of Venezuela in Carabobo. This business was closed by its former owners. The workers struggled for two years to keep their jobs and the business was finally expropriated by the state, with corresponding indemnification [of the former owners] and was put back into production under a co-management system. The almost 400 workers were forced to form a cooperative and to buy 49% of the plant, with the state holding the other 51%. That permitted the workers to receive credit from a private bank. The company also had administrative personnel and employees from an affiliate necessary to its functioning, and which it employed directly, but who didn't belong to the cooperative, bringing the total number of workers to 650.

The machinery in the physical plant was produced in 1957 and was totally obsolete and in deplorable condition. Production capacity [at the time of the state takeover] was 20%. There was also an attached electrical plant and periodic receipt of primary materials [presumably wood for pulping] from Argentina and Colombia. Losses were approximately two million Euros per year, and the business could only survive because of the support from the state.

The 51% the state owned gave it absolute control–the top manager, in fact, was the Minister of Labor—over the administration of the factory; it hardly supplied information to the members of the cooperative. Because the managers of the cooperative tolerated this situation, the members of the co-op elected new, more radical managers, who found themselves in constant opposition to the state-controlled administration of the factory; [but this] didn't substantially change the situation. The administration determined [things such as] the volume of production.

The workers in the cooperative had to, without supervisors or department heads, organize weekly meetings in every section, and were very satisfied with the work climate. The administration didn't interfere with this. But when at the end of 2006 the workers received a smaller bonus than they had the previous year (three months' wages versus four the previous year), the workers reacted angrily, and among other things blocked the streets. But none of them even thought of calling a strike, because in their situation a strike would have produced no pressure, given that the administration cared little about the volume of production. And the workers couldn't demand anything legally; they couldn't make wage demands because they were members of a cooperative and were working in the business as co-proprietors. There was no wage agreement. One could add that they all received the same wage, but not because of any concept of solidarity. The workers in fact considered equal wages unjust.

These are the consequences of forming a cooperative under pressure–which is how the INVEPAL workers felt. They put their hopes in the elaboration and enactment of the cooperative's statutes, which would someday clarify their rights. When we asked them their opinions about co-management, they replied: "It's like always. Exploitation is the same before and after [the management change]." As well, since the cooperative can't pay its debt to the bank, the owner, that is the state, has had to pay it. The result? Now the workers, the members of the cooperative, are in debt to the company.

Of the film, *Five Factories: Workers' Control in Venezuela*, which had been [in part] filmed in the factory, the workers had heard not a word.[344]

Short Circuiting Community Media

After the events in April 2002, during which Pedro Francisco Carmona Estanga, head of the business cartel FEDECAMARAS, "served" a few hours as de facto president in the course of the failed coup, the Bolivarian government conducted a communications offensive. In October it created the Ministry of Communication and Information which, along with the National Telecommunications Commission (CONATEL), unfolded a policy of financing and promotion of para-governmental media.[(345)] In 2002, the media was overall unfavorable to the government; that situation would be reversed in the coming months.

In October 2003, the Venezuelan government organized the International Forum on Communications Media in Caracas. At that event, President Chávez announced that he would supply an estimated $3.1 million (US) to create a community communications network. According to a report on the event: "Chávez received a wave of applause when, at the conclusion of a long critique of the big communications media, and especially of the television stations aligned with the opposition, he proclaimed that 'some day they will be the alternatives.'"[(346)]

Years later, in January 2007, the Minister of Communication and Information, Andrés Izarra, outlined the government objective of constructing a new hegemony in communications, in which one of the pillars would be alternative media: "In the communications hegemony there are going to be several levels: integration of systems of public media; articulation of a strategic plan that permits [our] orient[ing] of these media; the creation of a national system of community and alternative media; the impulse toward independent production."[(347)]

In this manner, and with funding from petroleum resources, by 2009 the Bolivarian government had tilted the media balance in the country in its favor. According to an investigation conducted by professor Marcelino Bisbal, the state controlled 36 television outlets, some with national and international scope, such as Telesur, VTV, Ávila TV, ANTV, Vive TV, and TVES. It also had influence in 73 community periodicals that circulated in Caracas and other cities in the country. The state's tentacles also reached 227 AM and FM radio stations, many of which were commercial while others presented themselves as community radio.[(348)]

The "community" and "alternative" media that developed over the years that Chávez has been in power have become para-governmental media with restricted autonomy, and which focus more on spreading propaganda than on building independent, high quality journalism. Two large consortiums comprise the majority: the Venezuelan Network of Community Media (Red Venezolana de Medios Comunitarios), which was created in 1999, and the National Association of Free and Alternative Community Media (ANMCLA—Asociación Nacional de Medios Comunitarios, Libres y Alternativos), created in 2002. However, the relationship between these two organizations is not cordial, with the principal source of antagonism being the subsidies provided by the state. At the same time, both organizations have reproduced the political practices that, in theory, they want to overcome. In March 2007, a large number of community media outlets announced their secession from ANMCLA. They made that secession public in the "Manifesto of Charallave":

> For us, these letters—ANMCLA—constitute an accord based on solidarity, trust, and maximum respect between the collectives. We were growing rapidly and all of us [made] errors, which were unleashed in the painful national crisis in 2006. Given the urgency of rescuing what we had constructed, the best of us proposed to immediately change the mistaken model that had been dragging us along, and we proposed to return to the rotation of duties and to better the sharing of information, among other things. Nonetheless, the lack of will and political maturity of some comrades from Caracas, who didn't rid themselves of the customs of elites and partisan vices inside the organization, and who definitively did not permit the collective reflection that could have saved us, impeded the internal debate. They preferred to defend the flag of the letters [ANMCLA] and the benefits obtained under its name, in order that it be administered under their discretion. They completely forgot that it's the people, with their loves, joys, struggles, and pains, who give legitimacy, by the principles of the accord, to the words, names and acronyms.[349]

In June 2009, the Municipal Council of Caracas presented the Fabricio Ojeda Municipal Prize for community media, and while doing so gave a special mention of President Chávez "for being a great, revolutionary alternative communicator," which is indicative of the use of terms such as "alternative" by the state, and the confusion in their use.[350]

There are two primary focal points of the Bolivarian government's "alternative journalism." The first is Mario Silva, the host of the daily TV show *La Hojilla* ("The Razor Blade"), which also appears in a weekly printed version. Its methods are similar to those of the brown-nosing press ("prensa chicha") that sucked up to corrupt, currently imprisoned former Peruvian president and war criminal Alberto Fujimori. The purpose of the "prensa chicha" was not only to ridicule, but to criminalize the opposition. Silva's purposes are similar. He uses recorded phone calls, photos, and a production team to not only mock the opposition, but also to attack tendencies within the Bolivarian Movement that the government disapproves of.

Mario Silva openly brags on *La Hojilla* about his relationship with the government's political police, DISIP. In March 2009, he boasted on the air about the commendation of merit he had received from DISIP during a ceremony celebrating the organization's 40th anniversary, and proudly displayed the certificate and medal DISIP had given him.[351] Nestor Francia, a Bolivarian intellectual who, along with Silva, created *La Hojilla* in 2004, left the program a year later owing to the relationship between Silva and DISIP. He issued this convoluted but still revealing statement on the APORREA web site:

A few days ago, because of circumstances that are not worth mentioning, there was an interrogation with police-like characteristics (in fact with the participation of police officials) that in my opinion gave the appearance of irregularity, as regards the methods and place in which it took place, even though the legality or lack of it is not what concerns me regarding *La Hojilla* . . . but rather the fact that members of the program staff participated in that interrogation. This, in my opinion, is a consequence of an ongoing chain of events, as well as personal involvements, and the surreptitious relationship with police officials, and in consequence the creation of a police circle tied to the program."[352]

Some supporters of the Bolivarian Process have registered alarm about the dangerous influence of the program. Antonio Marack, on the Fuerza Socialista web site, stated: "I insist that *La Hojilla* has been showing fascist traits and that it's necessary to correct them immediately."[353] Despite such opinions, high government officials, including the president himself, have reiterated their support for Silva. In March 2008, then-Minister of Information and Communication, Andrés Izarra, stated that "[T]here are many people, including adherents to this revolutionary process, that have asked that *La Hojilla* be taken off the air. I am absolutely against taking *La Hojilla* off the air because it's a tool in the media war, in the political war . . ."[354] In the 2008 regional elections, President Chávez named Mario Silva as a candidate for the governorship of the State of Carabobo, despite the facts that Silva was not a resident of Carabobo and that he had not been selected by popular vote.

The second reference point is the APORREA web site, which calls itself the "billboard of the revolutionary process." Two militant trotskyists created the site in 2002. Martín Sánchez, the Venezuelan consul in Chicago, provided the technology and financial resources, and Gonzalo Gómez, presently a member of the PSUV, assembled and coordinated the team that generated its content.[355] In a 2009 interview, Gómez said of the site: "It's a space with an irreverent character, where criticism is permitted in an atmosphere of support for the revolutionary process. The path of the revolution is debated, the errors and problems of the Bolivarian Revolution are criticized. All of these [positions] are taken openly, from the most moderate to the most radical, which in many cases are contrary to the positions of important figures in the Bolivarian government, but always with the intent of defending the revolutionary process."[356]

However, this idyllic vision does not correspond to reality. Miguel Ángel Hernández, a historian and professor of sociology whom I interviewed for this book, was one of the trotskyists who participated in the creation of APORREA in 2002. Along with Orlando Chirino and other militant workers, he founded the Unitary, Revolutionary, and Autonomous Class Current (CCURA) as a trotskyist tool in the union struggle, just as Left Socialist Unity is a trotskyist tool in the political struggle. Due to their defense of union autonomy and their questioning of the PSUV's intention to absorb all of the social organizations that were part of the Bolivarian Movement, [Hernández and his comrades] began to distance themselves from the political postures of Gómez, a split which deepened when they called for abstention in the voting on constitutional reforms in December 2007. As a result, Hernández told me, he and six members of his group were expelled from APORREA, and their ability to post information to the site was eliminated with no prior notification.

But by 2005 there were already indications of what level of radical criticism APORREA would tolerate. The documentary film maker Gabriel Muzio, one of the producers of *Nuestro petroleo y otros cuentos*, told me of his experience with the "irreverent" web site:

It has left a very bitter taste in our mouths, not because of the opinions expressed, because everybody has a right to say what they want, but because of the absolutely abusive, absolutely unacceptable way in which they manage the space [site], which supposedly is a collective [web] page of revolutionary information. They're monopolizing this [site] . . . [W]hen you went to the site, this article that criticized *Nuestro petroleo y otros cuentos* was on the home page for two weeks. . . . [M]any people wrote to APORREA protesting against it [the article and its prominent placement] and giving their own reactions to the video, but almost none of their comments were posted. [APORREA] only posted three of them, but we received copies of many more which were never posted. So there's a censor, a filter. And even the three comments they posted were put in the normal posting area, which is to say that they disappeared after only one day, in contrast to the critical article which appeared on the home page for two weeks. To me this appears completely unacceptable and deserving of criticism, because they're exploiting their position of power.

At the same time that the above-mentioned problems still exist in the para-governmental community media, there are also tensions and cracks within it that sometimes lead to greater independence. David Berrios, educator, journalist, and coordinator of the Social Communication Program of the Bolivarian University of Venezuela, Mérida campus, states that "one observes degeneration" in the sector, since "those of us who believe in communication as a means of legitimizing, promoting, and consolidating popular organization cannot allow ourselves to be held back by those with the power to grant licenses and financing."(357) But the principal means of self-restriction is entrapment in the false dichotomy of Chávez versus rightist opposition, which indefinitely postpones meeting the needs and demands of those involved in the community media in order that they immediately comply with the political agenda imposed from above.

A clear example of this was the active involvement of the para-governmental community media in the fight of governmental and oppositional elites over the licensing of Channel 2, Radio Caracas Television (RCTV), which lost its license in 2007. As we explained in Chapter 3, the principal beneficiary of the shutdown of RCTV was Channel 4, Venevisión, owned by the tycoon Gustavo Cisneros. The intense mobilization on the part of the community media to shut down RCTV was a step toward achieving the dream of every capitalist [in this case, Cisneros]: monopoly through the elimination of competition.

However, the limitations of the para-governmental community and alternative media are not imposed solely through political orders from above. The journalistic and communications practices of these media are qualitatively no different from those of the commercial media. This poverty of language and form reflects the isolation, immaturity, and weakness which have plagued the development of Venezuela's social movements since 1999.

In the state-supported community/alternative media, the lack of systematization and reflection upon their practices keeps them stagnating in the primitive notion that their audiences are empty boxes to be filled with their messages, with no capacity to analyze and reflect upon the information presented in light of their own experiences. This is what "obligates" them to balance the slant of the commercial media with a slant in the opposite direction.

RAFAEL UZCATEGUI ◆ 194

This is very much in line with the comments of author Ken Knabb:

Leftists often imply that a lot of simplification, exaggeration and repetition is necessary in order to counteract all the ruling propaganda in the other direction. This is like saying that a boxer who has been made groggy by a right hook will be restored to lucidity by a left hook.[358]

---

301. Hugo Chávez Frias, *La propuesta de Hugo Chávez para transformar a Venezuela*. Mimeo: Caracas, 1998, p. 11.

302. *El Mundo*, "Entrevista a Guillermo García Ponce," July 30, 2001.

303. PROVEA (1999), op. cit.

304. Pilar García-Guadilla, op. cit.

305. Raúl Zibechi, *Dispersar el poder*. Ediciones Abya-yala: Quito, 2007.

306. Blanco Muñoz, op. cit.

307. *Aló Presidente*, No. 71 (June 2001) http://alopresidente.gob.ve

308. PROVEA, *Informe Anual octubre 2000–septiembre 2001 sobre la situación de los Derechos Humanos en Venezuela*. PROVEA: Caracas, 2001.

309. Luis Bonilla Molina and Haiman El Troudi, *Historia de la Revolución Bolivariana. Pequeña crónica 1940–2004*. Ediciones Gato Negro, 2004.

310. Radio Alternativa de Caracas, "Rodrigo Chaves describe el trabajo de los Círculos Bolivarianos" (April 2003) http://www.aporrea.org/actualidad/n6266.html

311. "Circulos Bolivarianos" http://www.efemeridesvenezolanas.com/html/circulos.htm

312. *Aló Presidente*, No. 99 (June 2001) http://alopresidente.gob.ve/

313. Francisco Sierra, "Primer Congreso Ideológico de los Círculos Bolivarianos" (December 2003) http://www.aporrea.org/actualidad/n6248.html

314. Radio Nacional de Venezuela, "Designado nuevo Director General de la Disip" (July 2009) http://www.radiomundial.com.ve/yvke/noticia.php?29760

315. Alejandro Botía, "Culmina activación de comandos Maisanta." *Ultimas Noticias*, July 2, 2004.

316. Alejandro Botía, "Círculos Bolivarianos parecen burbujas en el limbo." *Ultimas Noticias*, March 20, 2006.

317. Aram Aharonian, "Venezuela cambió para siempre" (September 2004) http://www.voltairenet.org/article122162.html

318. For Albert's account of his visit, see http://www.zmag.org/znet/viewArticle/5077.

319. Article 6 of the Law of Local Public Planning Councils (Ley de Consejos Locales de Planificación Pública). (Link no longer available)

320. Maria Pilar García-Guadilla "El poder popular y la democracia participativa en Venezuela: Los Consejos Comunales" (September 2007) http://www.nodo50.org/ellibertario/PDF/consejoscomunales.pdf

321. Juan Carlos Rodríguez and Josh Lerner, "¿Una nación de Democracia Participativa? Los Consejos Comunales y el Sistema Nacional de Planificación en Venezuela." *SIC*, No. 693, 2007.

322. There are dozens of possible ways to translate "Jornada Nacional Moral y Luces," as "jornada," "moral," and "luces" all have multiple meanings.

323. Fundación Biblioteca Ayacucho, "Todos los motores a máxima revolución...¡rumbo al socialismo!" http://www.bibliotecayacucho.gob.ve/fba/index.php?id=102

324. Jesús Alberto Machada, *Estudio de los Consejos Comunales en Venezuela*. Fundación Centro Gumilla: Caracas, 2009.

325. "Transferirán Bs. 2,2 billones a los Consejos Comunales" (February 2006) http://www.aporrea.org/poderpopular/n73099.html

326. Pilar García-Guadilla, op. cit.

327. Agencia Bolivariana de Noticias, "Consejos comunales de Caracas y Disip iniciaron red de inteligencia social" (July 2009) (Link no longer available; agency has been renamed Agencia Venezolana de Noticias: http://www.avn.info.ve/)

328. Agencia Bolivariana de Noticias, "La Milicia no busca militarizar a la sociedad, sociabiliza nuestra Fuerza Armada" (September 2008) (Link no longer available; agency has been renamed Agencia Venezolana de Noticias: http://www.avn.info.ve/)

329. Ministerio del Poder Popular para las Relaciones Interiores y Justicia, "Manual de Normas y procedimientos del Servicio de Policía Comunal"

330. Steve Ellner, "Un modelo atractivo con fallas: los Consejos Comunales de Venezuela" (July 2009) http://www.rebelion.org/noticia.php?id=87637

331. Nelson Freitez, "Alcances y límites de la economía social de la Venezuela Actual" (May 2009) http://www.convite.org.ve/Publicaciones/publicacion5.pdf

332. Comité de Víctimas contra la Impunidad–Estado Lara, "El CVCI-Lara toma la palabra." El Libertario, No. 54, September-October 2008.

333. PROVEA (2007), op. cit.

334. Betsy Bowman and Bob Stone, "La revolución cooperativa de Venezuela (August 2006) http://www.aporrea.org/endogeno/a24649.html

335. Freitez, op. cit.

336. Ibid.

337. Radio Voces Libertarias 100.3 FM, "Las cooperativas del Municipio Libertador a la opinión pública" (July 2008) http://www.aporrea.org/contraloria/n115412.html

338. Agencia Bolivariana de Noticias, "INE: Censo Económico ha abarcado 200 mil establecimientos" (September 2007) (Link no longer available)

VENEZUELA ♦ 195

339. Ernesto J. Tovar, "Solo 22,2% de las cooperativas de Vuelvan Caras II están operativas establecimientos." February 6, 2008, (Link no longer available)

340. Luis Alfredo Delgado Bello, "Venezuela: ¿Fracasaron las cooperativas?" (ACI Américas, May 2008) http://www.aciamericas.coop/spip.php?article1530

341. PROVEA (2008), op. cit.

342. Pepe el Toro, "Entrevista con Teófilo Ugalde, Cecosesola." *El Libertario*, No. 57, May-June 2009.

343. See http://www.azzellini.net

344. A version of this report was published in *El Libertario*, No. 51, November-December 2007.

345. CONATEL, "Un cronograma detallado de la capacitación y recursos cedidos por CONATEL a los medios comunitarios" (May 2003) http://www.aporrea.org/imprime/n6688.html

346. Yensi Rivero, "Chávez financia medios alternativos." IPS Noticias, October 2003. http://ipsnoticias.net/interna.asp?idnews=24449

347. Raisa Urribarrí, "De comunitarios a gombunitarios: los medios alternativos en tiempos de revolución" http://www.nodo50.org/ellibertario/PDF/raisaurribarri.pdf

348. Gustavo Gil, "Advierten que el gobierno pretend cubanizar el escenario mediático," *El Nacional*, May 18, 2009.

349. The complete document and names of the community media entities that signed it are available at http://www.aporrea.org/medios/n91809.html

350. Mariela Acuña, "Anuncian premios de periodismo." *Ultimas Noticias*, June 23, 2009.

351. Laclase.info, "Mario Silva condecorado por la DISIP" (March 2009) (Link no longer available)

352. Aporrea.org, "Néstor Francia renuncia a 'La Hojilla'" (May 2005) http://www.aporrea.org/actualidad/n59693.html

353. Antonio Marack, "La Hojilla, el Presidente y el proceso revolucionario" (March 2008) (Link no longer available)

354. Agencia Bolivariana de Noticias, "Programa La Hojilla es herramienta contra guerra mediática" (September 2008) (September 2008) (Link no longer available; agency has been renamed Agencia Venezolana de Noticias: http://www.avn.info.ve/)

355. Martín Sánchez, "El reto venezolano es cambiar las turbinas del avión en el aire, sin que los pasajeros se den cuenta" (March 2007) http://encontrarte.aporrea.org/hablando/60/

356. Yásser Gómez, "Globovisión sirve para defender a los violadores de los derechos humanos" (August 2009)

357. Urribarri, op. cit.

358. Ken Knabb, "The Joy of Revolution," available at http://www.bopsecrets.org/PS/joyrev.htm

Photo by Lorenzo Labrique

The author (right) with the two survivors of the El Amparo Massacre,
Wolmer Pinilla (left) and José Augusto Arias (center)

CHAPTER 7
The Challenge of the Future

Journalist Jóse Roberto Duque, a defender of the Bolivarian Process, says in an article published in December 2008 that the future of the revolution lies with the popular, pre-Chávez social movements:

> These forms of organization, whose signature feature is informality, were born before Chávez [came to power] or at the margins of the Chávez government and will therefore survive him; they did not form an original or substantial part of his project. The same thing [survival after Chávez] will not happen with the Community Councils or Bolivarian Circles, much less with those creations of the state, the missions.[359]

Let's look at this statement. The most important thing in it is the recognition that the grassroots organizations formed over the last ten years are not revolutionary, not an abrupt break with the past.

At the same time, we need to state that not all of the Venezuelan social movements have been coopted, not all are following the political agendas of the governmental or rightist opposition. There are initiatives—invisible because of the Chávez/opposition polarization and the communications media that promote this polarization—that have risen from below and that have conserved their capacity for self-organization and independence. As a concrete and significant example, let's take the Committee of Victims Against Impunity in Lara State .

The Committee was formed in November 2004 in Barquisimeto, the capital of Lara State, when a group of people from the barrios who were victims of police abuse, or family members of people murdered by the police and military, and who lacked the money to hire lawyers, decided to organize themselves to demand justice. In other words, the Committee came together to make use of the law in an unusual way: creating and issuing accusations, mobilizing in order to pressure institutions, sharing its knowledge as a means of seeking justice against police and military extortionists and murderers.

In March 2008, *El Libertario* interviewed Ninoska Pifano, a member of the Committee, who described its form of organization:

In the beginning we had a very important discussion: whether or not the committee had to have a legal character. . . . We decided not to have a legal character, and that's how we'll continue. It was a decision about the direction we would take based on our own experience. It was not imposed from the top down, but something we ourselves were constructing. We organized ourselves in weekly meetings. We're keeping the organization independent, grassroots, and politically and economically autonomous.[360]

According to a 2008 report from PROVEA, the state police in Lara were the worst in the country, having murdered 31 persons. This situation occurred in the generalized context of the degradation of police bodies in Venezuela. According to figures provided by the federal Treasury, and forwarded to us by the Committee of Victims, between the years 2000 and 2006, of the 211 homicide cases [in the state], 60.6% involved members of the police. Some of these cases were taken up by the Committee of Victims, with the active participation of the victims' families.

Since 2004 the Committee has been meeting weekly, and despite all of the police maneuvering against it, both on the national and local levels, it has maintained its capacity for self-organization and its demands for justice. In 2007, it erected, on its own, a monument to 57 victims of the region murdered by the police. The monument, a monolith and a gift from the artist, is located in Santa Rosa, which borders Barquisimeto. Santa Rosa was the home of José Luís Prado, a 25-year-old man with mental disabilities who was "disappeared" by the police in 2005.

As well, the Committee has held dozens of organizing workshops, has issued publications, posted flyers, and has organized demonstrations in both Barquisimeto and Caracas. On May 15, 2009 it organized a human-chain demonstration in which 200 people, from popular organizations in the region, took part. The human-chain circled the court building in Barquisimeto, the Palace of Justice. At the event, Ninoska Pifano took the microphone and stated: "[T]here are sixty-seven hundred cases in the country of extra-judicial killings at the hands of the police that have not been pursued by the justice system."[361]

The Committee of Victims Against Impunity has investigated the causes of police/military impunity in the country, and has reached conclusions that point to one thing only: "The numbers indicate that during the so-called [Bolivarian] Process the police have committed more murders than during the presidencies of Rómulo Betancourt and Raúl Leoni, whose regimes are remembered as the most repressive governments of the Fourth Republic." The Committee named Air Force Lieutenant Colonel Luís Reyes Reyes, governor of Lara State from 2000 through 2008, as the person responsible for the degeneration of the state's police forces. According to the Committee, Reyes allowed the formation of police death squads that, among other things, carried out five massacres during his time in office: Rio Claro, November 2004, four dead; Barrio el Tostao, June 2005, four dead; Quibor, January 2008, five dead; Loma de León, February 2008, four dead; Chabasquén, October 2008, nine dead. The modus operandi was the same in all of these cases: [murder by gunshot] from commando groups wearing masks, and with military arms.

Despite these crimes and the accusations stemming from them, the officials involved have ascended further up the state pyramid. The most outstanding example is Luís Reyes Reyes, whom Hugo Chávez named Minister of Popular Power for the Office of the Presidency in December 2008. Reyes Reyes is now Chávez's Minister of Health.

Obstacles to Autonomy

If the existence of popular organizations such as the Committee of Victims is an exception that points out the lack of autonomy and combativeness of the social movements in Venezuela, what are the reasons for the immobilization of the other grassroots movements?

In the first place, there's the heavily promoted political dichotomy of the government versus its rightist opposition. This false dichotomy has been accepted and internalized in both Venezuelan society as a whole and by the grassroots movements themselves.

This false dichotomy is not unique to Venezuela. It's been used by politicians from Lenin to Mussolini to George W. Bush: "You're with us or you're against us," in the words of Mussolini, or, to use the words of Bush, "Either you are with us, or you're with the terrorists." Such false either-or "choices" are very useful to the powers that be in that they short circuit criticism. They falsely imply that only two positions are possible, and that if you don't support the government you're either "counter-revolutionary" or "with the terrorists" (depending on whether the government invoking the false dichotomy is leftist or rightist).

Also, the dichotomy is false in the particular case of Venezuela in that both sides adhere to the same "civilizing" and "modernizing" model for the country, basing it on the insertion of Venezuela into the globalized world market as a safe and secure source of energy resources.

This Chávez/rightist opposition dichotomy, which in reality exists only in rhetoric, has been very effective in that a good number of the social movements have accepted it in the context of a confrontation of forces, in electoral contests, and as the logic of the lesser evil. This manicheism means that anyone who questions the Bolivarian government can be [and probably will be] accused of being a coup plotter, a counter-revolutionary, and an ally of imperialism—regardless of his or her actual position.

This deliberate polarization has fragmented and divided the [political and] social network constructed in Venezuela since the mid-1980s, in which social activists have worked together for years; but since some took up the banner of one of the opposing sides [the government's], it's been impossible for them to work with their old collaborators. And this is deliberate. Several researchers have established that, as a result of this polarization, there has been a narrowing of perspective, a break with common sense, and the extreme simplification and stereotyping of causes of conflict.[(362)]

As we've seen, the Bolivarian government has rolled out concrete initiatives to foment a social movement controlled by the state. These attempts have had varying degrees of success, and they have even included attempts to foment "Bolivarian anarchism." In 2004, Luis Bonilla, president of the Miranda International Center, which is attached to the Ministry of Education, and Haiman El Troudi, who has held various posts in the Chávez government, including Minister of Planning and Development (2008–2009), stated in their book, *Historia de la Revolución Bolivariana*, that "*El Libertario* [the Caracas anarchist paper] has been assuming a visceral anti-Chávez position that moves it away from its [self-]definition as popular and liberatory." In the following paragraph they added, "We're convinced that in the near future protagonism of leftist positions will coalesce around what today we know as the Chavista left, the social movements, the revolutionary organizations, and new anarchist expressions."[(363)] Since Bonilla and El Troudi wrote these words, there have been various initiatives that call themselves "anarcho-Bolivarian" or "anarcho-chavista." These initiatives come from government officials or from beneficiaries of the missions, and their principal activity seems to consist of personal attacks upon anarchists via the Internet.

In the second place, the demobilization of social movements has happened because of the application of what Canadian author Naomi Klein calls the "shock doctrine" to the country following the attempted coup d'etat in 2002. Klein theorizes that governments take advantage of national traumas, such as the 1973 Chile coup, the 1982 Falklands War, the 1989 Tiananmen Square massacre, and the 9/11 attacks in 2001, to impose regressive social, political, and economic policies upon the shocked, disconcerted populace that is more open to manipulation and more prone to obey than before the "shock."

In Venezuela, the 2002 coup attempt and the very brief [two-day] "presidency" of Enrique Carmona, the head of FEDECAMARAS, Venezuela's Chamber of Commerce, have served to limit the demands of the popular movement that supports President Chávez under the excuse that such demands "revive the ultra-right and [the possibility of] coups," whose plotters are permanently conspiring to violently overthrow the Bolivarian government.

The utilization of the theme of being victims of a coup attempt, as well as the reiteration and manipulation of the events which resulted in the breaking of the constitutional thread, have been one of the factors that have permitted the implementation of policies that, ten years earlier, would have involved a very high social and political cost. These measures include the implementation of a value-added tax, the imposition of mixed enterprises in the Venezuelan petroleum industry, and presidential decree 3110 in 2004 that permitted the logging and mining of the Imataca preserve (which environmentalists managed to stop in 2007).

We must be clear about one point: As we've made clear in these pages, the coup d'etat tactic has been employed throughout the history of Venezuela, and groups and extreme tendencies exist now, as they did in 2002, that would cheer on the armed forces if they'd overthrow President Chávez.

However, these tendencies, despite their stridency, have been slowly displaced from the center of the political stage, with the social democratic parties now being the strongest players in the electoral opposition to the Bolivarian government. The important thing to understand is that the attempted coup d'etat in 2002, as well as the impunity of those who took part in it, has been utilized politically to channel and in some cases to stop initiatives and demands from grassroots social forces.

(It's worth noting that months after the coup attempt, several social organizations and human rights groups in Venezuela called for the establishment of a "truth commission" to investigate, in an independent and transparent manner, the events of the coup, and to establish responsibility for it, and for the deaths that occurred during it. This proposal was strongly rejected by both the elites of the Bolivarian government and the rightist opposition political parties. This suggests that the actual chain of events corresponds to neither that advanced by the Bolivarian government nor that advanced by its rightist opposition.)

In the third place, the weakening of the social movements has been achieved through adoption of language that masks the government's project of domination and the construction of a new hegemony in the country. Since

2006, by decree, all government institutions now carry the words "of popular power" in their titles. This is ironic in that those words convey exactly what has been lost in the "Bolivarian Process": the possibility of decision-making and control from below. The term itself, "popular power," emptied of all revolutionary content, now serves the same propagandistic purpose as the old politically correct euphemism, "dictatorship of the proletariat." Both terms signify one thing and one thing only: domination of the majority by a managerial, bureaucratic minority.

In fourth place one finds the various impediments imposed on the development of autonomous social movements by the Bolivarian government. The first of these is the wide popularity of President Chávez, based in good part on his personal charisma, which is reminiscent of the charisma of other South American political figures. The second is the organization of a series of civil groups and organizations that are given military training as well as funding and military armaments. These groups watch over social sectors with a proclivity to generate conflict (workers, homeless persons, street vendors, etc.), through what is called "social intelligence"; they also harass such people psychologically, and in some cases, confront them physically.

But if the above-mentioned factors do not suffice to contain social conflict, the Bolivarian government's response is the same as that of every other government in the world: repression. Since 2008, after Chávez lost the referendum that would have changed the Constitution, there has been an increase in the number of demonstrations demanding social rights—from 1,521 in 2007 to 1,763 in 2008.[364] And the use of the police and military to repress these demonstrations has caused the death of a number of demonstrators: Douglas Rojas, 25, a student in the University of the Andes, was killed by Mérida State police during a demonstration in July 2008; Mervin Cepeda, 18, was killed by the National Guard and the local police during a demonstration in Ciudad Bolivar in November 2008; two workers, Gabriel Marcano Hurtado and Pedro Suárez, were killed by police during the peaceful occupation of a Mitsubishi assembly plant in Anzoátegui State on January 29, 2009; Jean Carlos Rodríguez, 13, was killed by Caracas Metropolitan Police during an eviction on March 19, 2009; José Gregorio Hernández, 23, was killed by Anzoátegui State Police during a street-clearing operation on the El Tigre-Ciudad Bolivar highway on March 20, 2009; the student Yusban Ortega was killed on March 30, 2009 by Mérida Police [during a demonstration demanding] improvements in the Ejido Technological Institute; Rony Antonio Canache, 31, was killed on July 3, 2009 by Miranda police during a street-clearing operation on the Petare-Mariches highway.

One indication of the weakening of the horizontal ties between the different Venezuelan social movements is that none of these deaths resulted in street protests.

The Domination of the Spectacle

Guy Debord was a critic before his time. A revolutionary, philosopher, writer and film maker, he was also a member of both the Lettrist International group and Socialism or Barbarism, and the founder and chief theoretician of the ultra-left marxist Situationist International, which existed from 1957 to 1972. In 1967, he wrote his best known text, *Society of the Spectacle*, whose influence would be recognized decades later by the activists who opposed in the streets the G8 and G20 meetings of the world's power and economic elites.

Debord observes:

Capitalist production has unified space, breaking down the boundaries between one society and the next. This unification is at the same time an extensive and intensive process of banalization. Just as the accumulation of commodities mass produced for the abstract space of the market shattered all regional and legal barriers and all the Medieval guild restrictions that maintained the quality of craft production, it also undermined the autonomy and quality of places. This homogenizing power is the heavy artillery that has battered down all the walls of China.[365]

After reading everything described in this book, with all of its absolutely verifiable facts, figures, and dates, how can anyone maintain that what is happening in Venezuela is in any real sense a revolution? But surely it will continue to be called one, despite this and any other book written by anarchists. And it's there that the category of "spectacle," as developed in the works of Debord, helps us to comprehend why people will call it such. Because it is only the hypnosis of a spectacle, divorced from the material conditions of daily existence, that allows anyone to include the words "Bolivarian Process" and "Revolutionary Venezuela" in the same sentence.

The Bolivarian epic combines insurrectional posturing with an elected government that is financed by the world oil market—a government with incendiary self-referential proclamations, giant billboards of the leader, sad imitations of Cuba's "Fidelismo," and a rationale anchored in the Cold War. This epic production, as regards the unstoppable flow and flux of capital in the world economy [of which Venezuela is a part], is a mere diversion. A spectacle.

The Bolivarian Revolution, in the terms with which it defines itself, is a separate pseudo-world, an object of mere contemplation for its followers, who gather together as spectators and supporters of the media spectacle of the Chávez government. From this flows the long speeches, the never-ending display of urban housing projects, agricultural co-ops, and factories managed by their workers—all of which disappear when their actors march off the sides of the television screen.

The separation between those who give orders and those who take them, and the progressive accumulation of power by a single person, is maintained thanks to appearances—to the use of spectacular, inflammatory, self-referential language [see Chávez's weekly, multi-hour TV show, *Aló Presidente*], the premeditatedly "irreverent" gesture captured photographically, the witty phrase at a presidential summit immortalized on YouTube. The Bolivarian spectacle is oil capital transformed into image. This explains the government/opposition false dichotomy. As Debord said, "the unity of misery hides beneath spectacular opposition."

The concept of "spectacle" helps us to understand the reason why a government which has had tremendous economic resources at its disposal has produced such meager physical results, and the reason why, despite those meager results, it has raised such hopes throughout the world—a frenzy produced in proportion to the crisis in revolutionary theory following the downfall of all of the certainties that flowed from scientific positivism and the industrial revolution. In the face of dizzying new situations, many have chosen to cling to the illusory lifesavers of old, discredited beliefs.

The situation in Venezuela is changing at the very moment in which these words are being written, and this book, like any other, is only a pallid reflection of the situation it describes. The Bolivarian hegemony reached its zenith in 2007 when it hit its electoral ceiling—seven million votes—and in 2008 when it hit its high point in income. The electoral defeat of the Constitutional referendum in 2007 revealed the separation from reality of the Chavista elite. [Given the government's advantage in the media, one would have expected the referendum to pass if it was truly in the interests of the vast majority of Venezuelans.—tr.]

Since then, the quality of support of the majority of Venezuelans for the Bolivarian Process has turned from unconditional blind support to ever-more-visible demands for concrete, palpable results. As well, fissures have opened inside the Bolivarian Movement, originating with the appearance and subsequent distancing of a "post-Chávez" intellectual class. These individuals supplied intellectual justification for the dominating populist charisma of

President Chávez during his first years in office, but broke with him when the weight of the contradictions in the Bolivarian Movement became too great to bear. [Of course, these intellectuals have not passed over to the rightist opposition, as they're to the *left* of Chávez.] These individuals include Margarita López Maya, Miguel Ángel Hernández, Javier Biardeu, Roland Denis, Victor Poleo, Douglas Brava, Francisco Prada, Antonio González, Tito Núñez, and Edgardo Lander.

As well, the opposition rightist parties derive their power from economic sources that are in decline because of economic globalization. In addition, they have no intellectual capacity and have lost the capacity to regenerate themselves; they are part of a past that will not return, no matter how much their mouthpieces want it to.

This is why the false dichotomy—the Chávez/rightist opposition false dichotomy—is showing signs of exhaustion. Add to that the diminished resources to pay for the wide government net of cost subsidies to its clients, and you'll find the catalysts of a crisis in the democratic model installed in 1958—and which yet persists—as well as the catalysts of impossible-to-predict popular reactions, and a new cycle of anti-systemic movements.

The Crisis of the Left

It's predictable that the unease and combativeness of those at the grassroots will not be understood by the international left, which has religious faith in the Bolivarian government. In this situation, Debord's *Society of the Spectacle* maintains its relevancy: "[W]ith each downfall of a personification of totalitarian power, the illusory community that had unanimously approved him is exposed as a mere conglomeration of loners without illusions."

The world's leftist intellectuals, who have mistaken their desires for reality, cannot in their myopia decipher testimony such as that of Migdalia Figueredo, a humble inhabitant of the decrepit Nueva Tacagua housing development in Caracas,[366] who for 20 years has been demanding her right to decent housing. In an interview conducted by Lexys Rendón for this book, Migdalia recounted her history, which comprises the remainder of this section:

Since I was twelve years old I've been working in this process through the Movement Toward Socialism, through José Vicente Rangel, who I saw in the Plaza Bolivar and gave him a kiss and a hug. Later I went home and then brought him a bite to eat, which I gave to him when I had the opportunity, in the Avenida Bolivar de Catia. And this dog, after he because Vice-President of the Republic, didn't even remember us, didn't even fix the elevators in our buildings. We struggled for MAS, which was created to aid the people and so contributed to the construction of internal revolutionary movements, because the people were waking up to the fact that a future [revolutionary] process had to come–a process of beneficial change, a process to support the poor and needy. But the result of this process was to destroy the poor and needy, to aid those who had the most, to mix, to involve the Fourth Republic in a Fifth Republic disguised in red. What are now the Community Councils were in the Fourth Republic the OCV [Civic Organization for Housing]; what today is the Robinson Mission was in that time the ACUDE [Cultural Association for Development]; what today are the Integral Diagnostic Centers (Barrio Within II), were in that time the dispensaries; what today is scholastic aid existed then too, with the black shoes provided by [former president] Carlos Andrés [Pérez] that most certainly damaged my feet. (Laughs) Seriously, [they provided] some black shoes and a blue blouse that I didn't like wearing to school. Today it's the same blouse, but red, with the difference that they no longer give shoes, but only the blouse and scholastic uniform that are given meanly; they no longer give crayons, protractors, pencil sharpeners, a pencil and a couple of books. But it's [basically] the same thing. I don't see a process of change.

Am I disillusioned with this revolution? Yes, I am disillusioned. I first worked in MAS, then I was involved in the MBR-200. I supported Chávez when he passed through the Propatria-Catia [district]. We hid Freddy Bernal in Nueva Tacagua when there was the first coup attempt. And what have they offered us? And [it's more galling] because some of those who provided them help were [the people of] Nueva Tacagua.

[When] I was very small, I remember that the older persons inside the process brought along the youth. And I supported them in this, believing that we would be able to have a better quality of life. I was very happy because, I told myself: "Shit [will happen] if a revolutionary government comes [into power]." And many others fell into the same trap. Today it's become a total disaster. You go to the ministries, the people [working there] are discontented. You go to the Metropolitan Police, and there's discontent. You go to the barrios, the Community Councils, and they yielded to the first idiots who showed up there, they gave them a blank check, some of them robbed them, and now they [the people in the barrios and CCs] are also discontented.

And where is the progress in the country? Progress begins with the hands of those qualified to work; all of the countries have them, and so do we; [but] we have so much potential that we could be a world power. And the sad thing is that, with whatever leader rules the country, we still are so lazy that we applaud them and hand them the flag. My struggle is against this. We've constructed the true empire under the colors of red (PSUV), white (AD), and green (COPEI).

This is a capitalist empire that exists here, and it's destroyed all of our interests: the interest to live better, the interest in better birth conditions, the interest that no Venezuelan woman will have to give birth to five children, that when your child is ready to go to college [s/he can, because] today he or she has to have financial resources. Or that he or she graduates next year from secondary school. In a mission, this is impossible, because they provide bad education.

If we're talking about equity and equality, we're talking about an equity and equality of rights. Everything comes from below, and I haven't seen a president who hasn't left office with full pockets and who hasn't enjoyed it [those full pockets]. [For example], there's Carlos Andrés Pérez lying in bed; there's Jaime Lusinchi [Venezuelan President, 1984–1999] lying drunk. And there are so many people who have done so much damage, and who have not received their just desserts. And if that ever happens I'm going to run for president. (Laughs)

I can't go on believing in such a person—President Chávez, with his anger and intolerance--only because he talks like me. Follow him fanatically only because he talks like the common people? This has to end. There has to be a change. . . . Where is the equity? Where is the equality? Where is my equality as a human being? Where are my rights as a person? Where is all of this? Socialism speaks of the social, the humanist, of what you need, of what I need, it's a pact with the people. Where is all of this? [The present system] makes me dependent; it makes me dependent on Mercal [state-run food delivery system] . . .

But this fanaticism [in support of the government] is going to change. A moment will arrive which will determine many things in the country. There are many new movements that will bring about this change—in Zulia, Miranda state, the Capital District, Valencia, New Sparta. These states are important, because they're the political base of the government. And there it's weakened. And you're going to tell me it's not going to weaken more if every day things get worse? It is worse and worse. [The government is] weakened by lack of response, by lack of conscience, by its failure to deliver on political promises. President Chávez might have had good intentions in his first three years—and delivered upon them—but in the last seven years what has he done? Where are the [deliveries on] the promises? [He's delivered on] the promises to Cuba, to Nicaragua, but what about those to Venezuela?

The Challenge for Venezuela's Anarchists

After more than a decade of Bolivarian government, the Venezuelan anarchists have a four-part challenge: to participate in the reconstruction of autonomy in the combative social movements, which is a precondition for the spread of anti-authoritarian ideals in the country; to actively resist the renewal of the influence of the inheritors of the traditional political parties (AD, COPEI, PSUV, Primero Justicia, among others); to participate in the impending implosion of the [traditional] political-cultural matrix, of which Hugo Chávez is an heir, and to support new values in a collectively constructed alternative society, based in liberty and social justice.

If we understand the Bolivarian government to be an expression of crisis, we can also take this situation as an opportunity. Without forgetting history and the lessons of the emancipating movements of the past, we can undertake the urgent task of recreating a revolutionary theory and practice in the face of globalized capitalism. In this collective task, it's necessary to ridicule the emperor with no clothes, despite the fact that the mummified left insists a thousand times that he's clothed. In the case of Venezuela, among other things we must question the clothing of the naked concept of "process," which hides the reification of that "revolutionary process" and the emptying of meaning of words which until a few years ago signified a break with the past.

It's clear that some government policies, in concrete terms, signify advances for the popular sector; even if they don't signify the end of the state and capitalism, they're still beneficial. In Venezuela, Colombia, Spain, or the U.S.A., it's clear that the construction of a school in a poor neighborhood is a good thing, an advance for those who will be educated within its walls. This is obvious. Anarchism is not devoid of common sense. However, we maintain that social change cannot be calibrated by differences in living conditions between countries, between, for instance, Haiti and Venezuela. The achievement of such comparative improvements does not constitute revolutionary change. If some want to maintain that Hugo Chávez is better than George Bush or Barack Obama, without stopping to think about the situations that make both governments possible, and make this emotional attachment to Chávez the center of their advocacy, we wish them all the luck in the world. The logic of anarchist thought and action is different. As Daniel Barret said, anarchism is not a theory of comparative advantages, but rather, among other things, a libertarian ethic.

Along with that departed Uruguayan anarchist, we believe that anarchism and its practices do not constitute a previously foreseen succession of historical changes, but something decidedly different. A social anarchist creation cannot be conceived as being a result of a nebulous historical process, nor as a design imposed from above, nor as an engineering project resulting from central planning, nor as a happenstance, nor as a virgin birth. A free society can only be the result of deep autonomous decisions and of an interminable succession of struggles and initiatives that take form over time in the folds of the collective consciousness. We're at the same time anti-capitalists, anti-statists, and anti-authoritarians. We know that without any more than this we can leave behind the "intermediate" objectives and confront imperialism, neoliberalism, fascism, and globalization. We can sum it up in one sentence: The anarchist knows that the important thing is not to arrive but to keep moving.

359. José Roberto Duque, "El futuro de la revolución son las organizaciones populares prechavistas." *SIC*, No. 710, December 2008.

360. "Entrevista con el Comité de Víctimas contra la Impunidad, Lara: 'revindicamos la organización autónoma económica y politicamente.'" *El Libertario*, No. 52, February-March 2008.

361. Rafael Uzcátegui, "Tomados y tomadas de la mano, convocando a la vida, rechazando la muerte" (May 2009) http://rafaeluzcategui.wordpress.com/2009/05/19/tomados-y-tomadas-de-la-mano-convocando-a-la-vida-rechazando-la-muerte/

362. Mireya Lozada, "Violencia política y polarización social: desafíos y alternativas" (June 2002) (Link no longer available)

363. Luis Bonilla and Haiman El Troudi, *Historia de la 'Revolución Bolivariana: Pequeña Crónica 1940–2004*, p. 210. Ediciones Gato Negro: Caracas, 2004.

364. PROVEA (2008), op. cit.

365. Guy Debord, *Society of the Spectacle*, translated by Ken Knabb. AK Press: Oakland, 2006.

366. Nueva Tacagua is a housing complex for poor families constructed toward the end of the 1970s in Caracas by the Venezuelan government. After hundreds of apartments were sold to an equal number of families, the buildings began sinking. This put their inhabitants at risk, and in 1993 the government ordered their relocation. This task was not completed in the following years. In 1999, following his electoral triumph, President Chávez announced that all of the inhabitants would be relocated within a year. While a large number have been relocated, a decade after Chávez made his announcement 800 families continued to live in Nueva Tacagua, literally among ruins.

Photo by Rafael Uzcátegui

Migdalia Fernández being interviewed during a housing rights
demonstration in Caracas in 2008

EPILOGUE

"What's so exciting about at last visiting Venezuela [is that] I can see a better world is being created, and [I] can speak to the person who's inspired it."[(367)]

—Noam Chomsky, addressing President Hugo Chávez on Chomsky's only visit to Venezuela on August 24, 2009

"God grant that you'll help us to improve the situation and the relations with the government of the USA . . . We extend our hand to you and the people of the United States, recovering hope; God grant that we recover the level of relations that we had during the administration of Bill Clinton. We want to retake this road, God grant that we'll be able [to do so]."[(368)]

—Hugo Chávez, welcoming Ali Moshiri (President of Chevron Africa and Latin America Exploration and Production Company) while announcing the creation of a mixed enterprise to operate in the delta of the Orinoco, on February 10, 2010

Many things have happened since I wrote this manuscript until its appearance in English. All of these occurrences have pointed to the relevance of what I've said. In the first place, the role of Venezuela as an exporter of energy resources to the world market has deepened. On October 15, 2009, President Chávez dedicated the largest gas well in the country, located on the Paraguaná Peninsula in Falcón State, with the potential of producing eight trillion cubic feet of natural gas. The exploitation of this resource will be in the charge of a mixed enterprise in which PDVSA will participate along with the multinationals Repsol-YPF and ENI.

At the dedication event, called the "outburst [or flare-up] of the country," the vice-president of Repsol, Nemesio Fernández, declared that it was a source of pride that his company "could participated in this exploratory project" in the Perla I field, and that it could "contribute to the development of the gas industry in Venezuela." On the same occasion, with one of his usual verbal gymnastics, President Chávez stated that "These are great gas projects we're developing, and we'll recover control of our natural resources . . . It's indispensable that Venezuela not only become a natural gas power, but also a moral, political, and social power in this century."[369] As well, the Orinoco Socialist Project (Proyecto Socialista Orinoco), located in the Orinoco Delta, and destined to increase petroleum production by 1.2 million barrels a day, announced on February 10, 2010 that the contracts to develop the Carabobo Block I and the North Central Block were awarded to the transnationals Repsol (Spain), Petronias de Malaysia and Indian-owned ONGC, Oil Indian Limited and Indian Oil Corporation. Block 2 of the Carabobo reserve of the South, the North Carababo Reserve and the Carababo 5 reserves were delivered to Chevron, and Inpex, the Japanese multinational.[370] Chevron Latin America head Moshiri said, "We're happy with the notice and the prospect of negotiating a possible widening of our association with PDVSA and the Venezuelan petroleum community."[371]

Another complicating factor was the devaluation of the Bolivar versus the US dollar on January 8, 2010. According to the presidential announcement, the exchange rate converted from 2.15 Bolivars per dollar to 2.6 Bolivars per dollar as regards importation of essential goods, and 4.3 Bolivars per dollar for other transactions. The Minister for Popular Power for the Economy and Finances, Ali Rodríguez Aranque, explained that the monies generated through these manipulations were destined for the exportation sector and to the [internal] substitution [of goods formerly supplied via imports].[372]

This is self-contradictory, given that the devaluation is intended to increase exports, while on the other hand it presupposes development within Venezuela that would obviate the need for imports. As well, as many radical left groups have stated, this devaluation of the Bolivar translates into a reduction in wages for the Venezuelan working class. This neoliberal type devaluation has as its object an increase in the number of Bolivars received through energy exports in a National Assembly election year. [Translator's Note: Chávez's PSUV won the election, although it lost its super majority.] As regards neo-liberal economic policies, one might also mention the $425.3 million the government received from the IMF in 2010.[373] Finally, Venezuela, the country of the so-call Bolivarian Revolution continues to have the highest inflation rate in the region: 30.9% in 2009, according to official figures.[374] This rate is far higher than that of Nicaragua, which had the second highest rate of 13.7%. The high inflation rate in Venezuela has been a constant during the Bolivarian Revolution, and continues in 2010; the figure for the first six months alone was 16.3%.

A look at recent violent crime statistics also reveals a bleak picture. In the period January-September 2009, government statistics indicated 10,360 homicides, and the projection through December came to 14,467, which is similar to the number in 2008. As well, in 2009 there were 366 murders in Venezuela's prisons.[375] In that same year, 46 union leaders were murdered in workplace struggles. And four campesinos were murdered in land disputes, bringing the total of murdered campesinos to 215 since the passage of the Land Law in 2001.

The harassment of autonomous social organizations escalated last year as well. On November 26, 2009, Mijail Martínez, 24, a videographer and a member of the Committee of Victims Against Impunity in Lara State, was shot to death at his door by a thug. The murder appears to have been an attempt to silence Mijail's father, Victor Martínez, a former National Assembly member and a founding member of Chávez's MBR-200, who had denounced police crimes and murders in the city of Barquisimeto. On July 3, 2010, in that city, Victor Martínez was handing out flyers denouncing the murder of his son when a general in the National Guard, and his escort, came across him. For the crime of denouncing the murder of his son, members of that escort brutally beat Martínez. If the publication of this book in English serves any purpose, let it be that it serves notice that any additional violence against the family of Mijail Martínez or against the Committee of Victims Against Impunity of Lara State is the responsibility of high civilian, police, and military officials in the region.

After more than a decade of the "Bolivarian Process" government, the expectations created by the bureaucratic makeover in 1999 seem to be dissipating; this has translated into a significant increase in protests in favor of popular demands. The 2009 report on social conflict issued by PROVEA and Public Space (until then the only group conducting daily monitoring of conflicts within the country), showed that there were at least 3,297 demonstrations in 2009 in Venezuela, an average of nine per day. During that year, seven demonstrators were killed, four by the state security forces and three by individuals. The four murdered by state security forces were Alexander García and Pedro Suárez, who were killed in the midst of conflict with Mitsubishi company over renewal of their union's collective bargaining agreement; Yusban Antonio Ortega, a university student in the state of Mérida; and José Gregorio Frenández a resident of Anzoátegui State, who was killed while demanding decent housing.

As well, the facts give lie to the government line that a majority of protests are called by the rightist opposition over matters such as nonrenewal of licenses of the rightist broadcast stations. In contrast to this assertion by those backing the government, monitoring by independent human rights groups reveals that 67.3% of the protests had as their objectives social, economic, and cultural rights; and the largest percentage of these protests were over labor issues, which accounted for 30% of the total number of demonstrations in the country. The next leading causes of protests were decent housing and the problem of violence. And the increase in popular protests seems likely to continue. The cuts in supplies of electricity and water—due to deficient planning and lack of investment—caused street blockades all over the country in the first quarter of 2010.

Another factor is the criminalization of the new wave of demonstrations by the Bolivarian government. Ironically, the principal victims of this criminalization are Chávez's grassroots supporters, who are trying to make concrete the official discourse about social justice. These activists suffer long trials in the halls of "justice" and, as in the case of Rubén González, sometimes punishment behind bars.

González is an officer in the PSUV [President Chávez's political party], which called a called a strike in August 2009 at the Ferrominera Orinoco plant, which is located in Ciudad Piar, in the municipality of Angostura in Bolivar State. González was imprisoned in the month in which the PSUV called the strike, and remains in a cell of the regional police, Patrollers of Caroní, owing to the fact that the courts have refused to put him at liberty while he awaits trial. The crimes he's accused of are conspiracy, instigation to criminal behavior, and violation of a security zone. He could be sent to prison for five to ten years if convicted. (The author of this book had the honor of visiting González in prison in March 2010, after which Venezuela's anarchists undertook solidarity actions.)

This case is emblematic of those of dozens of other workers and union officials who have charges pending, but whose trial process is strung out for years. This, of course, vitiates their effectiveness in social struggles and also weakens solidarity efforts on their behalf. One example is the delay in the trial of 11 workers and three union officials at SIDOR, Venezuela's largest steel factory. The 14 men were charged with participating in a demonstration in September 2006. The charges against them could result in imprisonment of three to six years. At this writing, after four postponements, they have still not been sentenced.

This criminalization of popular protest would not be possible without the complicity of the state media and pro-government "alternative" and "community" media, which are subsidized by the state. As Radio Ecos (93.9 FM) stated in its letter of resignation to the National Association of Free, Community, and Alternative Media Association (ANMCLA):

It's telling that the communications media that call themselves "alternative" ignore the protests and proposals of the various actors [groups, movements] that at present find themselves affected by the sudden reversals of the government that calls itself revolutionary and socialist . . . We condemn the silence of ANMCLA . . . since this silence makes it complicit, for example, in the imposition of neoliberal economic measures against the interests of our people, of which we are part and [of which we are] expediters; we condemn the silence in the face of the illegal jailing of the union official Rubén González by a government that every day ties itself more closely to the interests of the capitalist exploiters."[376]

As well, [the primary pro-government web site] APORREA—a site that calls itself "billboard of the revolutionary process"—has been guilty of not posting information regarding the González case.[377]

The campaigning for the National Assembly elections held on September 26, 2010 marked the revival of electoral political polarization and the remobilization of citizens by the top echelons of the opposing parties. The government side is reviving the phantasms of imperialist aggression and threats against the life of the President in order to rally its followers. The rightist opposition has dusted off the threat of Castro-style Communism and has also called "free expression" demonstrations following the corraling [i.e., intimidation of, via license-renewal threats] of the opposition media. Both sides seek to portray themselves as victims in order to demonize their adversaries and also to spur their forces to turn out on election day.[378]

Nonetheless, the increase in nonelectoral social conflict related to nonfulfillment of the government's promises remains. This discontent, as a number of investigations have found, is not automatically covered in the opposition's media and does not fill its party files. According to an opinion poll held in October 2009, the popularity of both the Chávez movement and the rightist opposition had decreased. In contrast, the nonaligned sector, the "neither/nor" sector, came in at 60% of the electorate.[379]

Understanding the Present in order to Change the Future

One of the hypotheses aired in this book is that blind support of a figure such as Hugo Chávez reveals the worldwide crisis in revolutionary ideas—that it'a debacle in both theory and practice. However, all crises present opportunities. And in Latin America disparate individuals have begun to understand the role of "leftist governments" in the perpetuation of global capitalism.

To put a fitting end to this appendix, we'll comment on two texts whose authors are very far from the libertarian movement. The first of these is *De silencios y complicidad: la izquierda latinoamericana en tiempos posneo-liberales* ("Of Silence and Complicity: The Latin American left in Post-Neo-liberal Times"), by Pablo Dávalos.[380] The author provides a quick overview of the situation in Latin America, concluding that the region will be entering a "new epoch characterized by the recuperation of its sovereignty in a context of democracy, citizen participation, and political renewal, in which the new progressive, leftist governments attempt to recuperate their sovereignty." This is a good summation of the standard leftist pro-Chávez position, one which is repeated worldwide.

Nonetheless, this Ecuadoran economist and university professor notes, coinciding with our analysis, that governmental power is more attractive when it has the face of a progressive government: "In all of the progressive governments, there's a methodology in construction that sustains and supports in rhetoric the practices of resistance and social mobilization in order to manipulate and absorb them into the functioning of the new power." As we've done in this book, Dávalos describes the peculiar relations between the progressive governments and projects such as the Plan Puebla Panamá, IIRSA, agricultural monoculture using genetically modified organisms, the production of biofuels, and economic integration projects with politically correct titles such as UNASUR (Union of South American Nations). Dávalos maintains that "It's also strange that the forms of resistance and social struggle become invisible and subsequently criminalized and persecuted, and that [these things] do not incite solidarity from these progressive governments nor the left which canonizes them." The final pages of Dávalos' text coincide with several points we raised in this book:

> I'd call attention to the fact that the constitutional changes made in the region can be seen as points of arrival of the historical process, when they consolidate and ratify political and economic liberalism, and close off [or suspend] the liberatory goals of the people. However, the manner in which the debate, discussion and the critiques of the left on the continent are being closed off is alarming.

> The radical, leftist critique of the discourses of power now has lowered its banners of social criticism and attempts to justify the unjustifiable. The left that supports, endorses, and adheres to the political projects of the so-called progressive governments, has been converting itself into a strategic reserve of power to close the horizons of historic possibility and to permit the transition to post-neoliberalism.

Meanwhile, we maintain . . . a silence similar enough to complicity, [and] the entire continent is turning toward post-neoliberalism. [This is] a transition that would have been traumatic if it would have been effected by openly neoliberal governments, but which can be imposed without major trauma by the post-neoliberal ["progressive"] governments. [It's an] entrance into the post-neoliberalism in which the bourgeoisie of the region will accentuate the extractive and productive practices, the privatization of land, the criminalization of social [movements/protests], and will put the region in tune with the drifts and demands of globalization, with everything [marching] to the rhythm of "socialism of the 21st century."

A second voice that supports what we've said is from the book *Territorios en resistencia* ("Territories in Resistance"), by Uruguayan journalist Raúl Zibechi.[381] With the intent of systematizing some of the research conducted around the continent, Zibechi describes what he straightforwardly calls new forms of control in the region: We're traveling [toward] new forms of domination. It matters little that those coming to power call themselves leftists, because the new arts of governing transcend [such categories] and incorporate them at the same time." Zibechi makes some interesting contributions to the discussion, and admits that his traditional marxist background constitutes a straightjacket when trying to fully comprehend the new situations: "We often set limits on the creative capacity and that condemns us to reproduce what is already known and which has failed."

It's no coincidence that these new forms of domination have arisen in countries (Bolivia, Ecuador, Argentina, Venezuela, for instance) whose societies have a great capacity for popular mobilization and resistance to the implosion of the neoliberal policies. For Zibechi, the experiences in all of these countries have taught several things to those [pulling the strings of the government and economy]:

1) These popular movements cannot be defeated by repression–which would create new forms of resistance—without mass killings of their members;

2) It is possible to defeat them through the joint action of those on the left, the political parties, and nongovernmental organizations who would moderate the politics of and fragment these movements;

3) Finally, the powers that be need to co-opt or break the [leading militants] or collectives in these movements.

The author describes a permanent process of construction and reconstruction that cannot be understood as a mere response to the movements: "[There is] a point of intersection between the movements and the state, and beginning with this 'encounter,' this process of colliding with each other, new forms of managing states and peoples will be born." If there's something lacking from this hypothesis, it's that the old forms of governing, at least in the majority of the countries in the region, are in crisis.

Zibechi's concepts are an important. They lay before us the challenges and dilemmas that those of us working for the emancipation of Latin America must face. Like Zibechi, we hope to have aided in laying out the complexities of the debate, and to have generated more questions than answers.

To quote Zibechi once more:

> For this [task of facilitating economic globablization] the progressive governments [are most suited], because they are more capable, in the new situation, of disarming the anti-systemic character of the [social] movements, [and of] operating in the deepest parts of their territory and in the times in which revolt gestates . . .

> But this is a first step. The second step takes place when the left assumes the policies of the right, that is, when the left assumes the administration of portions of the state apparatus and in the process swerves to the right, leaving the social movements without a compass, given that [the leftist government] arrived in this space via the promise to satisfy popular demands. The ideological and political disarmament this produces adds up to an organizational crisis, given that those charged with carrying on the policies of the right in the institutions, in the name of the left, are precisely the leaders of those movements, carrying the endorsement of their base. This triple dismemberment (ideological, political, and organizational) of the movements assumes the form of a beheading of the popular struggle, which the grassroots experience via the cooptation of what remains of their movements. To put this another way, the policies of the leftist parties achieve the same objectives that repression could not: a historic defeat [of the popular movements], without massive repression but with a destructive power very similar to that which in other moments was wielded by the authoritarian actions of the state.

Fortunately, if the paths of liberation are sinuous, so are those of abjection and submission. And if there's one thing that we can count on while men remain men and women remain women, it's that where there is injustice there will be rebellion. This is the path we're walking in Latin America.

367. See http://www.youtube.com/watch?v=M 1FDT2C9SI

368. See http://www.aporrea.org/tiburon/n150883.html

369. Telesur, "Chávez inaugura el mayor pozo de gas del país y uno de los más grandes del mundo" http://www.telesurtv.net/noticias/secciones/nota/59710-NN/chavez-inaugura-el-mayor-pozo-de-gas-del-pais-y-uno-de-los-mas-grandes-del-mundo/

370. Agencia Bolivariana de Noticias, "Gobierno adjudica Bloque Carabobo en la Faja Petrolífera del Orinoco" (Link no longer available; agency has been renamed Agencia Venezolana de Noticias: http://www.avn.info.ve/)

371. "Chevron Awarded Rights to Develop New Venezuelan Energy Project" http://www.chevron.com/news/press/release/?id=2010-02-10

372. Agencia Bolivariana de Noticias, "Excedentes del nuevo esquema cambiarlo se destinarán al fortalecimiento de exportaciones" (Link no longer available; agency has been renamed Agencia Venezolana de Noticias: http://www.avn.info.ve/)

373. *Ultimas Noticias*, September 9, 2009, p. 20. "FMI repartirá hoy otros $33 millardos."

374. Inter Press Service, "Tasas de Inflación en América Latina" http://ipsnoticias.net/inflacion.asp

375. Observatorio Venezolano de Prisiones, "Situación Carcelaria de Venezuela," 2009 report. http://www.ovprisiones.org/pdf/INFOVP2009.pdf

376. Radio Ecos 93.9 FM, "Renunciamos al silencio que mantiene la Asociación Nacional de Medios Comunitarios Libres y Alternativos (ANMCLA)" (Link no longer available)

377. See http://rafaeluzcategui.wordpress.com/2010/04/21/de-como-aporrea-org-mantiene–preso-al-sindicalista-ruben-gonzalez/

378. The electoral struggle has already produced its first fatalities. On January 25, 2010, two students were killed during demonstrations in Mérida State: Yosinio Carrillo Torres, 16, and Marcos Rosales, 28; one of them was identified as a Chávez supporter, the other as an opposition supporter.

379. Datanálisis, "Baja la popularidad de Chávez en las clases populares" (Link no longer available)

380. See http://alainet.org/active/34795&lang=es

381. Raúl Zibechi, *Territorios en resistencia. Cartografía política de las periferias urbanas latinoamericanas*. La Vaca Ediciones: Buenos Aires, 2008

ACRONYMS

AD—Acción Democrática (Democratic Action party)

ALBA—Alternativa Bolivariana de las Américas (Bolivarian Alternative of the Americas)

ALCA—Area de Libre Comercio para las Américas (Free Trade Area of the Americas)

ANMCLA—Asociación Nacional de Medios Comunitarios, Libres y Alternativos (National Association of Free and Alternative Community Media)

APORREA—Asamblea Popular Revolucionaria Americana (American Popular Revolutionary Assembly)

BID—Banco Interamericano de Desarrollo (InterAmerican Development Bank)

BR—Bandera Roja (Red Flag)

CAF—Corporación Andino de Fomento (Andean Development Corporation)

CAOI—Coordinadora Andina de Organizaciones Indígenas (Andean Coordinatorship of Indigenous Organizations)

CC—Conosejo Comunal (Communal Council)

CCURA—Corriente Clasista, Unitaria, Revolucionaria y Autónoma (Unitary, Revolutionary and Autonomous Class Current)

CECOSESOLA—Central Cooperativa de Servicios Sociales Lara (Central Cooperative of Lara Social Services)

CEJAP—Comando Específico José Antonio Páez (José Antonio Páez Commando Unit)

CICPC—Cuerpo de Investigaciones Científicas, Penales y Criminalistas (Body of Scientific, Penal, and Criminal Investigations)

CIDH—Corte Interamericana de Derechos Humanos (Interamerican Court of Human Rights)

CLPP—Ley de los Consejos Locales de Planificación Pública (Law of the Local Councils of Public Planning)

CNE—Consejo Nacional Electoral (National Electoral Council)

CONAC—Consejo Nacional de la Cultura (The National Council of Culture)

CONATEL—Comisión Nacional de Telecomunicaciones (National Telecommunications Commission)

CONVIVE—El Consejo Nacional Indígena de Venezuela (National Indigenous Council of Venezuela

COPEI—Partido Social Cristiano de Venezuela (Social Christian Party of Venezuela)

CSR—Colectivo Socialista Revolucionario (Socialist Revolutionary Collective)

CTPJ—Cuerpo Técnico de Policía Judicial (Technical Body of Judicial Police)

CTV—La Confederación de Trabajadores de Venueela (Conferation of Venezuelan Workers)

CVA—Corporación Venezolana Agraria Lácteos, S.A. (Venezuelan Agrarian Milk Products Corporation)

CVCI—Comité de Víctimas contra la Impunidad (Committee of Victims Against Impunity)

DIM—Dirección General Sectorial de Inteligencia Militar (General Sectorial Directorate of Military Intelligence)

DISIP—Dirección de Inteligencia y Seguridad Policial (Directorate of Intelligence and Prevention Services)

FAP—Fuerzas Armadas Policiales (Armed Police Forces)

FARC—Fuerzas Armadas Revolucionarias de Colombia (Revolutionary Armed Forces of Colombia)

FEDECAMARAS—Federación de Cámaras y Asociaciones de Comercio y Producción de Venezuela (Venezuelan Federation of Chambers of Commerce and Manufacturers' Associations)

FOBOMADE—Foro Boliviano sobre Medio Ambiente and Desarrollo (Bolivarian Forum on the Environment and Development)

FSTB—Frente Socialista Bolivariano de los Trabajadores (Bolivarian Socialst Workers Front)

IIRSA—Iniciativa para la Integración de la Infraestructura Regional Suramericana (Initiative for the Integration of Regional Infrastructure in South America)

INE—Instituto Nacional de Estadística (National Institute of Statistics)

INVEPAL—Industria Venezolana Endógena del Papel (Venezuelan Endogenous Paper Industry)

MBR-200—Movimiento Bolivariano Revolucionario 200 (Bolivarian Revolutionary Movement 200)

MEP—Movimiento Electoral del Pueblo (Electoral Movement of the People)

MIR—Movimiento de Izquierda Revolucionaria (Movement of the Revolutionary Left)

MVR—Movimiento V Repúblicano (V [Fifth] Republican Movement)

OCEI—Oficina Central de Estadísticas e Informática (Central Office of Statistics and Information Science)

OMAL—Observatorio de Multinacionales de America Latina (Observatory of Multinationals in Latin America)

PCE—Partido Comunista de España (Spanish Communist Party)

PCV—Partido Comunista Venezolano (Venezuelan Communist Party)

PDVAL—La Productora y Distribuidora de Alimentos (Producer and Distributor of Foodstuffs) PDVSA–Petroleos de Venezuela, Sociedad Anónima (the Venezuelan state oil company) PPP–Plan Puebla Panamá

PROVEA—Programa Venezolano de EducaciónAcción en Derechos Humanos (Venezuelan Program of Education/Action on Human Rights)

PRV—Partido de la Revolución Venezolana (Party of the Venezuelan Revolution)

PST—Partido Socialista de los Trabajadores (Socialist Workers Party)

PSUV—Partido Socialista Unido de Venezuela (United Socialist Party of Venezuela, President Chávez's political party)

RCTV—Radio Caracas Televisión

SUNACOOP—Superintendencia Nacional de Cooperativas (National Superintendency of Cooperatives)

TVES—Televisora Venezolana Social

UBE—Unidad de Batalla Electoral (Unit of Electoral Battle)

UNT—Unión Nacional de Trabajadores (National Union of Workers)

UJR—Unión de Jóvenes Revolucionarios (Union of Revolutionary Youths)

BIBLIOGRAPHY

Arenas, Nelly & Calcaño, Luis Gómez. *Populismo Autoritario: Venezuela 1999 – 2005*. Caracas: CENDES-UCV, 2006.

Atencio, Heraclio. *Pobreza, reto del siglo XXI*. Caracas: Alfadil Editores,1996.

Blanco Muñóz, Agustín. *Entrevista a Herma Marksman* "Chávez me utilizó". Caracas: Fundación Cátedra Pio Tamayo, 2004.
—*Habla el Comandante*. Caracas: Fundación Pío Tamayo, 1998.

Briceño-León, Roberto & Fuenmayor, Olga. *Inseguridad y Violencia en Venezuela. Informe 2008*. Caracas: Editorial Alfa, 2009.
—*Violencia en Venezuela. Informe del Observatorio Venezolano de Violencia 2007*. Caracas: Laboratorio de Ciencias Sociales, 2007.

Cabrujas, José Ignacio. *El mundo según Cabrujas*. Caracas: Editorial Alfa, 2009.

Castells, Manuel. *The Information Age*. Wiley-Blackwell, 2009.

Debord, Guy. *Comentarios a la Sociedad del Espectáculo*. Barcelona: Anagrama, 1988.
—*Society of the Spectacle*, translated by Ken Knabb. Oakland: AK Press, 2006.

Fernández Durán, Ramón. *Capitalismo global, resistencias sociales y estrategias del poder. En Globalización capitalista, luchas y resistencias*. Barcelona: Virus Editorial, 2001.

Fernández, Frank. *El anarquismo en Cuba*. Madrid: Fundación Anselmo Lorenzo, 2000.
—*Cuban Anarchism: The History of a Movement*, Chaz Bufe, tr. Tucson: See Sharp Press, 2001.

Ferrero, Mary, ed. *Chávez, la sociedad civil y el estamento militar*. Caracas: Alfadil Ediciones, 2005.

Fundación Venezolana Positiva. *Sembrando el petróleo: 100 años de historia.* Caracas: Fundación Venezuela Positiva, 2001.

Gallegos, Rómulo. *Doña Bárbara.* Ciudad de México: Fondo de Cultura Económica, 1954.

García Guadilla, María P. (2009). "Ecosocialismo del Siglo XXI y modelo de desarrollo bolivariano: Los mitos de la sustentabilidad ambiental y de la democracia participativa en Venezuela." *Revista Venezolana de Economía y Ciencias Sociales*, vol. 15, n° 1 enero – abril 2009

Hardt, Michael & Negri, Antonio. *Multitude: War and Democracy in the Age of Empire.* Penguin, 2005.
—*Empire.* Cambridge Massachusetts: Harvard University Press, 2001.

Hernández, Pablo. *El verdadero golpe de Pdvsa.* Caracas, 2006.

Holloway, John. *Change the World Without Taking Power: The Meaning of Revolution Today.* Penguin, 2005.

Instituto Latinoamericano de Investigaciones Sociales. *Balance y perspectivas de la política social en Venezuela.* Caracas: Instituto Latinoamericano de Investigaciones Sociales, 2006.

Knabb, Ken. *Public Secrets.* Bureau of Public Secrets, 1997.
—*Situationist Anthology.* Bureau of Public Secrets, 2006.

Lander, Luis. "Petróleo y democracia en Venezuela: Del fortalecimiento del Estado a la subversión soterrada y la insurrección abierta." *Revista Galega de Economía, vol. 14, núm. 1–2*, 2005.

López Maya, Margarita. *Del Viernes Negro al Referendo Revocatorio.* Caracas: Editorial Alfadil, 2005.

Maza Zavala, Domingo. (2008). "Diagnóstico crítico de la economía venezolana en el período 1982–2007." *Nueva Economía*, Academia Nacional de Ciencias Económicas, Año XVI, N°28, Caracas.

Observatorio Venezolano de Prisiones. *Informe 2008. Situación del Sistema Penitenciario Venezolano.* Caracas: Observatorio Venezolano de Prisiones 2008.

Oilwatch *Chevron, mano derecha del imperio. Informe de Chevron, Texaco, Caltex y Unocal.* Quito: Oilwatch, 2005.

Otero S., Miguel. *Casas Muertas.* Caracas: Los libros de El Nacional, 2008.

Provea. *Informes Anuales* (1990-2009). Caracas: Provea.

—*Las estrategias de la impunidad. Nueve años de lucha por la justicia en El Amparo*. Caracas: Provea, 1997.

Reimers, Fernando. "Educación y democracia. El caso de Venezuela." *La educación, Revista latinoamericana de desarrollo educativo*, Nº 116, 1994.

Sanjuan, Ana María. "La revolución bolivariana en riesgo, la democratización social en cuestión. La violencia social y la criminalidad en Venezuela entre 1998-2008." *Revista Venezolana de Economía y Ciencias Sociales*, septiembre – diciembre 2008, volumen 14, número 3, 2008.

Simone, Bruno. "En América Latina se agrieta el sistema de dominación de Estados Unidos". *Diagonal*, marzo 2006, pp 4–5.

Vallenilla Lanz, Laureano. *El cesarismo democrático*. Caracas: Libros de El Nacional, 1999.

Yoris-Villasana, Corina. *18 de octubre de 1945: legitimidad y ruptura del hilo constitucional*. Caracas: Universidad Católica Andrés Bello, 2004

Zibechi, Raúl. (2008). *Territorios en resistencia. Cartografía política de las periferias urbanas latinoamericanas*. Buenos Aires: La Vaca Ediciones.

—*Dispersar el poder*. Quito: Ediciones Abya-yala, 2007.

—*La mirada horizontal. Movimientos sociales y emancipación*. Montevideo: Editorial Nordan, 1999.

NOTE: Many articles from *El Libertario* are cited in the text. For online versions see http://www.nodo50.org/ellibertario/archivoliber.html.

INDEX

NOTE: In this index, to make matters easier for readers who do not speak Spanish, we're following the common but incorrect practice of using initial articles as the first word in terms; for example, "El Libertario" is listed in the "E" section. As well, in order to keep this index at a reasonable length, for terms which have acronyms, we're using only the acronyms. If in doubt about a term or acronym, consult the acronym appendix on page 221.